"The secret to happiness is freedom,
and the secret to freedom is courage…"
                                        Thucydides

FREE AS A WOLF

A quest for happiness through shamanism

Frédéric Calendini

ACKNOWLEDGEMENT

The English version of this book would not have been possible without the support and encouragement of my dear friends Barbara Clark and John Cali. Thank you so much for all your invaluable help and guidance.

Thank you also to Emma Parry, who encouraged me to translate this book and make it available to a larger audience.

And, of course, all my gratitude goes to my wife Stéphanie. Thank you for your unconditional love and support. I am blessed to have you in my life.

Table of contents

To Mum & Dad,
thanks for everything

INTRODUCTION

This book recounts forty years of a spiritual quest. Forty years of evolving, growing, searching and experimenting. I do not have any pretensions, of course, of presenting here a universal Truth, as there exist as many paths as there are people, and each of them is literally endless.

As far as I am concerned, I have no method to sell, no dogma, no miracle product. At this stage of my life, I simply want to share my journey and experiences in my quest for happiness—my challenges, my doubts, my questions, my breakthroughs and failures... Everything that makes me human, with my strengths and weaknesses. In short, to be only a reflection in which anyone might find a resonance, a point of comparison that will perhaps help in his or her own evolution. Even if it means taking a path diametrically opposed to mine as a result.

To be honest, it is a bit of an intimidating exercise that does not really fit with my nature, which is rather private. Writing a book about myself is not easy, as some personal anecdotes are not those that you would usually share with your neighbor or even a friend. My writing here involves an intimate exposure, which many people may consider uncomfortable at best. But to achieve the goal of this book, which is intended to be a sincere and honest account of my journey, it is just impossible to write it behind a carefully constructed mask.

So why do this, you may ask? Because after many years of self-questioning and exploration, I've been able to find answers which have helped me heal my wounds, and be happier. Of course, self-discovery is an ongoing process, always rich in new learnings and challenges. But today, I feel much more at peace with myself, and I would like to encourage and support all those who are in a similar research.

Speaking of the lessons learned during my journey is simply my joy. Having already shared this perspective many times, I know the positive effects it can have. If through this work it can be useful, even for only one person, I will be completely satisfied.

But where is this happiness after which everybody chases, and which seems more and more inaccessible today? Moreover, isn't the "perfect happiness" we are constantly being sold a naïve and reducing vision of an infinitely more complex exploration? If someone asks me today what is the best way to live my life, I would gladly answer this: The best way is simply to let go, to stop wanting to control everything, and to finally be yourself. Simple answer, even banally obvious, and yet so out of step with the typical behaviors of our anxious society.

In this time when the image of success and social pressure are an integral part of our lives, what greater achievement could we conceive of, if not living in acceptance of ourselves, and in gratitude for what we already have? No great destiny, no achievement that will go down in history, no exceptional career or perfect social life. Just the permanent and conscious choice to always act freely, in joy, in the moment. And above all, in accordance with our deep nature.

I am now sure of one thing: Happiness doesn't depend on external things. It is not a slave to the goodwill of our friends, our family or our partners, and even less to fate, destiny or karma. It is neither the guaranteed result of our professional journey or our financial situation. Happiness is within each one of us, simple, pure, immediately accessible and unconditional.

The idea of this book is above all else to recount how, while living a so-called "normal life," I finally managed to reconnect myself to this truth, through a mix of personal exploration, meditation and shamanic traditions. Rather than write a book on personal development, in which I would be tempted to share direct conclusions of my research, I chose to write about the steps that led me progressively to these insights. Besides, whatever the final destination may be, only the journey counts in the end.

Finally, I would like to highlight that everything I describe in this book is exactly as happened. Only certain names and places have been slightly modified to protect the anonymity of the people concerned.

BEGINNINGS

I was born in May 1973 in a provincial town of the French Riviera, in the South of France. I was the last "little one" with a large age gap between me and my brother and sister. In fact, my parents had waited eight years before deciding to have a new baby, but I also had the luck of knowing I was wanted, and even longed for.

First of all, I would like to make it clear that I have a deep and true love, and the greatest respect, for my mother and father. Even if certain passages of this account might appear to challenge this, there is no question. I am forever grateful to them not only for giving me life, but equally to have proven their love to me through their unfailing support over all these years. They have always been responsible parents. But obviously, each human being has their own journey, and this influences how they teach and bring up their children. I would then like to put in context the environment in which I grew up, simply to shed some light on my psychological profile, and to explain some of my future motivations and reactions. Everyone knows the importance these first years have on the rest of our lives.

My father can certainly attest to this. His childhood was in fact marred by the behavior of his abusive mother, who treated him badly at every occasion. When he was seventeen, he left home, trying to forget so many years of humiliations. My mother didn't grow up in a serene environment either. As a little girl born in a rural area, her father often showed very unstable and violent behavior. From this, she developed a fragile and hypersensitive character.

My parents recently celebrated their 60th wedding anniversary, and it is obvious they are perfectly compatible. Loyal companions, each of them has learned how to deal with the wounds of the other. With two such characters, so affected by their upbringing, the atmosphere in the house was often quite tense. Daily conversations were ruled by the indisputable authority of my father, and the complete acquiescence by my mother. Obviously, as a result of his childhood, my father couldn't stand to be opposed. For him, any contradiction implied a sign of disrespect and questioned his intelligence.

At the time, this feeling created a constant pressure amongst the family. While we felt like we could act as we pleased, we couldn't question him directly for fear of causing a big blow-up. My mother, therefore, went from an overbearing father to an oversensitive husband, who at any moment could get upset instantly. The result was the same, needing to always watch your words for fear of setting off drama, especially as it could sometimes result from a completely random event or comment.

Living on a volcano always ready to explode was one of the main aspects of our upbringing. Each time we were doing something silly, or even if we gave the impression we might contradict our father, Mum would say to us with fear in her voice: "Shhh...! Dad will hear you!"—with all the unspoken consequences it implied. This long-term conditioning significantly affected my personality and future behavior. Yet on reflection, I wasn't ever mistreated by my father. But on the several occasions when he behaved this way during memorable blowups, it was enough to depress my spirits. When he wanted to show us who was the boss, he only had to use his icy look and tensed-up jaw to nip in the bud any rebellion.

I really think he wasn't conscious of the environment this created at home. Especially since he was, on the other hand, a loving father—even if he was far from being a demonstrative man —and very generous, always helpful and protective. Yet, for as long as I can remember, this tension was always present in all our daily activities and interactions with him. I was so scared of his reactions that I was constantly afraid when the family went out, fearing he would start a fight with anyone triggering his anger.

My mother, on the other hand, was a housewife, and what

people might call a "mother hen." She loved me very much, and in return I was very attached to her. Starting nursery school was tough, and going to classes each day was heartbreaking for me, as it forced me to leave the security of my family cocoon.

My school years, whether in nursery or primary school, passed relatively smoothly. I received good grades and my parents pushed me all the time to try my best. Yet I developed anxieties, which sometimes turned into nervous tics or a severe skin rash. I remember particularly one class in my eighth year, when I couldn't stop blinking my eyes. I sometimes had these blinking issues so badly that I couldn't do my homework in the evenings. Since these issues passed on their own with time, we never looked into any steps to fix them. But it was clearly a warning sign of my sensitivity, which was not really going to improve during the following years.

It was when I was in sixth grade that things started to deteriorate. We had moved to another area and I found myself in a different school, without any of my friends from primary school. To say that I found this new universe hostile would be an understatement. Moreover, I must admit it, I was still a "Mummy's boy," wanting to hide behind my mother's skirts.

I won't go into detail on events in this period, other than to say it was surely one of the most trying times of my life. Everyone can remember with more or less fondness, or anxiety, their adolescence and all its complications. But I had a few handicaps which made my existence difficult. If I was to draw a self-portrait at the time, I would describe myself as an introverted boy dressed in an odd way, and with a submissive attitude that wasn't exactly glamorous. My mother had decreed pretty early on that jeans would be avoided, and that she would only buy me polyester trousers, with the pleat from ironing still clearly visible. This original style you can get away with in primary school. But in college, where everyone compares themselves with each other, you can quickly be seen as a nerd. That was definitely what happened to me.

This sounds a bit funny, when we see the independence teenagers, even tweens or younger kids, have today. But thirty years ago, parents still had a real say in the way their children dressed. Moreover, my mother never stopped saying that I looked stylish and, every time I tried on a simple pair of jeans, she never missed the opportunity of letting me know that I "looked like a tramp." And I believed her. I know for sure she only wanted me to be happy, and she was doing this with a good heart. But she never realized it made me so out of touch with the way other kids dressed in my school.

I was totally submissive, not only to my parents, but equally to the entire world. For me, rebellion wasn't even an option. I thought that I simply didn't have the right to speak. Someone could have put underwear on my head and clown shoes on my feet, and I think I would have accepted it without challenging anyone, even if it caused me constant suffering.

To sum up, I was the dream target for all the bullies in the playground, whose scapegoat I quickly became. I had to put up with daily bullying and humiliations, mainly related to the way I looked. Insults, mockery, objects being thrown at me during lessons, and even intimidation and physical threats. I kept this from my parents, as I was sure this would have caused my mother a lot of pain, and I was afraid that my father would consider me a coward. As a result, I endured this in silence.

Even if my education and family environment were clearly very important to my psychological development, I suppose I could have found the strength to reject this, or even used my differences as a force instead of a handicap. My older brother was a good example. He distanced himself at a very early age, despite even tougher relations with my father, and was always for me a symbol of freedom, audacity and self-confidence. However, he always maintained a more distant relationship with my parents, which I'm sure helped him cut the ties with them more easily.

When it came to me, saying "no" to them would have been the same as disowning them, like telling them they were wrong and didn't have a clue. I had to choose between the love I had for my parents, or the external pressures I was facing. In other words, agree with my closest family or with the thick-headed brutes in the playground.

Of course, I could never resign myself to choose the second option. My home was, after all, the place where I felt the most secure, and I didn't want to lose the only support I had at that time. Entering into conflict with my parents would have been like digging my own grave.

Unfortunately back then, I didn't possess such awareness, and this situation seemed way beyond my comprehension. I just couldn't understand it. Why were other people so nasty to me? It was still a mystery to me, and I was in danger of adopting the typical "poor me" stance: "It really is so unfair!"

Since I was convinced my look wasn't necessarily going to win me any friends, I did my best to develop as nice a personality as possible, characterized by a good sense of camaraderie and a slightly caustic sense of humor as a counterbalance to the rest of my image. Even if it could mean turning into a "people pleaser" most of the time.

However, during this period, I was fortunate to meet several people who saw through this first layer of my personality. In fifth grade, I had the pleasure of meeting Jeff, who would very quickly become a loyal friend, to whom I am still very close today. He also had a few concerns about his own popularity, and we quickly became inseparable, developing an understanding that bordered on telepathy. I owe him a lot, as he is one of those rare people who offer you long-time friendship, despite life's uncertainties.

I continued to struggle with these concerns until I was fifteen. It was also during this year that I had to choose which career path I was going to follow and which subjects I was going to study. Since I really hated math, I chose literature and specialized in languages, with a vague idea of becoming an interpreter.

Unfortunately, the next year was far from great. Even though I was happy enough with the subjects I had chosen, I wasn't very enthusiastic about my career prospects. At the same time, my interest in computer science, that I had discovered a few years earlier, and which was only beginning to emerge, was becoming all-consuming. I had to admit, I was made for it.

Unfortunately, the academy didn't really get it, and a scientific degree was deemed necessary to take technology studies. So my only option was to change direction and retake my first year. I wasn't over the moon about having to take math here, but I realized my vocation required this sacrifice.

And this was certainly a blessing in disguise, since it was here that I made the most important encounter of my life, with the person I consider to be my soul mate: Stéphanie. Obviously, I am convinced there are no accidents. We were destined to meet, especially when you consider she also had changed path at the last minute and found herself in the same class as me.

Another unexpected benefit of retaking the year was a new level of confidence, as I was older than most of my classmates. In addition, this finally broke my image of an "egghead," and made me seem imperfect, which I liked a lot. I was no longer from another planet and I even took on a new look, of which the prerequisite "jeans and sneakers" were a major part! I'm laughing to myself at the thought of what must seem ridiculous today, but which had ruined my life for all those years.

In any case, I must say it was love at first sight when I met Stéphanie. We quickly became friends and, after a year of getting on really well—and me very attentively (but a bit chaotically) pursuing her—we started to go out together more seriously.

To sum up, at almost seventeen years old, and despite a recent improvement in my social life, several key points in my personality were then clearly identifiable:

- I didn't trust others; in fact, I was clearly afraid of other people. For me, they represented a danger, an uncontrollable threat who could at any moment decide to make me suffer.

- As a result, I internalized all my emotions, fearing that if I showed any weakness, it would be noticed and used against me. No matter what, I always tried to put on a good show.

- I felt more at ease with adults, who seemed more reasonable to me than young people my age. When people asked me about the kids at school, I never really visualized them as charming innocent angels. Quite the opposite—they were sociopaths who got their kicks from pulling wings off flies!

- Also, I wasn't at all sure of myself and clearly suffered from an inferiority complex.

- I tried to deal with this by responding positively to anyone who spoke to me, in an effort to achieve rapport. This created a strong need to please other people, and never contradict them. Certain persons could then easily impose their influence over me and, of course, some took advantage of this.

- I reacted instinctively to what was happening to me, feeling like I couldn't control any of it. When I saw other people around me, seeming to handle their lives better than I was, their emotions and their rapport with others, I felt I had lost the manual for my own life.

All this resulted in a deep uneasiness, a need to change and to stop going through this every day.

However, it was this same year that I took my first step towards my personal evolution. Today, I look back on my adolescence as having played a major role in my search and questioning, and being the founding point of my future spiritual exploration. But the first real step on this journey of transformation was when I met my classmate Michel.

FIRST CONTACT

Michel was a big guy who gave an impression of calm and self-confidence. His sturdy constitution was softened by his relaxed manners—his ponytail, round glasses and goatee gave him a rather charming artistic look, which he seemed careful to maintain. We were not exactly friends, and we actually never became close. But on that day, in the classroom, we were sitting next to each other. I can't say what made us begin a conversation, especially regarding this specific topic. But he started telling me about a personal development seminar he had recently attended, and that he was heartily recommending to me.

It was the Silva[1] method, which I had never heard of before, but that is now internationally renowned. Needless to say that at this time, in France and especially in a small town, it sounded a bit weird—the New Age movement was still relatively unknown at that time. The fear of cults was often linked to new practices, which were easily associated with charlatans wishing to control poor and vulnerable victims.

Michel eased my mind immediately about this, assuring me that it was not a cult movement. I was clearly intrigued. I was so desperately looking for more self-confidence. Was it something I could benefit from? Michel seemed so calm and peaceful. Could I

---

[1] The Silva method (formerly known as Silva Mind Control), was developed in the 1960s by José Silva, as a commercial tool to promote mind control for companies and individuals. This method is available in more than 100 countries and counts millions of "certified students." It is delivered through books and seminars, with the contribution of many instructors.

become like him by following this seminar?

With a new-found enthusiasm which I was not really used to, I decided to give it a chance. I talked to my mother about it. She seemed interested too. Of course she had her own emotional issues, and the promise of a new serenity was especially attractive.

So we registered for the seminar, which was held in a hotel near a commercial area of the town, over two full weekends.

The method itself relies on two main principles: techniques to induce relaxation and a light trance; and auto-suggestion through the use of affirmations, in order to create a kind of "mental reprogramming." These affirmations are practiced during deep meditations to make them more efficient.

During the first session, the instructor explained how the seminar would be organized, and the methodology that would be implemented. He would guide us through a set of visualizations, while listening to a specific recorded sound which was supposed to help us reach a natural alpha state.

I clearly remember this first session, which had a very strong impact on me. I was surprised to see the room was full, proving that word of mouth was working efficiently. Edouard, the instructor, started playing the recorded sound. It was made of a very specific, cyclic background noise. It's difficult to describe, but it was close to a muffled, distorted washing machine sound.

Edouard gave instructions to help us reach a deep state of relaxation. It was supposed to be a simple introduction exercise, but had an unexpected effect on me. While doing this obviously harmless meditation, I began to feel worse and worse. I had the impression of diving into the depths of the sea. I heard my muffled breathing, as if I was scuba diving, and felt a growing pressure in my eardrums. I felt strong heat waves, and I sincerely thought I was going to faint. At the back of the room, I heard someone suddenly rush to the adjacent bathroom to vomit. Apparently, I was not alone…

This created a sufficient distraction in my concentration, so I was able to control my own bodily reactions till the end of the session. My mother, sitting next to me, was surprised to hear the experience had been so intense for me. During the meditation, she had only felt a slight dizziness, and had enjoyed the calm voice of the instructor.

The next day, I was a bit concerned by my overreaction to this exercise, and asked Edouard about it. He took a minute to reflect on it, and said I didn't need to worry, it was certainly due to a big release of stress. Indeed, I felt as though I had released a lot of pressure out, rather like a relief valve suddenly opening up. I certainly had a lot to let go!

The rest of the seminar went without incident. We studied topics as diverse as lucid dreaming, memory training and global health improvement. Even if this was an introductory work, I must admit this had a significant impact on my inner state. I was extremely receptive to the "positive thinking" message, and there was finally hope again. I was having a glimpse of the life user manual I thought I had lost. Now I had something to relate to, and the constructive and optimistic approach made sense to me. I was bolstered by this experience, so much that Stéphanie hardly recognized me on Monday morning. I felt as if a weight of ten tons had been taken off my shoulders. I was totally unconcerned by others' judgment, something unthinkable for me just a few days before. I would never have thought such a change could have occurred overnight. New perspectives were opening up!

I would like to say this state of mind lasted long after the seminar, but unfortunately, it did not. The techniques I had learned proved very useful to me, even years later—especially to reach a deeper relaxed state before going to sleep. But the initial effects slowly faded, to get lost again among the issues of my daily life. However, it undoubtedly represented the first significant step on this new path.

And most importantly, during this same seminar, I had the chance to hear about a writer who would literally change the rest of my life: Carlos Castaneda.

THE SORCERER AND THE APPRENTICE

Carlos Castaneda is the famous author of a dozen books, which tell about his initiation by a Yaqui shaman—or sorcerer, as he called himself—from Mexico, whose apprentice he finally became in the sixties. His work was a resounding success, and made him an icon of the American counterculture. It has always been controversial though, especially after his death in 1998, when his detractors increasingly attacked his credibility.

I won't get into this debate. I prefer to value the global message those beautiful books deliver, rather than try to validate every small anecdote. Otherwise, it would be more about focusing on the details of those stories instead of their core teachings. What is certain is that his message found an immediate and perfect resonance within me. And as we'll see later, they were almost prophetic for me. I literally devoured those mysterious tales with great excitement and absolute fascination.

For those who haven't read Castaneda's books, it may be useful to explain the fundamental principles of his training, which his master Don Juan calls the "Way of the Warrior," believed to be linked to ancient knowledge from Pre-Columbian cultures. The "Way of the Warrior" is a set of complex shamanic practices and philosophical concepts. Their goal is to reach "Total Freedom"—to cheat death itself and transcend our human nature, to reach a superior evolutionary level, where the material world is replaced by pure, disembodied energy.

This ultimate achievement is reached of course through a life of strict self-discipline and deep exploration of human consciousness. Among the most prominent principles of this spiritual path are the following.

- The use of "teacher plants:" During all his training, especially at the beginning, Castaneda was introduced to visionary plants such as peyote, which induced altered states of consciousness that he described in detail in his first books. According to his master, their use is mainly necessary as a way to weaken and question his conception of reality, and thus open new perspectives for him. Castaneda was of course influenced by his academic approach—he wrote his first book as an ethnology thesis for UCLA, and needed extensive use of those plants to acquire the flexibility required by his initiation.

The success of his books during the 1960s and 1970s gave him an unfair reputation as a strong advocate for hallucinogenic substances. To get rid of this pro-drugs author image, he had to clearly state on numerous occasions that his repeated use of psychotropic plants was due to his own resistance regarding the overwhelming and abstract world of sorcerers. It was absolutely not an end in itself, but simply a way to shatter the foundations of his western and analytical belief system.

- "Cutting off the inner dialog:" Like other traditions, "The Way of the Warrior" involves the assiduous practice of inner silence. This is a crucial element to open and have direct communication with "Spirit," which is the fundamental expression of All That Is.

This inner silence is therefore used to maintain, as long as possible, a state where the usual constant stream of thoughts is totally stopped. It is obtained with a set of techniques, mainly dedicated to overloading human perceptions, to the point where no room is left in the mind for analytical thoughts. It is undoubtedly the centerpiece of the training Castaneda received during all those years.

- Letting go of self-importance: another central concept of the teachings of Don Juan. The loss of self-importance focuses on the ego and the tendency to take everything so seriously, especially ourselves. This practice is therefore a constant monitoring of our thoughts and behaviors to identify and get rid of the complacency and heaviness that unfortunately characterize many human reactions.

- The confrontation with "Petty Tyrants:" The concept of "Petty Tyrant" is particularly interesting, and has a really practical application in our current society. Overall, the apprentice must find an individual with a despotic personality, preferably having maximum power and authority. Ideally, someone who would have the power of life and death over him, even if this turns out to be increasingly difficult to find nowadays. The goal, then, is facing this challenge, implementing a strategy to overcome it and win the confrontation. This involves a range of behaviors, such as humility, cunning, an ongoing evaluation of the forces in action, and the weaknesses of the opponent. This approach, which could appear as pure masochism, has the ultimate intent of totally breaking down the ego by resorting to extreme situations and reactions. It gives access to total self-control and detachment towards events we would usually flee or dramatize.

- Dreaming is another fundamental element of Don Juan's teaching. Castaneda devoted an entire book to it, "The Art of Dreaming." The principle consists in becoming aware we are dreaming and, without waking up, interacting with our dreamlike environment which then becomes surprisingly real. This technique is commonly called "lucid dreaming," and promises many exciting explorations for those who practice it regularly.

- Finally, the last crucial item of this short presentation, and surely the most confusing at first glance: the "Assemblage Point." Sorcerers, who claim to be able to see the energetic body of human beings, describe it in the form of an egg or luminous cocoon composed of light-like filaments. On the surface of this cocoon would exist a more brilliant point, which is usually set on a specific position.

Sorcerers claim this point of light, called "Assemblage Point," guarantees the stability of our perceptions when it is immobile. But under some circumstances, it can leave its usual position and move on the surface of the luminous cocoon—leading to completely altered states of consciousness. Just like a radio that would pick up radically different information when you change frequency, switching from one reality to another in a second.

The ultimate goal of sorcerers is therefore to learn to voluntarily move this assemblage point, thanks to the techniques explained above, in order to achieve the ultimate perception: an extreme move that would allow them to even escape death, and thus achieve total freedom.

This concept is obviously fascinating and brings up a considerable number of questions on the nature of perception and the universe itself. A concept which in many respects reflects the scientific theories of quantum physics, involving consciousness as an integral part in the construction of our physical and tangible "reality."

Summarizing the rich work of Carlos Castaneda is of course almost impossible in so few words. But this brief summary should outline the concepts that I then decided to explore on my own spiritual journey, even if it meant adopting a mildly weird way of life.

For I have to admit my biggest interest was to gain access to the knowledge and powers described in those books. Those shamans appeared to be capable of such feats that I was excited at the idea of experiencing them firsthand. However, my primary goal was to acquire a better control of my life, rather than to deceive death itself—it still seemed extremely ambitious...

It is remarkable that I have never questioned Castaneda's writings, which always seemed to make perfect sense, despite the incredible nature of the reported experiences. Many of my friends had also read his books, and were charmed by the wisdom and relevance of those concepts. But they seemed to keep a distance that made them admit all this on a purely intellectual level, without considering them as practical teachings which could be applied every day. This was not my case. I took this testimony as a guide, a real map that would allow me to reach my full potential. I was so fascinated by these stories that the doubt thrown by some on their veracity seemed derisory, in comparison with all the information this tradition conveyed. After all, what were the risks of exploring this unusual path and seeing what I could do with it? And above all, what did I have to lose?

STOPPING THE INTERNAL DIALOGUE

This is how I devoted myself to this new project, naively hoping to obtain quick results. I do not think that, at that time, I knew the magnitude of the task I had set myself, nor the fascinating experiences it would ultimately allow me to live.

I began by focusing on a goal that seemed particularly important to me: stopping my inner dialogue. And I did not know yet how crucial this exercise would be for the rest of my explorations.

"I think, therefore I am," wrote Descartes. So if I don't think anymore, I die? I cease to be? For many people, stopping thinking means a kind of brain death, a coma depriving us of any will and turning us into simple apathetic vegetables. At the risk of incurring the wrath of all Cartesians around the world, nothing could be farther from the truth. I would say this is absolutely the opposite: The inner silence allows us to finally Be, fully aware of the present moment, while retaining our consistency and our strength of intention. But we must actually live it to be entirely convinced of this.

Now the big question is: How to halt this incessant flow of thoughts, this almost crazy machine which jumps ceaselessly from one idea to the other, and which seems to never want to stop? I didn't really know where to start, but Don Juan had given some tips to Castaneda on this subject, and I decided to implement them.

The first one... certainly was to have the intention to do so! It may seem pretty obvious, but this unbending intent, this constant attention on trying to stop this mental chatter—even just for a few seconds—is surely the indispensable foundation for finding the required dedication. When you are *really* determined to achieve silence, it already makes things much easier.

At the beginning, I was obviously not at all familiar with this state of inner silence. I could even say I had a very intellectual attitude, which was clearly not an asset, considering the goal I had set for myself. Because of that, I was easily fooled by my mind, which was using all the possible tricks to come forward again. For example, I started by saying firmly to myself: "Okay, I'll focus so I don't think any longer." But after a few seconds, I invariably heard my little inner voice ask, "So is it good, did I stop thinking? Is it genuine inner silence? How long will I be able to remain in that state? Did I do it properly?" And so on. My thoughts couldn't help but nag me over and over again, taking control back.

As mentioned above, Don Juan had given another crucial directive: focusing as much as possible on our direct environment, such as the street noises, the contemplation of a complex pattern, touching a rough texture, or even bending the fingers inward while walking. In short, trying to saturate the intellect with perceptions, in order to overload its analytical capabilities, and thus prevent it from going into endless reasoning. Above all, diverting its attention, and keeping it busy with something else.

For example, we could compare this state to what it feels like when, at night, we suddenly hear a suspicious noise. All our senses are alert for a few seconds, waiting for another sound so we know if this noise means potential danger, such as an intruder attempting to break into the house. The mind is alert, attentive, and remains silent to be sure not to lose any vital information.

The first risk of this type of training, and the first pitfall I was confronted with, is to get discouraged quickly. Indeed, our mind is so strong and persistent, that it is difficult to stop it. It is certainly highly trained and hard to ignore! However, we must keep in mind an absolutely crucial thing: *Inner silence builds up.*

Even if it lasts only a minute, or just a few seconds, it adds up indeed to all other seconds of silence we already have accumulated. The mistake would be to give up too early or criticize ourselves for not being able to maintain this state. Any effort, even minimal, adds to all the others. So with perseverance, we begin to store a capital of silence, which weighs more and more heavily on our mental habits, until it finally creates a kind of breach.

Furthermore, this idea allows us not to focus continuously on our results. That annoying little voice which always interrupts, asking "How long did it last this time??" is more discreet when there is no self-judgment. Everything is then acceptable, and creates time and space in our mind, little by little.

So I devoted myself to this task, accumulating these moments of pause in my usually hyperactive mental dialogue. Progress was quite slow, I have to admit. Particularly because Castaneda's accounts, as exciting as they were, were sometimes a bit esoteric. In the absence of a master, this required a personal exploration that took time. It required trying various methods to obtain one that suited me best. In short, an empirical progress, but one which was never really tedious or frustrating, as each new discovery was very rewarding. Moreover, I felt it had a lot of potential, and I should not give up.

The first benefit this state of inner silence brings, is the ability to break the incessant mental loop, to "stop the world," as sorcerers say, and to allow our consciousness to finally leave its rails and take a step back to examine itself. This self-awareness, which becomes more accessible as we practice, is essential to detect the routines and automatic behaviors we reproduce all the time, and which define our personality. I realized I would have to be extremely, even brutally honest to myself, if I wanted to flush out all these definitions which made my life so difficult. I knew I would have to avoid slipping into self-indulgence, reviewing myself in a fair but uncompromising way.

What struck me first, is how my self-importance was surprisingly developed. I had always seen myself as a humble person, who had been educated in the idea that it was bad to boast or to put myself forward. I realized with a certain annoyance that all my thoughts were still focused on me, Me, ME! How others were seeing me, if I was looking smart, if I was well dressed, if I was correctly meeting their expectations... When I had identified a concern, I found ten more hiding behind it, much as the tree that hides the forest. I began to wonder if I had ever really known myself, or if I had lived on autopilot all these years. My behaviors seemed neither in line with what I wanted to be, nor with my values.

This constant vigilance made me also realize how ego can use insidious tactics. For example, I had originally started a spiritual approach in order to no longer suffer from people I felt as hostile towards me. But as this way would supposedly make me stronger, I was switching from a stance of victim to one of arrogance—by thinking I had understood everything, and feeling a certain contempt for my former tormentors. As if my ego, to keep control and remain at the forefront, had said, "Very well, victimization does not work anymore, let's try pride and haughtiness."

While continuing to dissect my thoughts, I began to understand how my mind always managed to toss me like a pancake, by juggling with a broad range of reflexes—generally neither very glorious, nor very noble.

INNER CHILD

Obviously, during this period of self-analysis, the world had not stopped turning.

Stéphanie and I had settled in the city of Marseille. Stéphanie had started working, and my intention was to continue my studies in computer science. Doing military service is no longer mandatory in France, but at the time, it still existed, and represented a terribly frightening prospect for me. It was a pretty ridiculous thing inherited from the past, as the French army was already professionalized for a long time. Moreover, I had absolutely no intention in pursuing a military career. But it seemed I would not be able not escape it. Fortunately, I had obtained a postponement to complete my university education, but it left no room for failure: If I had to retake a year, I could not finish the curriculum I had set for myself. I would have to interrupt it to go and play toy soldiers for eighteen months instead.

To top it all, the training I had chosen involved the use of intensive math, the same mathematics I had hated throughout my schooling. I then realized my terrible shortcomings in this area, compared to other students in my class, and I doubled my efforts to overcome this huge handicap. In the end, I felt a tremendous pressure on my shoulders, since failure was not an option.

After three exhausting years of hard work, I finally got my diploma. However, this success was then partially spoiled by the imminence of my military service. Unfortunately, my only option seemed to get over it, and perform my duties with total resignation.

What I had not expected, though, was the price I would have to pay for all the stress I had imposed on my body. The same day I passed my exams, I went home, and when removing my shoes, I saw my feet were abnormally swollen. I decided to not pay attention to it, but over the following days, the situation worsened. Not only were my feet swollen, but my legs were also beginning to swell. Finally, I decided to consult a doctor, and was quickly diagnosed with nephrotic syndrome.

Nephrotic syndrome is an autoimmune disease, which means that an individual's immune system goes haywire and starts attacking the body it is supposed to protect. In my case, my antibodies were attacking my kidneys, and were destroying their filtering walls. The usual result is renal inflammation, but also a porosity of these filters which don't retain the proteins in the blood, and let them go into the urine instead. This malfunction also causes water retention, which in my case made me gain twenty-four pounds in a single week. I went to bed at night, and by the force of gravity, the water spread in my body, especially towards the head. I woke up then on the next morning with a goiter, which dissipated during the day when all the water was falling back down to my legs.

The "good" news was that, due to the seriousness of this kind of illness, I was quickly excused from military service. It is also evident this disease had not occurred by accident. And even if at that time I had not linked it to my apprehension regarding the army, it worked out well. Obviously, I was not aware of the exorbitant price this relief was going to cost me.

I followed the opinion of specialists, who explained that this type of problem could be treated in two different ways by allopathic medicine: As symptoms result in inflammation of the weakened organs, a treatment with cortisone is generally used, ingested in large quantities in an attempt to generate a "drug shock" and reverse the situation. In case the first solution did not work, a treatment with immunosuppressive drugs would be tried— which, as their name suggests, are designed to strongly weaken the immune system, so that it can no longer attack the body so violently. Both treatments, hard on the body, are generally taken with significant doses of diuretics, and involve a strict salt-free diet to compensate for the water retention effects.

I, therefore, began the first phase, based on high doses of cortisone. Side effects quickly manifested, and proved to be particularly unpleasant, creating tension and irritability, and a constant sense of hunger. And of course, a typical swelling effect resulting in a puffed-up face. I confess that, at this moment, I did not worry that much. I put my fate in the hands of a higher authority, doctors in this case, and accepted my situation with certain passivity, hoping that the treatment would be effective.

Unfortunately, after several months, and despite massive amounts of cortisone, the results were hardly encouraging. I began to realize that, in the absence of substantial progress, I risked a renal insufficiency condemning me to dialysis for the rest of my life.

During this same period, I found my first computer job fairly easily. I still carried many burdens inherited from my childhood and my adolescence, and the world of work didn't seem more welcoming than the world of my studies. Even though I enjoyed my job, I was still anxious to please and be acknowledged as a model employee. In addition, my permanent fatigue due to my disease did not really make the situation more enjoyable.

At that time, I was already aware that my state of health had nothing to do with an external cause, and that this pathology had been entirely created by messy emotional behavior, and excessive stress. When I presented this hypothesis to physicians, they usually laughed at me, telling me they themselves had undergone periods of stress without developing a nephrotic syndrome. This beautiful confidence crumbled a bit when I asked them where this disease could come from then. I usually got an evasive answer with a shrug, "We don't really know... maybe an insect bite that would have triggered an overreaction of your immune system?"

I would have not been too distressed by the weakness of this explanation, if I didn't have to suffer from the violence of the drug treatments that were prescribed to me. After the failure of cortisone, immunosuppressive drugs had also proved as hard on my body as they had been ineffective in my healing. I began to feel like an experimental guinea pig.

After two years of this, my body was in quite a miserable state. The situation became more and more disheartening, and I seriously started to doubt the ability of medicine to cure me. Especially since doctors appeared totally closed to an alternative view on the root causes of my health issues, merely prescribing treatments to eradicate the symptoms and not the source of the problem.

Yet in continuing my study of shamanism, which I had never really stopped—and which had indeed helped me hold on—I became interested in other practices from Asia, such as Do In. Do In is a healing technique based on the flow of energies in the body. By tapping on precise locations, it flushes out all energy residues that might be blocked in the muscles and joints. This science is based on the use of energy meridians, in a manner similar to acupuncture. But despite my commitment and my various explorations, I saw no particular progress, which led gradually to a dangerous sense of resignation.

I must say this process was partially disrupted by a fast-moving professional life, leaving me with no real breathing space. Indeed, the small company I worked for in the South of France had just been taken over by a much larger entity based in Paris. I then found myself facing the choice of moving to the capital, or losing my job. I was not fond of the idea of leaving my homeland, especially as my vision of Paris was not especially flattering— local chauvinism certainly helped portray it in a negative way. After much consideration, however, we decided to take our chance. The small-town guy would soon land in the wonderful Parisian corporate world.

After moving, I did my best to adapt to this new life, still characterized by constant stress and pressure—pressure which, of course, was self-imposed most of the time: I could not help but suffer from an inferiority complex, typical of the "rookie from the South," lost among all those seasoned managers and suited businessmen in the "La Defense"[1] district...

And then one day, seemingly by accident, I made a crucial connection on an Internet forum. His name was Ross Heaven and he was living in the UK. He is now a renowned author, of course, but at that time, he was still working on his first book. He had been practicing shamanism for quite some time, and hosted an online community dedicated to this subject. In the course of a conversation, I described my health problems to him, and he kindly offered to attempt a distant healing experiment. I found the idea

----

[1]   La Défense is a famous business district in Paris

interesting, and eagerly accepted to give it a chance.

Shortly before, I had read a book dealing with "Soul Retrieval[1]," a shamanic technique aimed at healing people who have "lost" a part of themselves due to trauma, depression or a series of painful events. The shaman enters an altered state of consciousness, and embarks on a shamanic journey. She tries to make contact with the lost part of the patient, usually the inner child, whose candor and positive energy left in favor of the adult self, generally more austere and grim. This practice is thus dedicated to healing on mental, emotional and physical levels, in a holistic approach where individuals finally restore their completeness, and can again operate with all of their resources.

Ross first sent me a letter containing some instructions and a small stone he had infused with positive intention. I had to relax in a quiet room where I would not be disturbed, and hold the stone. We had agreed to a time at which the session would begin, and when he would start his shamanic journey.

I settled comfortably, burned a little incense to create a peaceful atmosphere, and lay down while trying to calm my mind and put myself in a receptive state.

During the session, I felt a few physical effects, including heat sensations around my belly. However, once the work was completed, I didn't feel fundamentally different. Simply quiet, and with the feeling I had done what was needed.

Surprisingly, Stéphanie told me later that our cat had been extremely agitated throughout the session, running and jumping everywhere, and finally stopped suddenly at the end of the healing, in perfect timing.

Ross wrote me a few days later, to give me an account of his experience. What he had written was surprisingly relevant and had a huge impact on me. Here is the message he sent me[2]:

---

[1] "Soul retrieval: Mending the fragmented self", by Sandra Ingerman

[2] Ross published his first book two years later, where he told this experience in detail, while modifying my name and my nationality to preserve my anonymity. *A Journey To You, A Shaman's Path To Empowerment.* © 2001 Ross Heaven.

"During my journey, I had the vision of an injured little boy, nine or ten years old, who represented the part of your soul you had obscured, and which contained the emotions you felt at that age. You felt alone in a world without support, and exposed to anger and aggression of a violent family life, with parents constantly having tense relationships. Your father was always on the nerves and shouted, while your mother remained passive and never really interfered in your favor. The young Frédéric felt betrayed and abandoned by adults who ruled his life, very alone in a world of suffering.

"When I proposed this boy to accompany me and come back with me, he was really not enthusiastic and asked why he should. I explained that the older Frédéric now had a disease, that this child could help heal. He was not impressed—after all, no adult had never really taken his side.

"I sat next to the child, and I put my arm around his shoulders, fully aware of his sadness and sorrow. I explained as simply as I could that the adult Frédéric loved him a lot, and that he was expressing this love by asking me to be here at this time. All things are connected, I said, and if the adult Frédéric could heal, his child self would also be helped as he would never have to face the disease later in his life.

"The child was moved that someone, finally, cared enough about him to begin this positive approach—but he was still suspicious and wanted assurance that the 'big Frédéric' would take care of him if he was coming back with me. I explained that at this same time, 'big Frédéric' was meditating for this purpose—how to make the world more welcoming for him—and that he would be loved, protected and considered if he would return with me.

"Hearing this, he became happier and more open, a vision of the happy child he was before living the events that had led him here.

"He began to play and asked me if I wanted to see bits of his life. I answered 'Yes, please,' and he showed me some scenes of his home, very quickly, just flashes, but the general impression was a very critical father and a mother who did nothing to support the child—not really rallied to the ideas of her husband, but without doing anything positive either, as if she did not actually feel involved.

"I reassured the young Frédéric again that things would be

different now, and we played a moment before returning home."

I was flabbergasted by the accuracy of Ross' vision. However, by reconsidering my childhood today, I realize my parents' behavior was much more loving than this bleak description might suggest. For example, I know now that my mother was too afraid of my father's reactions to contradict him, and it absolutely did not reflect a lack of love towards me, but rather a fear of conflict which was too difficult to overcome. And I also know the tension my father was expressing was in direct relation to his unhappy childhood, but it did not bring into question his attachment to me.

However, my feelings when I was nine certainly must have been much closer to what Ross described, compared to my current, more mature understanding of the situation. I realized how that part of me had seen this environment as hard and hostile—and this perception had been intensified by my extreme sensitivity.

But the last paragraph Ross included in his message had the biggest impact on me:

"Oh, one more small thing. My personal guide, the spiritual entity who travels with me in my journeys, suggested that your state of health was linked to the fact you were overprotecting yourself, literally. And that this overly powerful protection system was solicited to the point of threatening the body it was supposed to take care of. Out of this excessive behavior, it had then become the aggressor."

I was both moved and excited by the absolute relevance of these statements. That was exactly the point, without a shadow of a doubt!

Following this session, and to my great surprise, my health improved rapidly. In fact, the next day, I already felt an undeniable energy boost, after having endured this feeling of permanent fatigue for years, due to the treatment I had to take. In the following weeks, my blood analysis showed almost normal rates, to the surprise of my doctor, who didn't dare stop my medication too abruptly. The end of my therapy, however, was a formality and I finally regained the vitality I had missed so much.

I was extremely relieved and grateful, of course, but this very quick healing also raised many questions. Why hadn't I managed to recover earlier? After all, I had already clearly identified the source of the problem—heavy stress, accumulated for many years. I also had started Do In and other techniques to work on myself. What was the cause of this failure, and how had this shamanic ceremony made a difference?

It took me a while to understand the chain reaction that had occurred within me until my complete remission. First of all, the fact that Ross—through his guide—had suggested I was creating this state in an act of overprotection, had triggered a radical upheaval in myself. The idea that, while trying to stay safe, I actually shot myself in the foot, immediately pushed me to reconsider my priorities. I had a strong realization that no situation of my professional life, or any other area, could have justified the suffering I had endured during my illness. No despotic boss, no pushy colleague, no complicated or even unworkable project, could warrant the slow self-destruction of my body. So far, I had indeed been sensitive to what those around me were expecting from me. But there were limits, and I had largely overstepped them.

This recognition led naturally to another one: If my sudden recovery was finally due to the refusal of this perverse game, it also indicated that, until then, I had accepted this situation one way or another. And that my efforts at healing through alternative methods had actually been meager attempts, only scratching the surface of my real troubles. I had to be honest with myself: On some level, I had accepted my nephrotic syndrome. As I said earlier, it was quite convenient when it saved me from military service. Then I had dumped it on the medical profession, to whom I had entrusted the task of repairing the damages for me. And it was not my shy incursions into self-healing that could curb the effects of such a destructive behavior, which I had not changed in the slightest, and which I had perpetuated unmindfully all that time.

It took me an even longer time to realize what the last, and most important, part of this healing process was. Indeed, which element had created the final click within myself? After all, I could have accepted all Ross' explanations on a purely intellectual level. What gave me the impetus to suddenly change the situation and start my remission? The answer was simple: a renewed self-esteem, and a genuine sense of compassion for myself. Finally, I understood I had created this disease by always seeing myself as less than others. Their desires always prevailed over mine, naturally creating the stress that had led me to this dead end. In other words, not only had I discredited myself so much that I had destroyed my health, but also, once sick, I had simply continued to accept this as established fact. Through devaluation of myself, I could justify being in this extreme situation, and enduring such pain appeared almost normal.

When I finally understood the ordeal I had inflicted on myself, thanks to the estrangement caused by the vision of me as a child, I could empathize with my own fate, and decide to cut my losses in a responsible manner. Haven't we all witnessed the courage of people who, while facing disease, used their strength and determination to overcome it, and win a victory which attracts everyone's admiration? So what energy pushes them to hang on, if not the love of life, and most importantly self-love and self-respect? In my opinion, this is the first step to initiate a healing, and I understand now how powerful the "Soul Retrieval" technique is.

We are often ready to inflict the worst suffering on ourselves. We believe we can endure it, or even deserve it. But when we become aware of the violence of this abuse to the child we were, and who is still within us, it would be sadistic not to stop and take care of this fragile and innocent being who simply wants to be loved.

We could recognize Soul Retrieval as a potent practice, but based only on the psychological impact of the story the shaman tells when returning from her journey. However, it is important to note—and this is where this process becomes magical—that the results are also effective if the practitioner does not share the visions with the patient. As if during this ceremony, the shaman was operating as a mediator between different subtle, but very real parts of our being, at a higher spiritual level which is beyond our grasp in our everyday awareness. The healer "plays" the scene of reconciliation and, on an ethereal plane, truly reunites dislocated parts of our consciousness, or soul, for lack of a better term.

Ultimately, this action has only one goal: to give us back our love, consideration and respect for ourselves, as these are the prerequisites for our healing. One thing for which allopathic medicine will surely never have a cure, and which we may only achieve by ourselves. Once these feelings are found again, and self-destructive behaviors are finally overcome, our organism knows perfectly how to repair itself quickly and naturally. And of course, for those who prefer not to entirely discard regular western medicine, this state of love will be the crucial element which will enhance the effectiveness of the prescribed treatments and guarantee their positive effects.

THE LION'S DEN

This new-found energy was clearly salutary, and gave me the strength to embark on new professional adventures. I left my job to try, like many others, to conquer the new Eldorado at that time: the Internet. Actually, the small company I joined was not entirely dedicated to the Web, but the euphoria of the moment favored proliferation of startups, springing up like mushrooms. Only a few actually survived, but in 2001, everyone thought they had "the Idea" that would make them millionaires.

In hindsight, this was surely one of the most rewarding positions in my career, as it was related to various creative projects, and the small size of our team made us pull together. Of course, this involved a total personal commitment, where our time at work literally exploded—sometimes spending several days in a row at the office without going home. We had to sleep at our desks in the most critical moments.

Despite all these efforts, the company did not survive the market collapse, and was forced into bankruptcy in 2004. Although the beginnings were promising, several poor strategic decisions and risky economic partnerships led to our decline. I left this situation totally exhausted, which suggests I had not fully absorbed the lessons of my nephrotic syndrome. But I also felt more confident, and ready to face any professional situation, thanks to all the challenges we had had to overcome.

My tendency to feel like a victim was beginning to fade away, and I had a better comprehension of the "petty tyrant" concept Castaneda described so well in his works. The situations weren't necessarily a burden I had to suffer any longer, but could also be opportunities for growing and becoming stronger.

However, I have to admit I still didn't really like people. Behind affable behaviors—I always wanted to create an immediate climate of complicity between myself and others—I had a pretty cold heart, and a constant desire to keep everyone at bay. But even though I was wary of my neighbor, whom I still considered a potential threat, I could finally transform these interactions to harden my armor. Since I had to live in the midst of a supposedly hostile crowd, at least I could use it for my personal evolution.

Of course, I sometimes fell back into my old thought patterns, and my body quickly called me to order with a growing pain in my kidneys. I always took these warnings very seriously, and ultimately welcomed them as a sign that I lost myself again. I had paid a high price for this safety belt, and I would certainly use it wisely to remember the lessons of the past.

After a mandatory break to recharge my batteries, and a quick mission in the video games industry, I finally applied for a project manager position I had found on the Internet. The ad contained few details about the company. I later discovered with surprise that it was actually a very large French press group—let's call it "The Group"—which wanted to revive its activity on the web, in anticipation of the slow but relentless decline of the printed press.

On the technical and organizational level, everything was yet to be done, and pressure from the editorial side was already huge. Moreover, I would be in charge of The Group's flagship magazine, a world-renowned women's weekly. Needless to say, I was immediately thrown into a lion's den, where mass hysteria was omnipresent.

Those who have worked in this kind of sprawling business will understand the daily drama involved: a constant waltz of egos and power struggles; a pyramidal hierarchical organization with so many layers that nobody knows exactly who does what; decisions coming out of the blue from the highest executives and which are generally inapplicable or even inconsistent; a management by terror and recurring backstabbing from colleagues... In short, a climate of permanent fear and stress, where everyone tries to survive by protecting themselves as best they can—even if it means having to sacrifice their neighbor when heads begin to roll.

I did my best to adapt to this chaotic professional environment, clinging more than ever to the teachings of Don Juan. Who would have thought that theories from an old Yaqui Indian would prove to be so effective in the aggressive world of Western companies? Firstly, the concept of petty tyrant, which once integrated, can potentially transform each delicate interaction into an almost exciting challenge, even with the most despotic boss. Then the cutting of the inner chatter, which during unavoidable stress, allows one to reduce tension in record time. Finally, the loss of self-importance, which creates an even more striking contrast in such an environment, governed mainly by ego and appearances.

I won't say it was an easy ride, but at least these principles helped me hold on, despite the general panic. As strange as it may sound, I progressively earned the reputation of the "Zen guy of the office." As a consequence, people would frequently come and sit at my desk to confide in me and share their personal or professional problems—surely because I was one of the few people who actually bothered listening to them...

My main difficulty came from my role as a manager. I had already handled teams in my previous positions, but always in different, generally calmer or more "friendly" conditions. In The Group, I could hardly follow my supervisors' management techniques, which treated people more as cattle, rather than human beings with feelings and emotions. I sometimes felt I was asked to hound my team, even if it meant horsewhipping the less effective, instead of considering the personality of each individual with understanding and psychology. And if they did not keep up with the pace, I was asked to scare them. Add to this my longstanding issues of submission to others, which didn't really make me feel legitimate in imposing my views—or rather those of my bosses, which I did not even share with them. Therefore, and against the general practice, I favored a soft communication, convinced we get much more from people by rallying them to our cause than by threatening them with a club. And I think the positive results I obtained proved right.

Of course this tricky situation, this feeling of being constantly between the hammer and the anvil, exposed me sometimes to overwhelming stress. If I needed coaches to train me to manage my emotions, I had found the masters. And I must admit they filled their role perfectly, by forcing me to find the faintest places of calm in myself, so I could handle the incessant pressure. I thank them today, because they allowed me to achieve moments of inner silence which I had never experienced before, proving that it is not necessary to go into exile at the top of a mountain to reach this kind of inner state. The advantage is that, having established this meditation in spite of a hectic urban life, it becomes possible to maintain it under many circumstances, even the most disturbing ones.

Thus, in the evening, still facing the tensions I had felt during the day and which kept going round in my mind, I set the intent to cut this inner chatter—which strangely seemed to take a malicious pleasure in maintaining my suffering. After a while though, by focusing on this intention and the present moment, without ritual or specific procedure, the silence literally took me over. At the beginning of my practice, years ago, I scrimped on every second of peace. It felt like maintaining balance on a tightrope, to finally tumble and resume the never-ending flow of my thoughts. But a significant shift seemed to have finally occurred. The silence came almost effortlessly. Instead, it wrapped me completely, as if I had "fallen" into it, and could stay there without struggling.

This progress was certainly due to my sustained efforts at shutting my mind off whenever I had the opportunity, but also to a few other elements which I have not yet spoken of. First, I was interested in a series of movements that Carlos Castaneda had promoted shortly before his death. He called them "Magical Passes," or "Tensegrity," and they were supposed to come from his teaching of the Toltec tradition. These movements, if properly executed, were intended to bring health and well-being. But they also had to cause a shift of the "Assemblage Point"—i.e., a shift of consciousness in the practitioner, to access untapped resources of the energy body. I have to admit the practice of these movements, which were precise and dynamic, had a powerful effect on my inner silence. After a session of about thirty minutes, they allowed me to feel an energy vibration throughout my body, and my head was totally empty of any thought.

I can't say if this shift of consciousness was caused only by these specific movements, or if simply practicing complex sequences was sufficient to overload my attention and stop the flow of my intellect. It worked beautifully though, and only a lack of self-discipline prevented me from exploring those techniques even more deeply. I imagine that Tai Chi, Qi Gong or most Yoga schools operate on the same principle, even if Tensegrity may sometimes seem closer to martial arts in its dynamic form.

At the same time, I found another major influence: Eckhart Tolle, who had written several books on how to reach inner silence. Two of his best-known works are *The Power of Now* and *New Earth*, in which he explains in simple and clear terms, how to achieve peace of mind. I guess that if I had had access to these writings earlier, I would have probably progressed more quickly. However, I do not regret anything, because my learning, although it was long, was now deeply rooted in me.

Despite these undeniable advances, I began to feel I was running out of steam. Indeed, the states Castaneda had described were empirically verifiable—this pragmatic validation had actually been my main motivation for walking that path. Yet, the most extreme, even magical, experiences told of in his works still remained out of my grasp. No vision of the luminous body, nor notable extra-sensory perceptions. I began to wonder if I had reached a dead end, and if the rest of these achievements would remain permanently inaccessible to me.

PARASITES

I must say that apart from these very pleasant quiet states, my mind still gave me some serious trouble. I had always been extremely analytical, up to the point of being tiresome. Stéphanie told me often that I was splitting hairs, and she was right. I couldn't help but dissect and examine everything in the light of my intellect. At that time, I didn't realize how this habit had become obsessive, and how it was powered by fear.

After thirty years of intense training, my mind was in great shape, and even overtrained. It could not help but step in, even in the most trivial decision-making.

However, there is a major drawback to this approach. Indeed, when the facts alone do not allow us to determine the best choice, it then leads to paralysis: As no certainty could result from our mental analysis, we end up doing nothing at all.

I was also fascinated, even appalled, by the negativity of this hyperactive mind. It never missed an opportunity to remind me how an individual or a situation was despicable or unsatisfactory—while promoting feelings of anger or resentment. The more distance from my thoughts I created through my inner silence, the more I realized that my ego was simply disgusting. I couldn't understand why I kept having such mediocre thoughts, which were at odds with my core values. Some kind of dissociation seemed to appear within me, like two people living in the same body: a good and loving one, wanting to evolve in a constructive manner; and the other one, focused only on negative considerations, similar to a malicious snake constantly whispering bad advice into my ear. I couldn't understand how I could live with such an inner conflict, and was desperately looking for an explanation.

At this stage of my life, I was clearly committed to Castaneda's "Way of the Warrior," which for me was a coherent and powerful approach—a philosophy that could be effectively applied to my life, involving humility, sobriety and determination. In addition, it had an esoteric and mysterious ancient traditions flavor, which stimulated my imagination. That's why I naturally turned to it again, in an attempt to find an answer to my questions—especially since my search for inner silence originally came from this same source of inspiration.

Carlos Castaneda had developed a theory on this subject in his final book, *The Active Side Of Infinity*. During his shamanic experiences, he told about his encounters with many typical entities from the traditions of native American and South American folklore. But at the end of his training, Don Juan had decided to reveal to his apprentice the ultimate secret regarding humanity. According to him, we were actually not at the top of the food chain. There were also ethereal creatures, existing on a more spiritual level, and which had established a kind of symbiotic relationship with the human race. While in modified states of consciousness, these beings could be seen by the initiated as vague black shadows, which fed on the energy of humans by using the ultimate deception: They were literally the mind of man, and the thoughts that we heard in our heads were not ours but theirs.

Fundamentally negative by their very nature, they thus constantly instilled ideas of anger, hate, sadness and self-importance, and fed on the energy generated by these emotional outbursts. Don Juan told Castaneda never to speak about it, simply because he would have been called totally insane. But for sorcerers, this represented an enemy to defeat at all costs in order to go beyond the ego. If I wanted to get off the beaten track, my wish was certainly granted!

Saying this abruptly and out of context, it might sound rather hazy, to say the least—or even completely crazy! However, since I didn't have any other explanation at this time, I was wondering... I had to admit that the concept was very well introduced, concluding a work of remarkable consistency on many levels. After all, there are many symbiotic parasitic relationships in nature. Why would we be exceptions? Only an appalling arrogance could make us believe in our absolute domination of our environment, protecting us from any predators. Moreover, it explained many things about the contradictory aspects of human nature, capable of acts of extraordinary beauty, as well as the most cruel and barbaric behaviors. This duality characterized in most religions, the idea of evil which must be constantly resisted, was it just a philosophical concept or something sadly concrete? Why so many people in the world were ready to believe in the devil, for example, and reject the idea of other possible sources of negativity for the sole reason they were less familiar in our traditional cultures?

These questions kept coming back into my life, from various influences. For example, Michael Harner, in his famous book *The Way Of The Shaman*, recounts very similar shamanic experiences about such negative entities. Eckhart Tolle, whose sobriety is exemplary, did not hesitate in his book *New Earth* to also define the mind as a true parasite. Even Hollywood had finally taken hold of this concept, with the well-known *Matrix* trilogy—replace the parasites with machines, and then set everything in a post-apocalyptic world, and you get this daring story which fascinated millions of moviegoers.

Obviously, we are venturing onto terribly slippery ground here. There is a huge gap between the pleasure of a science fiction story and its concrete application in everyday reality. We are leaving the rational world to study something much more hermetic and obscure—some would even say paranoid—considerations. Did I really have to go through this to find my answers? This theory would not necessarily have intrigued me, if it had not reflected the mental split I felt whenever I had to face the attacks—because they actually felt like attacks—from my mind. I ended up living between two alternating states: a relative calm tinged with silence, and waves of negativity I didn't even consciously support, and which seemed to be imposed forcibly upon my mind.

In all cases, real or not, the concept presented by Castaneda had the advantage of creating an even greater detachment from the ego, making its assaults more painful and strange, but also easier to anticipate and defuse. If it was a symbolic trick on the part of the writer to put a face on a too-abstract concept, I must admit it worked wonderfully and was particularly clever. Beyond the self-analysis tool it could represent, everyone was free to give it more credit or not.

I knew I could not honestly ask anyone to follow me on this path, which demands extreme open-mindedness. But for my part, I had to explain what I lived. And in the absence of better options, I had to choose between an outside influence and mental illness. As I felt overall healthy, rational and calm, I decided I had to leave that door open, and give Castaneda's stories the benefit of the doubt—stories which, until now, had proven to be valid and applicable empirically for those who would take them seriously. I had to move on, by exploring all the possibilities, at the risk of getting lost along the way.

EARTHQUAKE

As stated previously, and despite some valuable achievements which allowed me to maintain a certain balance, I began to stagnate in my evolution. This feeling of being blocked and no longer making significant progress manifested at all levels, professional and spiritual. I didn't really enjoy my job, whose prospects kept me barely motivated, and I got up reluctantly in the morning to go to the office. Yet I had a well-paid position, with high responsibility and varied content. Clearly, I had perfectly respected the goals I had been taught during childhood. Because even if I had always been passionate about computer science, I knew my academic background and career were a reflection of the values I had been repeatedly told over: Namely, that to be taken seriously, and not end up as a tramp under a bridge, I should pursue my studies as far as possible. "Diplomas are everything," my father constantly repeated. Which is a vision shared by many people, by the way, and I know he insisted so much out of fear that I might "waste my life."

However, I had to recognize this financial and social security didn't live up to its promises, and didn't bring me the happiness which was supposed to go along with this professional success. I felt useless, and was not really enthusiastic at the idea of managing projects all my life. In addition, professional development in this domain generally ends up in positions where acute "meetingitis" is the usual thing, and where actual production gradually gives way to pure politics. In short, a nightmare for me, who had considered this profession for its concrete and creative aspects.

Stéphanie felt for me, and supported me in this recurring jaded state, in which I wallowed sometimes. I haven't mentioned our relationship so far, but it was the basis of my daily stability. Steph was undoubtedly the love of my life, and we got along extremely well. We had fully compatible personalities, had similar personal stories, and we understood each other perfectly. We were a very close couple, and were lovers as well as friends. We did everything together with perfect mutual trust. She has always been a support for me, and I will never be able to thank her enough for this love.

However, I was so concerned about my own existential questions that I had not noticed the growing turmoil my wife was experiencing. She had a very secretive nature, keeping all her emotions to herself. However, several important issues in her life began to upset her greatly. The first one was not being a mother. Early in our relationship, we agreed that we didn't want children, a stance which is often criticized in our society. We couldn't spend a moment with "friends" without them raising this question. When we answered we were perfectly happy as we were, and that we didn't want to have a child, we systematically bumped into others' incomprehension. This was going from "Ha... I see...," followed by a silence that spoke volumes, to "But you'll see, it'll come one day!" Or even pure and simple judgments about our selfish nature, and the fact we only thought about ourselves. We then spent endless hours trying to justify a decision which seemed natural and honest to us.

Another recurring cliché came from our relationship, which had started early in high school. We didn't escape spiteful tongues, who said this kind of story rarely ended well, because the couple hadn't had time to live their youth. Of course, many were jealous of our happiness. But endless repetition of these judgments began to go round in Stéphanie's mind. Had she made the right choices in life? Wasn't she making a huge mistake by not wanting a child? The biological clock was ticking; was she going to miss the boat? Wouldn't she have been happier with someone else? All the doubts which had been insidiously instilled by her "good friends" made her think. And since she didn't share this with me, I did not realize the situation continued to fester.

In September 2008, events accelerated, making me feel as if a piano had fallen on my head. Stéphanie's behavior toward me had changed significantly, and I didn't really understand why. She was colder and more distant. She had stumbled upon an old acquaintance on the Web, with whom she always had a good relationship. As they reconnected, I understood this man was an attractive potential for her—another world where she might find a solution to her distress. Even though I initially decided to let her handle this situation, I began to get really jealous. In comparison, I felt I had become the boring guy, without spontaneity, nerdy, in other words, someone totally uninteresting.

Obviously, I had no desire to see my relationship implode, especially because of an individual who came out of nowhere, and who seemed light-years away from all the values Stéphanie claimed to appreciate—as far as I could tell. I imagine this is actually what made him attractive; he represented a totally opposite alternative to her current life, allowing her to know whether the grass was really greener on the other side of the fence. In that respect, he was just a symptom of a deeper issue. I knew it would be a mistake to melt down, and give in to anger, blame, or depression. I had to make a tremendous effort, and take the helm of a sinking boat, trying to remain the dignified and smart husband my wife would finally miss—at least that was the impression I desperately hoped to make.

With all these unsaid things, the silence became deafening. Our relationship went really wrong, and daily life became almost unbearable. Day after day, week after week, our marriage went to pieces, and it seemed that every stone of these apparently solid foundations was being crushed, destroyed. The shadow of a potential rival hung permanently over my head, and I could hardly manage my anger and jealousy. As a result, I felt completely lousy and uninteresting, and my self-esteem was down to zero. Of course, I was also mad at Steph, even though I knew that splitting up would be the biggest mistake we could ever make. We spent Christmas separately, in a particularly gloomy atmosphere. I did my best to somehow put on a happy face with my family by drawing on my last reserves. Upon my return to Paris though, we had to get to the bottom of our issues, and make a final decision, as I just couldn't stand it anymore. Stéphanie was also very affected by all this, and felt totally lost. Despite the emotional storm she was in, she finally realized she still loved me and wanted us to stay together.

Obviously, this kind of crisis always leaves a deep mark, and our situation didn't return to complete harmony as if nothing had happened, far from it. We had to rebuild everything, in particular the trust which had characterized our relationship. Stéphanie also was realizing the extent of the damage. She sincerely regretted that moment of doubt, which affected her a lot, and she began to sink dangerously into depression. She had feelings of guilt, of having made a big mistake and having somehow betrayed me, the obligation of having to live now with this malaise and suffer the judgment of my family, to whom she was very close: It was extremely hard for her. Yet, if there was a positive lesson to be learned from this painful story, it was that our relationship was the solid one we had always imagined it to be. And after having come so close to a possible separation, we realized how much we were attached to each other. We had, however, paid dearly for this.

If I recount these events, which are surely among the most intimate and painful of our journey, it is not to expose in an immodest manner a situation that I have no pleasure in remembering. However, Stéphanie and I believe this simple and honest testimony can help other couples have the courage of their convictions, and not have to suffer from the same negative influences which brought us to this difficult questioning. As we will see later however, this earthquake allowed us to unblock a totally deadlocked situation, and to initiate a complete and much-needed revision of our lives. Because the remedy was simply on the scale of the issues we had refused to heal, and that we had left rotting almost beyond recovery: We had needed a fantastic kick in the butt, and we had given it to ourselves unhesitatingly!

The most difficult thing, after this kind of ordeal, is having to come back to regular everyday life, knowing that those same daily patterns were the root of the problem. I came to hate the smallest routine, the smallest habit which previously seemed normal, and which I now suspected to jeopardize my relationship. I was getting paranoid and wanted only one thing: change. Yes, but, to change what? Apartment, work, neighborhood...? After almost losing the relationship on which depended my balance, and which was still very fragile, the prospect of also losing my job was not really comforting. I felt stuck, paralyzed, and anxious about the consequences of my possible inaction.

I was obsessed with the idea I had to act to save my marriage, but I didn't know how to reinvent things in a significant enough way, without destroying the few parts of our lives that remained intact.

Stéphanie was obviously as disturbed as I was. To tell the truth, she had even hit rock bottom. She was angry with herself, and had no idea of how to get out of her depression. She started getting bombarded with increasingly dark thoughts. However, as it often happened, she was the one who made the suggestion that would literally change our lives.

One day when neither of us felt well, she said to me casually: "At worst, we could do your thing... what was it called? Ayahuasca?" I was very surprised, to say the least. A few years earlier, in my research on shamanism, I had watched several documentaries about ayahuasca, a plant used by the shamans of the Amazon to heal their patients, physically and emotionally. The brew concocted from this plant was presented as a purge to eliminate accumulated inner negativity, which caused strong vomiting. Always fascinated by the use of "teacher plants," I had at that time expressed my unexplained attraction to this kind of exploration, stating that one day, I'd be curious to try the experience. Stéphanie had then clearly explained to me that I could go there if I wanted to, but it would be without her: Go and vomit in the jungle, in the middle of critters of all kinds… Thanks, but no thanks.

I was therefore surprised at this sudden turnaround, though it revealed a compelling need to change our life model, even if that meant taking paths which previously would have terrified us.

I know today Stéphanie's suggestion was not an accident, and that it was going to be the source of a radical transformation. I decided to give the idea a chance. "Desperate times, desperate measures," I thought... Despite the fact I was clearly unfamiliar with this kind of adventure—we were not really seasoned travelers, Steph and me—I seized this opportunity and dedicated myself to organizing this trip to the Amazon. More surprising were the enthusiasm and ease with which I set up this project, in an effective and smooth manner. Everything seemed much less complicated than I had imagined. At least I was able to act on something, whatever the final outcome would be, and I devoted myself entirely to this. Stéphanie, in the meantime, seemed passively resigned regarding her former reluctance. She was ready to try any solution, even the most desperate ones. She also wanted to go back to the way things were, to the time when we were happy and enjoyed each other's company without constantly questioning our relationship. If it could work, she was ready to sacrifice everything.

So I looked on the Internet, and after some research, I chose a site named "Ayahuasca Wasi[1]", which seemed simple and clear, and appeared to approach ayahuasca from a positive and spiritual angle. It felt more focused on personal exploration than tourist shamanic folklore and rituals, which felt reassuring to me. Above all, I just wanted to keep things simple.

But what exactly was this mysterious ayahuasca, subject of so many questions and prejudices? I could only rely on the stories of those who had already taken it, and which gave me only a very rough idea of this medicine—which didn't help a lot. Now ayahuasca tourism has literally exploded, and it is easy to find testimonials about it everywhere. But at the time, it was much less mainstream, and information and advice were more difficult to get.

The brew is actually based on the use of two plants, which can vary according to regions and traditions. One of the most common recipes uses the ayahuasca vine (*banisteriopsis caapi*) and chakruna leaves (*psychotria viridis*), which are boiled together for hours. Without going into too many technical details, the most common scientific explanation of the effectiveness of this decoction is as follows: The chakruna naturally contains DMT, a psychotropic substance which is believed to cause the visions and hallucinations. Normally, when one absorbs DMT, enzymes present in the human body are activated and quickly eliminate the DMT in the digestive system. However the ayahuasca vine contains beta-carbolines, elements that specifically inhibit the action of these enzymes. Thus, when the drink is ingested, the DMT elimination is put to sleep, and the substance remains active much longer in the body.

Obviously this "explanation" falls a bit short when we dig into

---

[1] "Ayahuasca Wasi" means "Ayahuasca House" in Quechua. Official site: http://www.sacredvalleytribe.com

the subject, as it is often the case when trying to analyze such subjective and complex processes in too mechanical a way. Indeed, one might think the truly active substance is the DMT coming from the chakruna, and that ayahuasca has only an inhibiting role. Yet some tribes exclusively use ayahuasca vine without chakruna, which may then seem to contradict the above theory. Moreover, mixing chakruna with other enzymes-inhibiting plants apparently gives neither the exact same therapeutic effects, nor the same type of visions.

The shamans of the jungle have a much simpler and pragmatic explanation: What makes this medicine so powerful and so beautiful, is the spirit of the vine, Ayahuasca. By climbing up to the sky above the canopy, it connects humans to higher spiritual planes, like a ladder between two worlds. For them, Ayahuasca is the mother of all plants, a maternal figure whose infinite love and wisdom are put at the service of healing, even if this means exploring the darkest recesses of our being to sanitize them. A purge in the truest sense of the term, which enables cleaning and eliminating painful traumas and deep wounds.

It is fascinating to think about the origins of this mixture. Given the thousands of plant species in the Amazonian forest, and given the necessary duration of preparation—it takes hours of cooking— we can wonder how the natives were able to invent this recipe. A headache for a rational spirit at least: Shamans just tell us candidly the spirits taught them how to do it a long, long time ago.

While organizing our trip, I developed a renewed interest in this fascinating plant, by watching several documentaries and TV shows on this topic. Some were really captivating, such as "Ayahuasca, the Snake and I"[1], or "Other Worlds."[2] Others were simply distressing—I cannot find another term. I thought I knew the shamanic culture reasonably well, and was appalled to see how certain mainstream national TV channels dealt with the subject. Hiding behind a pseudo-journalistic approach, ayahuasca and shamanism in general were systematically shown in a scary and

---

[1] *Ayahuasca, the Snake and I*, a 52-minute documentary written and directed by Armand Bernardi.
[2] *Other Worlds*, a documentary movie by Jan Kounen.

sensationalistic, or even ridiculous, way. This completely distorted the honest and spiritual approach of these men and women, and their quest for healing and transformation. They were therefore depicted as feathered and garishly made-up charlatans, adepts of animal sacrifices and abusers of fragile minds. At this time, I definitely lost faith in some famous shows which dared to present their work as "serious investigations," and which were ultimately an unbearable sequence of approximations and clichés aimed primarily at creating thrills among their audience. I dared not imagine all subjects I knew less about, and whose version I had accepted uncritically from the same unscrupulous media…

My parents, who knew we were getting ready to leave for the Amazon, had stumbled upon the same shows. It took all my powers of persuasion to reassure them their son was not going to South America to get killed by an evil and bloodthirsty sorcerer, and that everything would be all right. Of course, there are charlatans everywhere. Prudence is always good, especially with all the ayahuasca centers blooming every day in the jungle nowadays. But most of the time, a minimum of discernment helps find trustworthy people who have already proved their worth. This clearly seemed to be the case for those we had picked. The ayahuasquero[1] we were going to have this experience with was named Diego Palma: As far as I could see, he had received very good reviews from all those who had already participated in his ceremonies, and who had shared their feedback on the Internet.

The adventurer within me quickly reached his limits, though. I was concerned by my lack of experience as a traveler, especially heading to a destination as exotic as the Amazon. And in those cases, the Internet is not always your friend, as discussion forums are often full of conflicting theories and experiences, adding even more to the confusion. A typical example was about the vaccines. On the Ayahuasca Wasi site, it was made clear no vaccine was mandatory, not even the one against yellow fever—not a single case had been reported for ten years. Treatments for malaria were also inadvisable due to their side effects on the body, as they could spoil the whole experience significantly. I sent several emails to

---

[1] The local name for practitioners working with ayahuasca

Diego, whose patience I salute today regarding my anxious messages. He assured me that, contrary to what everyone said, no vaccine was necessary. I decided to trust him, even if I couldn't help but imagine the health authorities turning us back upon our arrival at Puerto Maldonado, without our international vaccination certificate.

This exhausting need to anticipate everything, and leave nothing to chance, consumed a lot of my time and energy. But June arrived quickly, and we were finally ready to go. We had scrupulously followed the instructions given on the Ayahuasca Wasi site, regarding a few rules to abide by before the retreat: avoid eating too much meat, in particular pork; reduce consumption of salt, sugar and spices; and observe sexual abstinence some time before departure, in order to have sufficient energy and live the experience in the best condition possible. Hopefully, everything would go well…

WELCOME TO THE JUNGLE

The trip didn't go *exactly* as expected. Our journey was rather long, the full trip including the following stops: Madrid, Lima, Cuzco then Puerto Maldonado. We could not do everything in one go, and therefore had planned to spend the night in Lima, capital of Peru. Always leery about potential trouble, I had combed through many hotels comparisons on the net, and had chosen a small hotel in the Miraflores district—reputed to be the safest of the city, and located by the sea. A taxi was supposed to pick us up at the airport and drive us to our hotel; and then bring us back very early the next day, for our departure to Cusco.

We arrived in Lima at the scheduled time, tired from the successive flights. We headed to the carousel, to retrieve our luggage... which was taking quite some time to arrive! Minutes passed, the carousel was now almost empty, and things began to get really suspicious. Our last hope disappeared completely when the carousel stopped and our suitcase had still not appeared. Obviously we were not the only ones. I headed to a desk next to the carousel, to line up with the other unhappy passengers, and explain that we were unable to retrieve our luggage. The person in charge didn't speak English very well, and communication was rather complicated. Also, he seemed pretty nonchalant and sometimes left his desk for a long time without telling us why. And then he was back again, making me repeat my explanation from the beginning.

Time passed, and I turned to see Stéphanie sitting on the edge of the carousel, her head buried in her hands, visibly desperate. Finally the company employee showed me a poster full of suitcases illustrations, and made me choose one close to ours. He then handed me a file, telling me I should call the relevant service in a few days. The document was entirely in Spanish, and the prospect of having to explain my situation on the phone in the same language appeared quite complicated to me, my Spanish being very rudimentary.

With all this, at least an hour had passed since we landed. Night had fallen, and we knew that our taxi—which was supposed to take us to our hotel—was long gone. When we exited the airport, an army of taxi drivers was standing there, calling us for a ride. We decided to cut our losses for the day, and walked to a fairly luxurious establishment located next to the airport. While the price of the room was clearly more expensive, we decided to mitigate this mess by enjoying a small pleasure, always a wise move in this kind of situation. The next day, we would be leaving in the early hours to spend a week in the Amazon rainforest—with only two t-shirts, two boxer shorts and panties, that Stéphanie had wisely put in our hand luggage. The rest of our belongings were in our suitcase. This may not have particularly worried experienced adventurers, but for our first trip to such a faraway country, it began rather badly. All the magnificent organization that had taken weeks to set up was wobbling dangerously.

In our hotel room, I felt a bit lost. I decided to call the lodge where we would spend the week. After several rings, a man picked up the phone, and to my surprise I heard:

- "Allo oui?[1]"
- "You... you speak French?"
- "Err, it seems so, yes..."
- "Oh my, you can't imagine how relieved I am!"

So I explained our misadventures to this person, who had a delicious Parisian accent—at least very pleasant to hear in these circumstances—and who was actually one of the lodge owners. I did not expect to find fellow countrymen in the depths of the Amazon, but the man was very reassuring, telling us not to worry.

---

[1]   "Allo, yes?", in French

Apparently it often happened, and they would take care of everything at our arrival.

The situation was improving, and allowed us to sleep better during the few hours we had before leaving. However, I still had a final concern: this damned vaccine that many people had told me was mandatory. I was hoping we wouldn't arrive at our destination and be refused entry, especially in those already complicated circumstances.

We took the plane the next morning and arrived at Puerto Maldonado a few hours later. I was hugging the walls, expecting to be chased by customs officers armed with giant syringes. Obviously, Diego was right, and there was nothing that could even be close to a sanitary booth. I do not know where people on the web got their information, but they obviously had to be taken with a grain of salt, like many things on the Internet.

Two people were there to welcome us and take us by minibus to the lodge office, which was in the city. We had already met some participants while waiting in the airport, and first contact had been very good. In any case, the small town of Puerto Maldonado was clearly exotic, with its typical appearance and its chaotic traffic. We were taken in hand by adorable people, who took our lost luggage file and promised to find our suitcase. There, we also met Tito, our guide. He was apparently native of the Amazon, about forty years old, and spoke several languages, including French. He turned out to be very helpful and considerate, and, while waiting for the rest of the participants to arrive, he drove us across town to do some shopping: essential items such as toothpaste, shampoo, and extra clothes.

After feverishly filling up a few bags, like good Westerners, our stay in the jungle seemed already less impressive. However, in our impromptu shopping session, we also heard we would take part in the first ceremony the same evening. We were quite surprised, especially since after watching some documentaries on the subject, I expected to do a preliminary diet by ingesting purgative brews meant to prepare us for taking ayahuasca. Apparently, it would not be the case, and I certainly wouldn't complain. This news was, however, made less exciting by the accumulated fatigue of our trip. We were exhausted, and to spend the following night vomiting was not exactly what we were dreaming of at this time.

Once the group of nineteen people was complete, we took a small motorboat to get to the lodge. Along the way, which took forty minutes, morale began to drop. The deadline was approaching, and everything seemed finally surreal. Stéphanie was sitting beside me, completely downcast, tears rolling down her cheeks. My neighbors discussed the giant spider they had seen on the ceiling of their bungalow a few days earlier, and I knew this would not help reassure my wife, who was probably wondering what she was doing here. In the face of this, I was keeping a low profile, and was fervently praying that all those efforts were not in vain.

We finally arrived at the lodge. The place was very cute, well maintained and comfortable. We then met Diego Palma and his wife Milagros. Diego was tall and very slim, with a clear complexion and shaved head. His calm attitude and smiling eyes inspired confidence, and reflected a gentle character. His wife had a more typical Peruvian appearance, with her dark skin and matted black hair. Despite her size—she was a five-foot-tall, slight woman—she exuded an extraordinary vitality. She spoke with an energetic voice, laughed out loud without restraint and had a playful look, like a child in an adult body. It contrasted with the quiet serenity of her husband, and they made a charming couple.

After a vegetarian lunch—we would follow this diet during our whole stay—we were told it would be the only meal of the day. The ceremony would take place the same evening, and we needed to attend it with an empty stomach. We were assigned our respective bungalows, and had the afternoon to get some rest. However, the prospect of the upcoming experience did not really help us sleep. Milagros visited each of us to exchange a few words, which seemed to help Stéphanie, whose apprehension kept growing.

At 6 p.m., Diego invited us to a small presentation meeting. He explained that, even though it seemed rushed, having a ceremony on the day of our arrival was ultimately preferable. This helped participants avoid over-thinking while waiting for the big night. Then all members of the group introduced themselves. Their personalities, ages and nationalities varied. They ranged from a young, twenty-five-year-old couple to a single woman in her sixties, and even a brother and sister trying a family healing experience. Although they remained mostly quiet about their motivations, we felt they were very diverse, either focused on self-discovery and self-exploration, or on a more pressing need to overcome the traumas of their lives.

Diego also gave us some brief recommendations on how the ceremony would take place. We were going to come before him, one-by-one, to receive our cup of ayahuasca. Once everyone had drunk, he would switch the lights off, and would start to sing shortly after. If after some time, we did not feel the effects of the plant, we could come back and take more. Apart from that, he gave us no specific procedure, as the experience might be quite different from one individual to another. However, he asked us to follow two golden rules: The first was to not speak out loud so as not to disturb other participants. The second was more advice on how to approach this common adventure. He asked us to "hold the space" during the ceremony, which meant to remain present, to commune with the group, so that it would become a collective experience where everyone would support the others by their intention.

Finally, if things were becoming difficult, he recommended keeping a simple idea in mind, which could be repeated like a mantra: "Nobody ever died from drinking ayahuasca. And it is an ephemeral experience which always ends sooner or later."

Once the meeting was over, we still had to wait until nightfall. Excitement and apprehension were increasing among the members of the group, and we tried to deal with them the best we could. Finally the crucial hour arrived: It was now 9 p.m. We took our pillows and blankets, and followed a small path into the jungle.

MEETING THE VINE

We walked about 200 or 300 yards into the jungle, on a trail lit by torches placed at regular intervals. We then arrived at the maloca, a circular building the lower part of which was made of wood, and the upper part of a mosquito net. A conical roof covered the structure, similar to a giant garden kiosk, but with the open section protected from insects. It gave the impression of being in nature, while maintaining a thin separation to prevent the intrusion of any unwanted nocturnal visitors.

Diego lit some candles and we sat in a circle on the floor of the maloca, on mattresses provided for that purpose, and next to which were placed small plastic buckets. Everyone was silent, and the atmosphere was very solemn. After a short ritual calling for the benevolence of Pachamama, the Mother Earth, the ayahuasquero took out a plastic bottle filled with an orange-brown liquid. Each person came in turn and kneeled before him to receive a dose. Just before drinking, we had to focus a few seconds on our intention for the ceremony—healing, self-discovery, the purge of a painful experience...

I was almost the last one. I knelt in front of Diego, who handed me the ceremonial cup. I set my intent, which was to get rid of all the negativity I had stored in my life—and God knows there was cleansing to do! I told myself that if I wanted to work in my house, I should first clean it thoroughly to create a healthy environment. I therefore addressed this prayer to the plant and swallowed the brew, whose taste was not very pleasant. Then I sat back at my place, and Diego blew the lights out.

We were now in the dark, surrounded by the jungle sounds. It took about twenty minutes to hear the first effects among participants. Some breathed harder or groaned softly. Others began to vomit. It was impressive to witness the violence with which some regurgitated. I remember one example in particular, where the person literally roared into her bucket. When you are in the middle of the Amazon jungle, in almost complete darkness, feeling the first effects of a substance you don't know anything about, and you hear screams that could have come straight out of *The Exorcist* movie, your heart is in your mouth! The most amazing thing was to realize, the next day, that these terrifying noises actually came from a small adorable lady with a baby face. But at the time, the dramatic effect was total.

As for me, I began to experience changes in my level of consciousness. Like a numbness accompanied by a greater sensitivity to light and sound. The crackling noise of nocturnal crickets literally filled my head, as if they were nestled inside my skull. I felt suddenly a wave of energy rise in me, an overwhelming pressure which took me over completely. I really began to be scared, and my mind screamed at me, "But what the hell are you doing here?!" Everything in me wanted to flee, but it was useless. Like when we ride a roller coaster, and we slowly climb to the top of the first steep slope, feeling the desperate desire to get off. We know we are already suspended in mid-air and we can't do anything about it. We'll have to hang on until the ride is complete.

I had, however, promised myself one thing, before embarking on this journey. Indeed, by watching some documentaries, it seemed that dark and terrifying visions could occur, such as snakes and spiders—and at that time, I was clearly arachnophobic. I had decided that my journey was not meant to scare me, but rather to move forward in my personal evolution, and that this should happen without drama. My intention was therefore to work with complete commitment, but on the condition that I keep things simple without transforming them into a horror movie.

I have to admit Ayahuasca responded perfectly to this request. The first visions came, representing various geometric forms, which I find hard to remember today, as the surge of energy gave me the feeling of being swept away by a tidal wave. I decided to stabilize as much as possible. I gradually managed to regain control—as far as it is possible with such experiences—and I blessed my efforts in learning how to stop my inner dialogue during all these years. Indeed, I was realizing that the negative visions, when they appeared on the edge of my consciousness, were the direct representation of my thoughts and fears. They did not exist as such, but were only a reflection of my own mind, which felt clearly threatened. Therefore, by stopping those thoughts and maintaining silence, these vivid visions vanished immediately.

I tried to keep this precarious balance, going through this tightrope-walking exercise throughout the night. Ayahuasca acted in waves: Pressure increased progressively, until it reached a critical threshold, making me vomit. I then felt immediate relief, as if a huge weight had been lifted from my shoulders. Eventually, after a pause, the plant got back to work and began a new purging cycle. It was fascinating to really feel this interaction with an entity, a fabulous consciousness whose wisdom and benevolence, strength and power, demanded absolute respect.

When the pressure was too great, I asked Her[1] to grant me a few seconds of respite, in order to regain a foothold. Then I told Her, "That's okay, bring it on!" And it started again, even stronger. It really felt as if I was working hand-in-hand with a surgeon, operating on me while I was telling her in real time where the pain was, in order to proceed with a removal. During that time, Diego played guitar and sang with Milagros mostly in English and Spanish. This had a very relaxing and reassuring effect. Their words were comforting and often evoked themes I was currently examining: We were all connected in a perfect choreography. Sometimes they would stop, and there remained only the silence of the night, punctuated by the sounds of the jungle and the expressions of the various participants—who seemed to have more or less pleasant experiences...

In any case, I had almost no visions. When I opened my eyes, I could see the flame from one of the torches outside the maloca,

---

[1] I will regularly refer to Ayahuasca using the feminine gender, as this medicine expresses a strong and loving feminine energy. Shamans call it "La Madre," "The Mother," and this absolute consciousness can often be felt as an almighty and caring Goddess.

creating a mesmerizing strobe effect. I also distinguished thin lines, like labyrinthine forms on top of my usual sight. Sometimes a face appeared fleetingly. At one point I even saw black humanoid silhouettes approaching me. They came to examine me, seemingly curious. I was not afraid, as I was in a state of pure understanding which allowed me to observe these phenomena with total detachment.

Hours passed and the cleansing process continued. I suddenly began to sob, and then to cry like I hadn't cried since my childhood. Surely because of a misplaced sense of virility, it is a behavior I didn't allow myself to have in everyday life. However, it seemed I had literally rivers of tears to evacuate. I cried without being able to stop, but what I felt was not sadness. Instead, it was a huge relief. I was getting rid of years of stress, and just like a pressure cooker, I was finally letting the steam out. The spasms from my sobs felt actually like breathing exercises which brought me well-being.

I had been so deeply immersed in my own experience that I had not been really aware of what was happening around me. However, I realized I had been really agitated, breathing heavily and moving my chest back and forth in a rocking motion that helped me manage the tension generated by all this work. However, when I began to cry, I heard Stéphanie sob next to me. I wanted to know how she was doing, and understood she interpreted my tears as a deep sorrow, which affected her in turn.

For her, ayahuasca didn't act immediately. She remained perhaps an hour and a half without feeling any specific effect, even though time is very difficult to track in this kind of situation. So she witnessed my own states for a while, which in this totally unfamiliar context, had surely been very disturbing—even downright scary. When she began to cry in turn, Milagros apparently felt her distress and came to kneel in front of her. She asked her to blow her nose, and seemed to make her smell the neck of a small bottle. After a moment, I could hear her breathe more strongly, visibly scared. She whispered to me that she was seeing a huge snake eye in front of her, staring at her, and she wanted it to go. Fear was clearly palpable in her voice. She also complained about strong nausea, and I encouraged her to vomit by promising her she would then feel much better. She resisted for a while, and I tried to calm her by stroking her back, and advising her to let go without holding onto negative emotions. Finally, she vomited for a few minutes, and I immediately felt her appeasement after this evacuation. She later told me that once her purging was finished, she blacked out.

Near the end of the ceremony though, her snake visions came back, but this time in a much friendlier manner. She was invited to climb on the back of the reptile, which led her to familiar and pleasant places of her daily life. It literally took her on a walk to reassure her and show her that she had nothing to fear, and all was done with benevolent intent. She also saw us both, walking leisurely on a sunny beach. This vision seemed to accelerate in time, like a film projected in fast motion: We continued to walk in love on this same beach, me with a white beard, and her with a long gray mat, with the promise of a long and happy relationship. Just before the ceremony ended, the snake simply asked her to promise that she would return for the next session, and she accepted.

Diego rekindled the lights. We had gradually regained consciousness, Stéphanie and me. It was about 2 or 3 a.m., but I had the impression of having spent a night in the drum of a washing machine: I was totally washed up, both literally and figuratively.

We didn't leave immediately, and spent a moment with the other members of the group, to prolong the experience and ask each other how things had been. Then we went out of the maloca, and somehow managed to get back to our bungalow, lighting the way with the flashlight we had been kindly lent—ours was still in our lost suitcase. We finally collapsed on our bed, and it didn't take long to fall into a restful, deep sleep, populated with strange sensations and dreams.

QUESTIONS

Against all odds, we woke early in the morning. I had thought I would suffer from the fatigue of the night, but I felt alert. We were, however, well aware of having gone through a very strong process, and to be honest, we considered stopping there and not participating in the following ceremonies. To use again the analogy of the roller coaster, just think of the time you get off the ride, still exhilarated and a little groggy by all these acrobatics. You are glad to have done it, but you don't plan to repeat the experience for a long time.

I felt good, relaxed and light. We met the other members of the group at breakfast, in a warm atmosphere. We had experienced a shared event, and it had obviously created bonds among us. Moreover, when one knows the determination—or even boldness—necessary to initiate this kind of approach, it naturally establishes mutual respect. We were now a kind of tribe, I would even say family, and it would be so till the end of the adventure.

Diego informed us that on the same evening, at 6 p.m., we would have a small meeting during which we could speak and share our experiences. But in the meantime, Tito, our guide, would take us on a walk in the jungle.

So we left in the early afternoon and went into the forest. Tito stopped often to explain the nature of certain plants and their role in the ecosystem, as well as their medicinal use. He seemed to have impressive knowledge on the subject. In fact, he looked as though he came straight out of *The Jungle Book*. He walked barefoot, a machete in hand, and appeared as comfortable as if he were in his living room. I would have not been especially surprised if he had also talked to animals…

I was actually astonished by my surroundings. I had always imagined the Amazon rainforest as a hostile environment, swarming with deadly creatures ready to bite you or jump at your throat. However, this was not the case at all, and even the mosquitoes didn't seem very motivated to attack us. Was it due to the time of year, and was June a particularly good month? The fact is that throughout our stay, we never had to suffer from the "wild" nature of the jungle, which instead felt like a real protective cocoon, filled with peaceful and harmonious life, and a mysterious atmosphere. After living such a genuine connection, it is very difficult to hear about Amazon deforestation without feeling truly heartbroken.

Later in the evening, our sharing meeting took place. Everyone tried to honestly describe elements of their experiences—or at least those they wanted to share with the group. However, some appeared to have difficulties putting precise words on something as abstract and elevated. But real wonder and gratitude already stood out regularly regarding the magic of this medicine. I personally had the impression of having undergone a ten-year therapy in one night. At the end of the meeting, Diego informed us that for the ceremony the next day, when coming before him to receive the plant, we should tell him if we wanted a greater or lesser amount than the previous night. The words "More," "Same" or "Less" would be sufficient to modify the dose accordingly. If we said nothing, he would choose for us.

In my hopeless need to assess all the consequences, I could not help but ask him if taking more would greatly increase the power of the experience. He took a few seconds of silence, as if reflecting on my strange question. Then with an amused and enigmatic half-smile, he simply replied, "Who knows..."

ALL ABOUT LOVE

The next day, we visited the Monkey Island, which as the name implies, is an island inhabited... by many monkeys. We appreciated Tito's knowledge, which was inexhaustible. During our excursion, I reflected on the ceremony which would take place later that evening, in particular my intention regarding Ayahuasca. In fact, my initial goal in coming to the Amazon was to get rid of all the "junk" I had in me. I had the impression of having accomplished this task—at least partially—with seriousness and application, and I was wondering what I could then focus on.

I was particularly intrigued by the sudden attraction I felt towards the people surrounding me. In short, I wanted to hug everybody! And I was so excited that I talked all the time—probably too much, actually. It was an entirely new attitude for me. In my everyday life, I already recognized I had never really felt affection for people. At best, some sympathy... But not the real attraction, the one that makes you feel a void when a person is not there, or when you truly miss someone you want to see again, have a drink, or enjoy a common activity with. This was not an emotion I usually experienced. Which explained why, apart from a few childhood friends, I had not really created tight bonds. Only my very close relationship with Stéphanie allowed me to really express my feelings.

Sensing a genuine connection with people in the group, and even with individuals I didn't know at all, made me wonder. I had the impression of catching a glimpse of something huge, and I decided to dedicate my second ceremony to this exploration. To fully dig into this topic, I would ask the plant to show me what unconditional love was, and teach me to forgive all those who had caused me suffering.

I then realized my desire to stop my ayahuasca experiences had vanished. I felt the benefits were too significant to stop there, and the upcoming roller coaster ride didn't scare me as much any longer. The day passed quickly, and the time of the ceremony approached. Apprehension was palpable among the participants, and we tried to support each other. Having already shared this adventure once made us stronger though. This time, we would go more aware of what the experience could be, and with our solidarity reinforced.

At 9 p.m., we reproduced the same moves as the last time: After picking our blankets and pillows, we headed to the maloca. The atmosphere was heavy... Suddenly someone burst out laughing, breaking the almost religious silence of our walk. I told myself it was a great way to defuse our fears, and took it as a reassuring omen.

After the short ritual Diego had followed two nights earlier, we again passed in turn before him to drink the brew. I decided to ask him for more. Not to prove anything, but since I was finally there, I wanted to live the experience fully. Even though I was still very far from an experienced user, I had felt in my first ceremony that the plant was open to a possible dialogue. If things went badly, I believed I could calm my emotions enough to keep them under control. Stéphanie opted for the same dose as the first time.

The effects of the medicine were almost immediate. Except that this time, they were not a mere wave of energy, but a real tsunami! I was literally washed away by an incredible force I couldn't even understand clearly. What made this experience bearable though, is the fact that this energy was just pure, intense Love. Torrents of love were literally pouring over me, inside me, through me, in a totally ecstatic experience. Obviously, no word is strong or accurate enough to describe this... I kept feeling this uninterrupted flow of unconditional love, similar to vibrating shocks flooding my whole body with sublime blissfulness.

This power, however, created a huge pressure on my body, which was not accustomed to handling such an overwhelming energy. I puffed and panted, and had to make a constant effort to regulate my breathing. I could hardly stand still and had to reproduce this balancing movement with my chest in an attempt to channel this giant wave which knocked me over. Someone next to me, obviously aware of the storm I was going through, whispered softly in Spanish, "my blessings go with you, my brother," and I felt infinite gratitude. I was at one with the Universe.

This love was so intense that I couldn't keep it for myself alone. I extended my consciousness to the other members of the group, and felt their energy. It was as if I could move instantly through the maloca, and stand beside the person I focused on. I heard participants crying, or at least I felt their sadness, and I sent them laughter and joy to support them.

I was filled with absolute compassion, and felt the urge to make an unexpected request: I humbly asked Ayahuasca if She would agree to heal people through me, by using me as her human vessel. I felt an acquiescence, and did my best to support others in their experience. Bill, a big guy, was sitting a few feet from me, and seemed to go through a difficult phase. I *knew* without a shadow of a doubt what he was going through, and that he was about to purge something particularly important he was struggling to get out. I could not tell how, but without having moved from my place, I was also sitting at his side. I perceived myself literally in two places at once, and I "remotely stroked" his back to help him expel a negativity discharge that I knew was imminent. He suddenly went through a violent spasm and began to vomit with unusual force. I cuddled him a little more, encouraging him and praising him telepathically for this success, then came back to my own individuality.

I saw the roof of the maloca as a sort of dome, and had a vision of all participants, or at least their spirits—or souls—ascending to this vault and communing in perfect harmony. It was an absolutely magnificent sight.

Then Ayahuasca began to give me very practical lessons. She was teaching me, as I had asked, what unconditional love was. These insights were like shocks of pure understanding about concepts I didn't need to intellectualize. It was wonderful to feel how the plant sometimes used the activity of the maloca to trigger a lesson, orchestrated in a perfect choreography.

Indeed, people came and went, some to go to the toilets, others to take an extra medicine dose... At one point, someone I recognized immediately passed before me: In a second, I felt the judgment I had experienced about her the day before, during the sharing meeting. I had found her confused, boring, visibly loving the sound of her own voice. I had the impression her speech would never end. In the second she entered my field of "vision," I vomited all those pathetic considerations in a burst, while receiving the following teaching:

> *"You will never be able to Love others if you keep judging them."*

Others would follow all night long, sinking directly into my core being:

> *"You can't Love with jealousy, as you can't Love if you don't trust your partner."*

> *"You can't Love people if you are constantly afraid of what they think of you."*

> *"You can't Love if you always expect something in return for what you give."*

This sublime understanding filled me with infinite gratitude. I couldn't stop whispering "Thank you, thank you, thank you," fully aware of being in front of something ineffable, that my poor intellect was desperately struggling to comprehend.

Then the communication with this divine consciousness calmed down a bit. I felt that in the middle of this indescribable beauty, a part of me, much viler, was trying to regain control—in vain. I looked at the bottom of my bucket, which I had purged into several times, and I perceived a repugnant presence. As if in this unfathomable darkness, in this bottomless hole, were lurking unspeakable creatures from which originated my primitive human behavior.

At the time, and as explained earlier, I still had in mind the image of Castaneda's "parasites," and I thought I had never been so close to feeling their influence: a pestilential negativity emanating from a revolting collection of pests swarming in black and vomit. I had the sensation of having snakes in my brain, trying by all means to clear a path in my mind, using an incredible arsenal of strategies and lies, each one more vicious than the other. I saw these reptiles sneak into my thoughts, and when they were blocked by my vigilance, go back and try a different route. By witnessing those treacherous moves, I couldn't help but laugh at such deviousness. I finally saw how my mind worked, and I could tell it joyfully, "Well tried mate, your maneuvers are really very clever, but you won't fool me this time!"

I knew that if I wanted to go to the bottom of this, I had to "dive" into my bucket, as Alice following the white rabbit. God knows what I would meet in that darkness, and finally I didn't have the courage to do it. I was just terrified about this idea. I still remembered the story of the anthropologist Michael Harner, I had read a few years ago. In his first book[1], he told about an ayahuasca ceremony during which he had seen very disturbing reptilian entities, and even communicated with them. Expressing an arrogant and overbearing attitude, they claimed to be the masters of humanity, which they had secretly enslaved. This was another experience which seemed to reinforce a disturbing theory, through the convergence of testimonies collected during shamanic journeys.

Were my own visions influenced by all my readings, or did these feelings have a very concrete origin? Whatever the answer to this question, my recklessness had its limits, and I didn't want to be the next to confirm the reality of such meetings.

Time passed, and I felt the ceremony would end soon. This made me uncomfortable, since I was still completely under the influence of the high dose I had ingested. However, I didn't want people to see me in this uncontrollable state, once the lights were on. I turned to Stéphanie, who seemed fully conscious, asking her to help me come down. She took my hand, which she patted a moment while speaking to me softly, but nothing helped. As soon as I started to come to my senses, a gentle torpor invaded me again, and I fell down into delicious, colorful visions, filled with snakes displaying fluid movements and magnificent pastel shades. I asked

---

[1] "The Way of the Shaman", by Michael Harner

Ayahuasca to leave me alone, telling Her that I really had to go. She seemed unwilling to do so, and redoubled with wonderful sensations that made me dive into an almost orgasmic well-being.

Actually, the plant gave me the impression of behaving like the lover you need to leave at dawn, and who tells you with a sweet and cuddly voice: "Come on... Stay with me a little more... Please... Just for a moment..." My resistance was the strongest though, and I managed to say "NO!" as firmly as possible. At that moment, I felt I was receiving one of the last lessons of the night about unconditional Love:

"To be able to love, you must not be afraid to say 'No.'
If you're afraid to deny something to others, it is because you're
actually afraid of their reaction, and this fear will prevent you
from loving them unconditionally. In an honest relationship, the
'No' is a healthy attitude, when it is practiced with respect and
integrity for oneself and the other."

Diego rekindled the candles, and I was still floating somewhere in the stratosphere. People from the group came to see me, and I somehow tried to talk with them. But the words echoed in my head as in a hollow shell, and I had the impression that someone else pronounced them—I still didn't quite inhabit my own body. When they saw that I wasn't really able to talk, they respectfully left to allow me to complete my experience. Then Diego came to sit next to me, to exchange a few words with my neighbor. I took this opportunity to tell him ayahuasca was still active, and that I now wanted to come down. If he had a technique or a tip to give me on this subject, I would be grateful. He seemed to think for a few seconds, as he always did before answering a question. Then he said softly: "Yes, I have a tip for you. This advice is: no plan. No plan at all." I looked at him, taken aback, and then thanked him with a smile. He was right, I was really obsessed with control. After all, if the experience was meant to last, so be it.

The big question was: How was I going to walk back to our bungalow in the middle of the night, since I could barely stand up? The maloca emptied gradually, and we decided to try our luck. Stéphanie, loaded like a mule, was carrying all our stuff, while I was already trying to carry myself, illuminating our way with our flashlight in a very approximate manner—I pointed the light as much to the ground as to the tops of the trees.

Steph told me to pay attention to the puddles littering the trail, which she had spotted earlier. Her sentence was punctuated with a big splash: I had just stepped into one with both feet. My good mood did not suffer, and I burst out laughing at the situation. At this moment, I certainly received the last conscious teaching of the night. As if I was totally detached from my ego, I observed myself from an external point of view, thinking, "This guy is nice, after all..." I felt a real tenderness towards myself. I had finally accepted to give up this incessant critical view of myself, and granted myself a bit of kindness and sympathy. And this is where the last lesson, the most fundamental one, came to me:

"You will never be able to Love others if you don't Love yourself too."

Still pondering this ultimate revelation, we reached our destination. I don't really know how, but I managed to get my clothes off, and collapsed on my bed to fall asleep immediately.

ARROGANCE

This time I had to catch up on my sleep after my last nightly marathon. Stéphanie got up long before me and, obviously feeling I was not going to emerge anytime soon, left with some members of the group for a walk in Puerto Maldonado. It was that day that she heard about the death of Michael Jackson. The "King of Pop" had such a worldwide presence that the news had reached even the depths of the Amazon jungle.

Steph returned early in the afternoon, announcing that our suitcase was still to be found, but it was obviously on its way. She also told me about her experience of the day before, which actually had turned short this time. Again, the medicine had been slow to act, and when the first effects finally could be felt, they took the form of visions populated with colorful geometric images. Then she saw the image of a path leading into the jungle, whose entrance was indicated by an arrow-shaped sign. She knew that if she continued, she would have to follow this path, which she refused categorically: She was too afraid of what she was going to discover. Following this decision, the plant seemed to respect her choice, and her state of consciousness quickly returned to normal. She spent the rest of the night quietly listening to songs from Diego and Milagros—and, incidentally, seeing her husband shaking like an epileptic beside her. She also confessed to me that my behavior was perplexing, even unsettling, which didn't really surprise me. But all in all, she had enjoyed this moment of respite, out of time.

Even if the ceremony had been mainly a restorative pause where calm and rest were predominant—and really welcome after those last difficult months—she seemed, however, to have received clear inspiration. In fact, she told me that during the night, and until we arrived in our room, she felt strongly that her purpose was also to support me and help me on my way. Something she had always done, actually. But that night, she had been shown the value of her contribution. This experience with the plant helped her transform a belittling feeling of uselessness into one of valuable support, giving her a sense of accomplishment. She had always thought that her participation was taken for granted, and was therefore of no real value. But she was now beginning to become aware of its importance for me and for our relationship. Our lively walk back to our bungalow on the last evening had been another nice example of this.

I guess that many people would have found that perfect. But I must confess that, oddly, I was a bit annoyed. Instantly, I foolishly interpreted this declaration as her way of transferring all responsibility to me, thus delegating the position of leadership in our marriage. Yet she seemed confident, and even relieved to have understood her role with such conviction—a role she now accepted without qualms. I had not yet realized at the time how right she was, and that our life together reflected this close partnership, where each one could always assist the other. And, of course, our relationship was not one-sided: If she was there for me, I was there for her, also supporting her personal evolution. We thus walked on the same path, side-by-side and hand-in-hand—in a deep and equal relationship, devoid of competition or dominance.

We did nothing special during the rest of the day, and enjoyed a well-deserved rest. It allowed me to chill out in my hammock and organize my thoughts. When I saw Diego walking nearby, I ran to hug him and thank him for his magnificent advice the day before. He smiled and said, "There is much more space now, right?" And indeed, I really felt lighter, less cluttered by my desire to control everything. Moreover, on a more or less conscious level, I knew I had worked on this theme during a part of the night, finally understanding this burden I had carried around for so long, unaware of its permanent presence.

If, after the first ceremony, I had already felt the urge to get closer to people, needless to say that with the night I had spent, I was in a state of almost perfect communion. I took everyone in my arms, and they gave it back to me, showing that I was surely not the only one enjoying the blessings of Ayahuasca. I just loved these people for who they were, without expectations or apprehension, and it gave me perfect happiness.

At nightfall, we began the second sharing session. I took this opportunity to tell about the wonderful teachings I had received, and I presented my sincere apologies to the members of the group for all the judgments I had felt about them. Again, participants had had varied experiences. Some were there for very concrete questions, and all seemed to have been given quite relevant insights regarding the approach they had chosen to explore. Diego announced that the next day, for those who were interested, they would organize an excursion in the natural reserve of Tambopata, through the forest to Lake Sandoval. He recommended we participate, especially if we wanted to reconnect with Mother Earth. He also reminded us that the last ceremony would take place later that day, and invited us to reflect on our intention. He suggested we give thought to our return to modern life, and how we could integrate this evolution into our daily routines.

Of course, we decided to follow Diego's advice, and the next day we were ready for our trip. Rubber boots were in order, as the path we followed in the forest was extremely muddy. We thus passed hours wading through slush, before boarding a canoe to sail on the lake. It was truly magical, and as we were promised, the connection with Nature was unique at the heart of this preserved environment.

However, I hadn't lost sight of the upcoming ceremony in the evening, and was thinking hard about what I could ask from the plant. As in a fairy tale, I had the impression I had been granted three wishes. I had one left, and had to choose it with the utmost care. My two previous experiences had gone exactly as I wanted, and I again began to drift dangerously toward this thirst for control I wanted yet to eradicate from my behavior.

What bothered me above all, was the apparent lack of results for Stéphanie. Of course, she seemed to feel a bit better. But compared to my own experiences, her sessions sounded less intense. I really dreaded returning to France without her taking the opportunity of creating a radical change in her perception. We had come here to seek solutions to our problems, and I wished we would both find as many answers as possible to give ourselves a second chance.

Moreover, Stéphanie had been suffering from various health problems for some time. After having recently healed from hyperthyroidism, which had lasted more than eighteen months, she was still subject to pain in the chest, at the level of the heart. This issue had been lasting for four years now. This wasn't really tachycardia, as her heart didn't exactly race. However, it pounded really hard, producing resounding "boom, boom, boom" vibrations, which made her teeth literally chatter at the worst of her crisis. She had seen several specialists who hadn't diagnosed anything wrong at the physical level, and she was reduced to taking beta-blockers whose effectiveness gradually decreased over time. It was exhausting for her, and she did not see what treatment could relieve her in the long-term.

In short, returning to Paris without having treated at least one of these problems seemed to me like wasting the opportunity we were given. Speaking of letting go, I obviously still had progress to make...

I therefore began to reflect on an intention that, properly formulated, would allow me to have it both ways: first, to help Stéphanie in her experiences, in order to reassure her enough so she could live them without restraint. Then, in the spirit of what Diego had suggested, focus on myself, asking the plant to show me visions of my future. I thought I got my magic formula, and therefore, was very pleased with myself. I was content, and felt prepared for our third ceremony.

Upon our arrival at the lodge, we were pleasantly surprised to find our beloved suitcase. Employees had been adorable, and had left it in front of our bungalow. We felt like two kids on Christmas morning. We would finally be able to put on clean clothes without worrying about cycling through the few we had—especially since the humid Amazon makes drying laundry almost impossible. However, inspired by the lessons I had already received, I couldn't help thinking this momentary loss was an obvious sign: a message to show me how my need to anticipate everything proved to be totally futile. Once the lesson was learned, and after having realized that I finally didn't care that much, the Universe had kindly agreed to return my possessions—or in less elegant words, all my big Westerner's junk—without which I thought I couldn't survive. However, after these somewhat destabilizing adventures, it was still good to return to these familiar objects which reconnected us to our comfort zone.

A GOOD SPANKING

I fine-tuned my intention for the evening a little more, and off we went for our ultimate ceremony. The fascination of participants was proportional to their apprehension: For many people, it was the big night. We settled in the maloca, and when it was my turn to drink the brew—the taste was definitely awful—I silently recited the magic formula that I believed to be as complete as possible. I had opted for an equivalent to the first dose, as the second one had proved to be extremely powerful, perhaps a bit too much. In essence, I asked the plant to allow me to join Stéphanie in her own visions, to support her in her process. And also to allow me to see my future after my return to Paris, because I did not really know how to reconcile what I had just received with my stressful corporate life.

I therefore settled at my place, and waited for the first effects to kick in. Well, they were not really what I expected...

In fact, the first manifestation was auditory, and on top of that, in English. I heard clearly: "You are dishonest." I was surprised, and a little worried—after the unconditional love experiences from the previous session, this kind of message seemed much more hostile. I decided to put it gently aside, and I began to concentrate on my first goal: connect to Stéphanie. A vision of her face came almost instantly in my mind's eye, with impressive clarity and stability. But the second after, I saw this image forcefully torn, as if someone held a big poster and reduced it to shreds. I received a very clear message: "For Stéphanie, I'm in charge! Take care of your own problems first, before wanting to fix others." There was no doubt for me: I had just been literally scolded by the spirit of the plant, putting me back in my place. Who did I think I was? I chose not to insist.

Fortunately, I had the second part of my great plan, i.e. the vision of my future. I started asking questions mentally:

- "Am I going to resign from my job?"
- "Yes."
- "Am I going to die?"
- "Yes."
- "Err, I mean, am I going to die *soon*?"
- "No."

Of course, everybody dies someday, my question was completely stupid... The more I asked questions, the more I wanted further confirmations, to be sure of the validity of the previous answers. In the end, I realized the complete inanity of this approach, mainly because I felt that nothing was written in stone, and that my future would be what I would make it. The more I insisted, the more I felt a kind of annoyance reflected by Ayahuasca, which seemed to tell me more or less nicely that I was a real pain in the butt, and enough was enough.

This perfect plan I had spent the day in forming had now gone down the drain. I made a final attempt, knowing that if I couldn't find anything relevant to study, it would all end up as a total fiasco. I ventured to ask the plant if I could work on the issue of my parents, but without much conviction. My request fell flat. Moreover, I felt I had pushed my luck a little too far, and the plant was now really upset with me. The medicine seemed to yell at me for a minute. But quickly, those harsh energies vanished and turned again into pure love. I had the impression of being an insufferable child who had received a good spanking from his mother, and was now taken in her arms to be comforted. I felt really bad for having been so pretentious and manipulative, thinking with all my arrogance that I could use Ayahuasca as a simple servant obeying my petty desires.

Following this realization, the effects of the brew ceased. I had the feeling that this fabulous ally had finally left me sitting there, like a poor imbecile digesting his lesson in humility. I was fully conscious and alert. Did my beautiful love story with Ayahuasca end that way? Had I messed it up? Yes, apparently, and I almost considered going back to our bungalow, still ashamed of my miserable failure. At the same time, I couldn't let Stéphanie down, as she counted on my support—as well as the rest of the group. I had to accept the situation, and spend the evening in the maloca while totally awake.

I was actually worried about Stéphanie, who began to breathe harder and cry. I heard her beg the plant to leave her alone, and tell Her that she didn't want to go on. She was becoming increasingly agitated and upset, in total resistance towards her experience. I thought this third ceremony was her "last chance," and that Mother Ayahuasca would not to let her go as easily as the previous times. It seemed that, like a doctor who had agreed to defer the due date of an operation repeatedly, the medicine considered now that She should act and proceed with a necessary intervention, even if Her patient was unable to bring herself to do it.

I saw my wife beside me, moaning and sobbing in the face of painful and frightening visions, with the certainty that the spirit of the plant would be uncompromising this time—for her own good, obviously, even if Stéphanie didn't seem to realize it. The night was definitely going to be long...

I tried to whisper gently to my wife, in an attempt to calm her down and encourage her to let go. She replied she felt a force which was trying to catch her and pull her up, and that she did not want to get carried away. I assured her there were no risks, everything was happening here and now, and there was nowhere else to go. But nothing helped. Her long struggle was very stressful, and I directly felt her emotions. In a desperate effort to help her, I tried another risky approach. Of course, I didn't want her to feel guilty, but I kindly explained to her that I was overwhelmed by her struggle, as did the rest of the group, and that her resistance was ultimately as toxic for her as for us all.

This had an immediate, almost miraculous, effect. Obviously, she agreed to suffer in agony, but could not bring herself to include others in this painful process. She calmed down quickly, her breathing became regular, and I felt a huge relief that she finally accepted letting go. I had remained very close to her for a while, whispering in her ear, and I could finally get back to a normal sitting position, and recover from all those emotions. I started to relax deeply, and it took me a while to realize the effects of ayahuasca had gradually increased again in intensity.

I saw a small red glow emanating from a kind of crystal, and I *knew* this crystal was Stéphanie's heart. I saw it compressed in a kind of straitjacket made of metal slabs and chains, as if it had been trapped in an armor much too small for it. This made me think of cars sent to the scrap yard, and which are then transformed into very compact metal cubes. I saw this straitjacket gradually disintegrate to reveal a completely withered and crushed heart, empty of its substance, much as a fruit squeezed to the last drop. I knew I had to somehow "inflate it," and I blew all my love into it—like into a balloon—in order to restore its original form.

When I thought I was done, I suddenly received an image: I saw Stéphanie, arms crossed, standing up in a proud and powerful stance. In the background was a giant pillar. The symbol was clear, and showed me that behind the illusion of fragility, my wife was deeply strong. Like us all, she could, of course, benefit from a healing, but this did not mean that she was weak. Yes, she was literally my pillar, and treating her with condescension would have been a monumental mistake.

The next series of events is a bit confusing, and it is sometimes difficult for me to remember them as a chronological sequence. I lay on the floor to have a break, and my visions consequently seemed to come more "down to earth." I saw the entrance of a tunnel, and was offered to visit the world of… spiders. I knew that this cave was going to take me there and, oddly, I had no fear despite my long-time arachnophobia. I accepted the offer, and then received wonderful visions of spiders, very colorful. I was fascinated by their perfect symmetry, by the beauty of their constitution. I felt that their nature was deeply loving and maternal, quite far from the role of merciless predators they are usually given. I would learn later that, in shamanic traditions, this totem animal is directly associated with creativity, particularly writing. Including the writing of one's own destiny, by the way.

After this fascinating demonstration, I went back to a sitting position, and the nature of my visions changed again. I was looking at a red wasteland, similar to the typical panoramic photos of Mars. I felt I was shown something important, and I knew at a deep level that it was related to the creatures I had already sensed at the bottom of my bucket. I saw beings resembling a crossbreeding between a vulture and an insect. At least that was the very nature they seemed to express: a hive of scavengers devoid of all empathy. I then heard the question: "Do you want to be shown how they feed?" In this role of observer, I was almost afraid to be spotted, but my curiosity was stronger, and I accepted.

I then saw one of these creatures, similar in appearance to a giant black wasp, jump on the back of a man and stab him with a kind of sting into the spine. I understood this was its way of instilling an idea into this person, an idea that would cause negative emotions—fear, anger, sadness—it would then feed upon. I was struck by the total lack of consideration this repugnant creature expressed towards human beings. This reminded me of a documentary I had seen on TV, and which showed chicken farm brutality: in slaughterhouses, an employee grabbed the poultry and threw them against the wall to put them to death. I wondered how someone could get up in the morning, and know the whole day would consist of throwing birds against a wall, in a completely barbarous act. This man had to be totally disconnected from the scope of his actions to be able to endure such violence on a daily basis. I felt the same disconnection with these creatures, this same lack of empathy that humans sometimes express too in their relationship with the animal kingdom: abuse, confinement, trafficking of species, massacres for pleasure or profit...

I started to feel a kind of familiarity, a different perspective that made me understand the nature of these beings. It was clearly negative, but it was simply their core essence, another facet of Creation. These were not "evil" creatures, filtered through my Judeo-Christian moral judgment, but beings operating at a very low level of consciousness, where empathy did not exist, and where only fear reigned—to the point of being their only means of survival. I saw them, lurking in the dark, terrified at the idea of being discovered and losing their only source of sustenance. Basically, they were pathetic, and I couldn't help but feel compassion for such a gloomy and absurd existence.

I decided I had seen enough, and I opened my eyes. I could hear the life of the jungle all around us, and I felt the presence of the forest spirits—benevolent, looking at us and protecting us. I perceived smiling faces coming towards me. At one point, I saw a character dressed as a pre-Columbian warrior, standing in front of me and staring at me. He had yellow eyes, like those of a cat. He had a fascinating presence and a really wild energy, like an indomitable animal. He stepped back and spread his arms horizontally: something came quickly out of them, as if they had turned into snakes or giant vines—hard to say, my vision began to fade away.

At that time, I was surprised to see Diego rekindling the candles. I was still totally in my experience. I was getting very clear, even compelling, messages, without having to interpret them. I simply *knew* beyond analysis. For example, I was told that a person in the group needed to be comforted, with such insistence that I couldn't ignore this information. I had to act on this, but I couldn't move: I was literally glued to the ground. I then asked Stéphanie if she could go and say a kind word for me, which she did with good grace. As soon as this was done, the message faded away.

I was in a state of absolute bliss, filled with love. The participants came to see me, and I tried to communicate this total love by holding them in my arms and kissing them. We were obviously connected, and shared powerfully emotional moments. Diego, seeing that some of us were still in their ceremony, continued to sing and play guitar for a while, which invited the other members of the group to sit in communion. It is impossible to describe accurately the sensations I was feeling. I just had the impression of blending with the surrounding Nature, which offered me a protective and reassuring cocoon. The ayahuasquero was right: Our day trip had allowed us to connect to Mother Earth, and I felt the impact of every step made in this almost organic mud.

I don't know if my state lasted so long because of my forced break during the session, but the effects decidedly refused to dissipate. Diego finally stopped and was about to go. I was still immobilized, and could not envision a return to our bungalow, even on my hands and knees. I would have normally been afraid to spend the night alone in the maloca. But this sense of protection and benevolence didn't leave me, and the idea didn't bother me at all. Stéphanie decided to stay with me, along with another member of the group, Samantha, with whom we had hit it off during the stay. She was actually the young woman who had roared ominously in her bucket at the first ceremony, and who had proved to be a lovely person with whom we had immediately sympathized.

Stéphanie was sitting to my right, Samantha to my left, and I was simply in the best place on Earth. We were sticking together in this empty maloca, lit only by the glow of candles, and I was constantly getting the same message, "You are safe, you have nothing to fear"—message that I kept repeating to my two partners as a kind of litany. We thus remained in this position for an indeterminate time. I was not asleep, I was just basking in the most perfect state of well-being.

Letting my mind wander gently, I could perceive some kind of disorder within Samantha, as if her stomach was totally knotted up. I saw her as an apartment in which all the furniture was stacked upside down. I began mentally to put things in order, and untie all these knots with an unusual confidence. I briefly informed her of my intervention, and she replied, surprised, that she actually felt better and lighter.

We remained silent for a while. Then something odd happened. Without knowing the source of this sudden inspiration, I began again to speak to Samantha. Spontaneously I told her:

- "Excuse me, but... Your father had problems with alcohol, no?"
- "Yes, indeed," she replied. "In fact, he was an alcoholic, and he committed suicide."
- "He is alive," I said without hesitation.
She thought that I had misunderstood her last sentence in English. She repeated:
- "No, no, he committed suicide."
- "What I mean is... He is alive, and he would really like you to forgive him."

And at this point, I sensed with absolute certainty her father's energy—or should I say spirit—and the remorse and regret he apparently expressed.

The words literally flowed from my mouth, without any control or censorship on my part. I was just in a state of absolute certainty, where doubt was not even an option.

Samantha seemed to reflect on this. I imagine that in other

circumstances, this abrupt statement might have seemed brutal and insensitive. Yet in this moment of direct connection, I was sure she understood what I meant. I did not know if her work during her last ceremony had actually dealt with this topic, but it seemed to make sense to her. Anyway, I didn't really control what I was saying. Even if I had wanted to add tact and delicacy, I would have surely been unable to do it.

A few moments later, I began to talk again:

- "Your mother has problems with her legs, does she?"

I had the sensation that she walked with crutches or was in a wheelchair. She replied, almost intimidated:

- "Yes... She recently underwent surgery for her leg, and the surgeon forgot an iron plate inside before the closing. It makes her suffer terribly."

- "And she filed a legal action."

- "Yes."

- "It will end up well, I see you at home celebrating her victory."

She thanked me, visibly troubled. She seemed to fall asleep shortly after. As for me, I stayed awake all night, not losing a second of this magical situation. Stéphanie was dozing intermittently beside me, and feeling her presence clearly participated in this happiness I wanted to last forever. We were out of time, and I hardly realized the day was slowly dawning. When the sun was high enough, I made an attempt to get up, and assessed I was stable enough to reach my bed.

I slept for a few hours, and then joined the rest of the group, who was having lunch. They were now my family, and I could hardly believe we were going to split up on the next day. Samantha pulled me aside to tell me that I really had a gift, and it was a blessing. I shrugged, as I didn't know what to think about it. I had never perceived myself as a psychic, and had actually never been confronted with a similar experience before. I was then baffled, even if I could not just discard what we had experienced that night. It had happened, there was no doubt about it, and I would have to integrate the consequences one way or another.

Indeed, there were many elements to analyze after this

extraordinary ceremony. First of all, I was fascinated by the absolute mastery of Ayahuasca: She had managed to fulfill my request, but by following a modus operandi that She had been the only one to decide—and which I would have never been able to imagine myself. Yes, She had allowed me to participate in Stéphanie's healing. Yes, She had given me a glimpse of my potential. But never in a form that my limited mind could have formulated, nor even merely conceived.

She first showed me my arrogance when I tried to control Her, and destroyed my delusion of grandeur when I thought I had mastered Her use. To teach me this, She had chosen to handle the session in a totally different way from previous times: no purge, no agitation, a prolonged period of full lucidity... She held the reins and decided what was going to happen, and when. Once the message had been clearly delivered, She had finally responded to my request, and even beyond all my expectations. She had allowed me to support Stéphanie, first in a lucid way, then showing me through visions what her heart problem was. And She had especially helped me understand my purpose in the best of ways. Not by just showing me pictures of my future, but by helping me live them literally. I knew now that my true nature was to assist and take care of people—not as the Savior, of course, but in a humble attempt to support them on a possibly difficult path. What She did that night was to make me feel how rewarding it could be, and who I really wanted to be, deep inside me. What a masterful lesson! I felt boundless gratitude...

I asked Stéphanie to tell me about her experience. She had taken a smaller dose than the first time, always wanting to stay in control: She definitely didn't want to let go. At the beginning of the ceremony, Ayahuasca had attempted to induce seasickness by sending her visions of rocking boats, in order to trigger vomiting. It had obviously worked, and she had started to purge. Then she saw herself sitting on a pontoon, waiting with a bit of apprehension for the following events. Then, she saw a white form move towards her, resembling a woman surrounded by a bright halo. She told me that a Roman Catholic could have easily associated Her with the Virgin Mary. This figure came forward again and placed Her hand on Stéphanie's forehead. By this contact, she purged again.

Then came scarier visions. She saw boats going down into an

underground cave. They seemed to descend into depths that she didn't want to explore at all. At this time, she went into total resistance, and that's when I heard her sob and ask the plant to leave her alone. Even if she tried hard to focus on the sound of my voice, she felt like vines or vertical forces were trying to pull her upwards. When I finally whispered to her that her agitation was so negative that it became potentially toxic for her and the other participants, she finally decided to let go. But then, instead of living these dreaded visions, she fell into a complete black hole. She had already done the most important thing: just letting go. There was nothing beyond.

She first thought she had failed her ceremony, which she expected to be some kind of visit to a purgatory of some sort. By experiencing this blackout, and then having soothing visions of boats floating on a quiet lake, she thought she had missed the ordeal she had to undergo. However, she had passed this test successfully, which was "simply" to overcome her fear of surrendering completely.

More surprisingly, after four years of daily heart palpitations, she felt no more pain in her chest—and that state would actually last for several months after our return from Peru. During all that time, her heart had been beating desperately in her chest, like an inmate who thumps at the door of his tiny cell. Through this desperate signal, it wanted to express the emotional confinement in which it was cloistered. She too was afraid of people, had no confidence in others, and had progressively sequestered herself in a dungeon— which initially was supposed to protect her, and had eventually become her prison.

We definitely had plenty to think about, and I was still pondering all these elements when came the time for our last sharing meeting. Each participant expressed gratitude towards the group, Diego, Milagros, and, of course, Mother Ayahuasca. My visions of predatory creatures were still going around my head, and I did not really know if I should talk about them. I came to the following conclusion: If I felt this apprehension, it was only out of fear of how others would receive this story. I was afraid they would see me as foolish or paranoid. But at the same time, was it not my ego pushing me to protect myself, and deny visions that had yet seemed very significant to me? I remained pragmatic:

Either these beings really existed, and maybe were influencing me at this very moment, pretending to preserve my reputation. Or they did not exist, and in this case... Well, I'd surely be seen as a wacko, and that would be it. It was ultimately a question of courage and integrity regarding my experience, and I decided that my self-importance did not justify suppressing information that I had received for one reason or another.

So I shared the nature of my visions, which left more than one dubious—I could see it on their faces. However, I was surprised by the reaction of some, who during my account claimed having had similar visions. They made reference to some sort of "mosquitoes," whose arrogant and overbearing nature closely resembled what I had felt myself. Nevertheless, I knew this was hard to swallow for someone who had not experienced this contact first hand, and I did not try to convince my audience. I simply added that if these creatures really existed, they represented a formidable challenge for human beings, where the balance of power was clearly against us. This is why it encouraged us to be even more forgiving with our relatives, our parents, and even our enemies, keeping in mind the overwhelming negative influences they could be subject to. We had to see beyond this mask of the ego, beyond the tyranny of the mind, to feel the magnificence of their profound being. And love them for who they really are.

We spent our last night together. We were tired and somewhat destabilized by all the things we had experienced. We knew that the next day, the separation would be difficult—even if somehow, we were happy to go back to our homes and daily lives. Lives that, obviously, would never be quite the same...

BACK TO THE TWILIGHT ZONE

The next day, we got up early to leave together. The atmosphere was tinged with joy and melancholy. Everyone exchanged email addresses and took final photos in an attempt to capture the last moments of this incredible experience. We boarded the boat that would take us back to Puerto Maldonado. As we moved away, it was difficult not feeling choked up, especially when seeing those who had welcomed us so kindly, standing on the dock and waving goodbye. By coming to the Amazon, I knew we were going to have a very nice trip, but I did not expect to have an exceptional human adventure there...

Again, our trip back to France didn't go exactly as expected: Our plane was forced to turn around in mid-flight, and after landing in Lima, I was able to email my office that I could not return the next day. To tell the truth, resuming my activity in my Parisian company seemed completely surreal to me, and this delay was definitely welcome. When we finally arrived in France, we were surprised to see once again that our suitcase was missing. At this moment, it sounded like a running gag, which made us laugh. Another way to observe a significant change in our attitude: Nothing seemed so serious after all.

Therefore, I took a few extra days off, firstly because I felt the strain of all the hours spent in airports, but also because I really needed to take stock of the situation. I felt a little lost. What was I going to do with everything I had received in Peru? Ayahuasca had been such a wonderful guide. How would I now go on without this precious help? The prospect of leaving this magical world, and returning to the drabness of my working routine, made me rather depressed. In truth, had I listened to myself, I would have run and bought a plane ticket, to go back there and become an ayahuasquero. But I knew that ditching everything would not be inconsequential. Life in South America is more rustic, and mastery of ayahuasca demands years of apprenticeship, diets and retreats in the jungle—at least according to the ancestral traditions of the shamans of the Amazon. Leaving my country, my family, my friends, and involving Stéphanie in this upheaval had huge implications for both of us.

The most frustrating thing was to know that the use of ayahuasca was totally prohibited in France, requiring me to go abroad if I wanted to continue exploring this path. It remains legal —or is at least tolerated—in other countries in the world, including a few European ones. But in 2005, the French authorities classified it in the category of narcotic drugs, because of the presence of DMT in its composition. Access to this medicine, even controlled, was strictly proscribed while ignoring its therapeutic character— character that makes it yet quite different from illicit substances that many take for recreational purposes. It has also been proven by scientific studies that it doesn't create any addiction: To the contrary, it is used in detoxification treatments in Peru, with very significant results[1]. It would seem that the perennial fight against dangerous cults, regularly waged by opponents of all kinds in France, also weighed heavily in this prohibition decision.

However, I am the first to say this is a very touchy subject. The power of this plant is clearly not to be taken lightly, and its use should be practiced in a controlled setting, with skilled and responsible facilitators. Ayahuasca is not "trendy," it is not "cool," and this really isn't the best way to have fun at a party. This is not "junky stuff," as some could easily claim. I personally never took

---

[1] TAKIWASI, created in 1992, is an officially registered non-profit organization and is recognized by the Peruvian Ministry of Health. Its broad objective is to revalue the human and natural resources of Amazonian traditional medicine, and to develop a true therapeutic alternative to face drug addiction. More information: http://www.takiwasi.com/

drugs, I don't drink, I don't smoke, I have a healthy diet, and I give the greatest attention to my good physical health. I would be the last to encourage regular drug consumption, whose damaging effects don't need to be proven.

However, here we are in a different situation, where the confusion with those harmful products is tempting. But such confusion is now unnecessary in the face of many serious studies. Why then continue to deny what has been repeatedly demonstrated? Simply because of a too big cultural gap with the traditions of another continent? I am convinced that ayahuasca represents an unprecedented opening in an often-overlooked aspect in our Western world, which prefers to focus on mechanical rather than holistic healing. However, used in a safe environment, the results are actually verifiable—and I don't speak here only about my personal experience. The testimonies of people who have benefited from this medicine, both physically and emotionally, are innumerable.

Everything is a matter of perspective. Hopefully, over time, attitudes and stances will change, allowing reconsideration of these hasty decisions that rob us of a valuable tool. Especially since scientific reports on the subject are not lacking, and would help constitute a very strong case in its favor. In 2008, Peru actually declared ayahuasca "a national cultural heritage," acknowledging its therapeutic qualities, and its ancestral cultural values. A stricter legal framework could minimize the potential risks, which have, of course, to be taken into account: intervention of reliable practitioners, physical and mental patient preparation, psychological counselling to understand the effects of the medicine, but also preservation of the plant, whose sustenance would be obviously threatened by a too intensive and unregulated exploitation...

Moreover, and to be perfectly honest, many excesses were recently witnessed in Peru, related to tourism developing uncontrollably around ayahuasca. To me, this can only plead for a deeper and more open reflection on all these questions...

Anyway, beyond all these considerations, I had to return to work. It was then with a certain reluctance that I proceeded to my company headquarters, on a Monday morning. My supervisor was smoking a cigarette with colleagues outside the entrance of the building. Seeing me, he couldn't help but have a jaded smile: "Sorry to welcome you with this, but you are expected..." He showed me a very upset email from the big boss, which he had received during the night on his phone. It was about the outrageous fact that the menu located at the top of the screen on our main web site was offset by a few pixels. For him, everything was "messed up" and, in essence, we were a band of amateurish incompetents. He had summoned me to his office, and I had to go and see him upon my arrival.

Please, kill me. Now.

Finally, I kept hugging the walls during the whole day, and managed to avoid a potential reprimand, probably because of an unexpected meeting that prevented ours from taking place. This did not stop my other colleagues from running after me, with a whole bunch of "urgent problems," that passed way over my head at that time. I had the impression of being in the Twilight Zone. I was seeing some of my closest co-workers—for whom I had a sincere affection—stare at their screen, grayish complexion and grim eyes, wondering how they were going to fulfill their objectives, each one more absurd than the other... and I really began to wonder what the hell I was doing here.

A few weeks passed, during which I could not help but feel this constant disconnection with my environment. Paradoxically, I felt closer to my colleagues, and my office regularly became a temporary refuge where they came to confide in me. I must say that I could hardly hide the impact our trip had had on me, and even though I was careful not to talk about ayahuasca at the coffee machine, the changes were too blatant to try to mask them—and I didn't want to play a character I no longer was, anyway.

The most visible element was surely my dress, which changed from the full black clothing I had always been wearing for many years, to the outfit of the perfect little adventurer: trekking pants, ankle boots and khaki shirt. I had carefully chosen a mortician uniform since my arrival at the company, believing surely that it gave me a sophisticated style, and found it now completely sinister. People seemed to actually enjoy my new look, and I was the first to be surprised. My recent assurance seemed to inspire my colleagues, who obviously welcomed any change, even the smallest one, like a breath of fresh air.

However, I had to accept the obvious: It no longer worked. I couldn't believe any longer in all those issues that once made me heavily stressed. I had always determined that if something disturbed me in my work, it would be an opportunity to acknowledge my weaknesses, and overcome them. Resigning would have then been considered a retreat in the face of adversity, which I didn't allow myself to do. But I had now reached a point where indifference had replaced apprehension. I felt like I had pressed the fruit to the last drop, and there was no more juice to extract from it.

Facing this realization, I resolved to go and see my supervisor, informing him of my desire to leave the company. As this departure was not due to a touchy reaction, but motivated by the simple fact that my job did not fit me anymore, I agreed to stay for six extra months. That would give the teams the necessary time to reorganize, and to recruit someone to replace me. I was in no hurry, just relaxed for having taken a decision in alignment with myself, without fear or resentment. It was as if my experience with ayahuasca had finally rid me of this paralysis which had been preventing me from changing track for so long.

By the way, this inner harmony allowed me to spend the best six months of my time in this company. Letting go, and not being afraid of what my professional environment was going to impose upon me, radically changed my relationship with others and my work. It wasn't just the relaxation that one sometimes feels by leaving a job, with a devil-may-care attitude. On the contrary, I had made it a point of honor to fully achieve my mission until the last day, but from a radically different angle, steeped in the teachings I had received in Peru.

I realized one thing had changed: my perspective on what this professional experience was supposed to be. If I had adopted this new point of view from the beginning, I would have learned as much, or even more, sparing me this tension and anxiety—and even this cynicism—that had characterized those last years. My relationships with others would have also reached another level. It was clearly obvious in the change of attitude my colleagues showed now towards me. My new openness, which was apparently contagious, automatically established a sense of trust in our interactions.

If I had a final lesson to learn from this work, it was the contrast between the situations I had experienced before and after our trip to the Amazon. A kind of ultimate demonstration that everything is subjective, and that each experience is literally constructed from our own internal state. Even the worst bosses can miraculously soften in contact with someone who exudes a genuine sense of peace. I do not say that life in the company was transformed overnight into the wonderful land of Care Bears. But undeniably, it had become much more enjoyable.

I must say my mental state had been deeply impacted. I felt regular "energy discharges," which sometimes put so much pressure on me that I had to take refuge in the toilets and calm down. It was not unpleasant—nothing to do with anxiety attacks—although this feeling would be difficult to describe. To take an image, it would be like exposure to bright sunlight, after coming out of a dimly lit building: We squint and put our head down, in front of this blinding light, and yet we can enjoy this comforting heat which always feels good. But, as one could guess, the suddenness of these changes was not always easy to manage. For example, when this happened in the middle of a meeting, I had to remain stoic, and do my best not to make involuntary grimaces generated by these rapid bursts of energy...

Another remarkable change: My mind had become very quiet. But where was this "parasite," which had made my life so complicated?

By the way, ask me today if I still believe that invisible beings exist, which would insidiously feed upon our energy by instilling negative thoughts into our mind, and I will answer that I don't—or at least that I do not know. After all, I have no way to confirm or refute this belief. I can only make a decision based on my personal convictions. All I know is that this concept now feels based primarily on notions of fear, and even paranoia. Lovers of global conspiracies will surely find this disturbing idea attractive, but this kind of approach no longer corresponds to what I want to believe.

Moreover, even if it has the great advantage of causing a very effective distancing with the ego, it can lead to a certain non-accountability of individuals: If I think negatively, this is not my fault, it's my parasite causing me trouble! I then react, in conflict with another part of myself, which may go against this desired inner peace. In short, this idea will have served me for a while to move forward, and explain an experience I had trouble understanding. If it still had to prove something, it would be that all approaches can lead to an expansion of consciousness. There are no good or bad ways, nor true or false paths, just an exploration that always benefits from a greater openness.

Then why did I talk about this disturbing theory, at the risk of losing some readers on the way, who may have considered all this as mere delusions from a nutcase? Well, because it actually contains a profound teaching. Indeed, as the Buddhists say so rightly, there are only relative truths. In other words, what is true for us is simply True. These certainties are going to affect all the perceptions of our earthly existence, and define the nature of our experience of life through the filter of our convictions. There is not one single reality, but as many as there are individuals.

And that's where the wisdom of Ayahuasca comes again into play. She could have tried to convince me that my thoughts were wrong. She might have wanted to force me to reject them in the name of Truth. But instead, She encouraged me to integrate them even further. As if She wanted to tell me, "Okay, you believe in the existence of these creatures? Then explore this path fully, because this belief is well worth another, and is finally equally applicable. But in this case, see these beings in a new light, and perceive their pitiful lives, hidden in the shadows, and immersed in an eternal fear. Feel compassion for these enemies, and realize that it is unnecessary to fight them. Understand their very nature and accept their behavior, by replacing revolt with acceptance."

It took me a while to understand this idea, which is of fundamental importance: For me, the art of Ayahuasca, and finally of spiritual evolution in general, happens through integration and not segregation. To be able to work on an issue, whatever it is, one must first own it, embrace it fully, even if it appears frightening or disgusting. Only by facing one's fears and weaknesses, and accepting them, can one hope to transform them.

The visions I had received had a simple purpose: to allow me to tame this rebellious mind, by literally understanding its point of view in a symbolic way. In order to make peace with opponents, one must first be able to understand their motivations.

Today I know that the virulence of my ego, and its sometimes overwhelming despotism, revealed its fear of annihilation. The mind is terrified at the idea of disappearing in favor of our spiritual evolution, and tries by all means to keep things under control.

To explain this concept more clearly, I would like to use an analogy from the corporate world. Imagine a head of department in a large company. This person is not especially competent in all areas, but by dint of intrigue and opportunism, he finally managed to reach this coveted leader position. He finally has control. And to keep that control, he thinks he has to handle everything, to secure everything, for fear someone notices his deficiencies and unmasks him. He exerts an absolute presence, and wants to participate in all decisions, all meetings, all projects. Does it ring a bell?

Now suppose that shareholders of this company decide, however, that this person needs help, and appoint a very competent and perfectly legitimate colleague to assist him. You can easily imagine the reaction of our man: With an obvious unwillingness, he will do everything he can to make this collaboration impossible, even by sabotaging the projects they work on. In other words, apply a "scorched earth" policy, where if he doesn't succeed with his methods, nobody will! Because if his gross incompetence is exposed in full light, thanks to the experience and the exceptional effectiveness of his new teammate, this will also highlight his own uselessness, and will result in an inevitable sentence: his dismissal. Which for him means death, the end of everything.

Then here is my conception of that duality, existing within each of us. On one side, we have our mind, literally scared to death and with limited means, but ready to use the most twisted maneuvers and most despotic behavior to stay in power. And on the other side, a much wiser and elevated aspect of ourselves, which relies on love and peace, and has the intuitive ability to solve many issues in a simple and elegant way—let's call it the "Higher Self."

In everyday life, our mind is naturally at work: It maintains its dominating position with an iron fist, and uses a whole bunch of tricks involving doubt, fear, anger, devaluation, which are all debilitating. It is even more inclined to do this, as it is itself inhabited by these same emotions of anguish, putting itself into a situation of absolute control where any failure can mean its own end.

Needless to say that when a person focuses more and more on her spiritual development, wanting to reconnect with her higher self, her mind doesn't agree at all. Its communicative fear redoubles, it begins to resist and panic, and inner conflict can grow. We can then witness this dichotomy I mentioned previously, the expression of two wills which seem diametrically opposed, and which can sometimes lead to an impression of split personality. This duality is so strange, that one can sometimes wonder legitimately about one's psychological balance—or even to build more speculative theories, such as energy parasites.

When we understand that those emotions of ill-being, fear, sadness, which can lead to real despair, are primarily generated by a conflict of interest between two aspects of ourselves, we gain access to an absolutely invaluable tool. As said above, we then realize segregation and struggle cannot lead to reconciliation: We must find common ground, where those different facets of our personality can be expressed in harmony.

Our mind also has its good sides, of course. Without it, our perception would not have this consistency and stability, and its analytical capacity is extremely valuable when it is used wisely. And the higher self is perfectly complementary, because it is designed to convey intuition, imagination and inventiveness. They are actually designed to work in harmony, something we totally lost sight of—especially through our rational education which gives full powers to our poor mind, totally overwhelmed by the weight of this responsibility.

As Einstein said: "The intuitive mind is a sacred gift and the rational mind is a faithful servant. We have created a society that honors the servant and has forgotten the gift."

For me, here is the secret to begin a journey towards a place of inner peace. The mind will probably not let go easily, and the best approach remains a pure and simple negotiation. In other words, as a business partner, explain to the mind all the benefits that it could gain from this association, while ensuring it that its role is valued and appreciated. And use the same arguments that could convince two entrepreneurs to merge their respective companies, to create a stronger and more prosperous entity under an agreement where both parties would win. I do not speak here of a mere philosophical thought: We literally need to make a strong plea to the mind, being sure to use the best arguments to persuade it that it is in its best interest to work hand-in-hand with the higher self.

I suppose it may seem a bit odd. Yet, when we accept that this recurring internal conflict stems from a lack of coordination between two aspects of ourselves—and that one of them feels so threatened by the other that it uses, as a dictator, violent coercive methods—we understand how our own being can become a battlefield inducing permanent struggle.

And that is what Ayahuasca had so subtly taught me through these visions: "Learn to love what you consider your enemy, to understand its nature and what motivates it. Then embrace it, and make it an ally." This understanding was not only an intellectual concept. It had offered me a silence and a calm I had never known before, and which I had previously attempted to reach through overly belligerent approaches. Acceptance, integration of all aspects of myself, this was the real centerpiece I had been missing all that time.

ROSS

All those realizations did not happen in one day. Even if I had understood what didn't suit me professionally, I didn't necessarily know what to replace it with, to continue to earn my living. I just wanted to be of service to other people, and finally feel useful.

In addition, I found myself facing another deeper apprehension, about how my family would judge my sudden change of course. Even if I was convinced this was the way to go—or at least the path I had followed so far didn't fit me any longer—I couldn't help wondering how to present this to my parents, among others. As I said before, I had always made a point of satisfying the hopes they had placed in me, and I can't recount all the times my father had encouraged me to continue my studies. I obviously understand the loving reasons why he insisted so much... So I had constantly put tremendous pressure on myself during my school career not to disappoint him, and I didn't want to start now. Despite being an adult, the filial love is always a very strong bond.

I have to admit, however, that this approach had failed to make me really happy—which was yet my father's intention when he advocated for my material success and my financial security. Because this vision of things had obscured a fundamental principle: It paradoxically brought me to sacrifice my well-being and happiness on the altar of social success. I could certainly shine in society, but inside, I had completely faded. And the worst thing was that I had not been aware of it until then. I was a prisoner of the values of my little world, where all this seemed perfectly normal.

I then hoped to preserve the support from my family, which was very important to me. Of course, upon our return from Peru, I had to explain my experiences to my parents, who were surprisingly understanding and open minded, especially for people who had never really heard about shamanism. Their concern before our departure was more due to the misinformation they had been subjected to, than to a real hostility towards a practice still pretty much unknown in our Western culture. I had done my best to tell them what I had experienced, in a sober and pragmatic manner, while trying to explain the enormous impact it had on me. And I realize now how grateful I am for their listening, and the respect and love they have always shown me.

But a few months later, with my recent resignation, I was undergoing a drastic transition. I was actually putting into practice realizations that, until then, could have been considered as mere whims—just a nice exotic experience to store in a corner of my mind, while continuing to live my regular Parisian life.

I had the feeling Ayahuasca had opened a door to a world so vast that I had only discovered a tiny part of it. And I still needed to learn how to embrace those radical changes, and explain them to those around me. I wanted to continue this exploration without, however, having to return immediately to Peru. I then began to look for possible alternatives in Europe.

To my surprise, I stumbled upon Ross Heaven's website, the shaman who had helped me ten years earlier to heal my nephrotic syndrome. And by a huge "coincidence," he had created a center in Spain the same year, where he organized shamanic seminars which included ayahuasca ceremonies. Apparently, Spanish law was still sufficiently tolerant to allow this type of activity. A retreat was organized in September, three months after our adventures in the Amazon, which seemed perfect.

Stéphanie was not very keen about the idea of repeating this experience so early, as it had been clearly tougher for her because of her resistance. Yet benefits were already apparent, and our home life had become much more peaceful—even if some ghosts of the past still occasionally showed up. We had understood our love was sincere, and that we were deeply attached to each other. We had allowed ourselves to be badly affected by many negative influences, which had created unbearable, and yet totally unfounded, doubt about our relationship. However, she said she still had many things to understand and integrate before undertaking another journey with the plant.

I seized this opportunity to invite Jeff, my childhood friend, to accompany me. My enthusiastic account of our jungle trip had definitely intrigued him, and convinced him to experience the blessings of this medicine. We therefore packed our luggage, and left for our guys' escapade. My personal intention was to use this new retreat to revive and develop what I had felt in the Amazon, especially during the last ceremony: a meeting with benevolent consciousnesses, or "spirits," and who had sent me precious messages and delicious sensations of love.

The seminar would last for five days, and include two ceremonies, interspersed with various teachings on shamanism. The center was in the region of Malaga, in the countryside, in the middle of olive groves. The place was very quiet, ideal for a meditative retreat—nature was still beautiful, and weather very pleasant, at this time of the year.

We were warmly welcomed by the members of the center, and could then see that our group would be more intimate than in the Amazon, limited to only seven participants from various places. I finally met Ross, who did not exactly match what I had pictured in my mind: The first time I saw him, he wore deformed sweatpants studded with bits of straw, a pair of plastic sandals, and had slightly bushy hair. He was kneeling in his garden, dealing with the many species of plants he had gathered. This neglected appearance was quickly forgotten as soon as the man addressed us. Indeed, he exuded a calm confidence and a typical British reserve, which gave a hint of the depth of his spiritual journey. He just seemed self-assured, and gave the impression of being totally unconcerned by what others might think of him. He spoke in a detached tone, in a slow voice that was almost hypnotic when we listened to him during our shamanic workshops.

As Ross had a more "Western" approach to shamanism, based on the use of the drum and light trance, our stay would be punctuated by sessions involving discussions and practical exercises, keeping the ayahuasca ceremonies for two special evenings. I confess I was impatient to participate in these ceremonies. Would they happen in the same way? Would the atmosphere of the Spanish countryside and the presence of another master of ceremony radically change the nature of the experience? Was I going to receive lessons as inspiring as in the Amazon? And what effects would Jeff also benefit from? So many questions for which I was burning to have answers.

The first day, Ross introduced us to various concepts, including the importance of the use of plants, considered by shamans as valuable allies in the process of healing and the communication of fundamental teachings. This session would therefore be dedicated to identifying our own teacher plant, i.e. the species directly connected to our being, and willing to help us on our path. Ross was going to play the drum for twenty minutes so that we could enter into a light trance, go through this shamanic journey, and obtain the vision of this particular plant.

The session began, and it didn't take long to achieve this state of slight trance. We were in a small, comfortable room located in an outbuilding of the property. I surrendered to the sound of the drum, and images came unexpectedly quickly. I was actually quite surprised, because I had already tried this experience at home with audio recordings of drumming sessions, but had a lot of trouble creating clear visions of my journeys. "Creating" is the important word here: I realize that my laborious efforts to shape mental images were finally the cause of my inefficiency. By letting go, and simply allowing a state of receptivity, visions generally come by themselves. If the intellect gets involved, wanting once again to control the process, it invariably trips over itself.

Thus, I clearly saw an olive branch, in front of a clear blue sky. I felt the roughness of the bark of the tree, its ancient nature, its gnarled and withered trunk, and its timeless personality imbued with wisdom. I felt a real attraction to the ideas of calm, stillness and grounding it evoked, and I spent a moment contemplating and immersing myself in its essence.

Then I returned to my original intention of better understanding the events I had lived in Peru, including the communication with "spirits." I had another spontaneous vision: a plant whose stem was splitting into several branches, like a chandelier, and tipped with small white bells. At the center of this plant, where the stem was divided into several parts, occurred a strange phenomenon: a repetitive pulse, similar to the very deep sound produced by a gong. Whenever this pulse occurred, it created a vibration that was going up along the stems, and shook the bells in a crystalline ringing—a "BOOOOOOOOM," followed by a "TINGLINGLING." Something told me that this plant, by this distinctive music, favored the communication with the spirits—these small bells being a way to invoke them, to invite them.

When the session ended, Ross asked us to share our visions, and then invited us to roam the countryside and look for our plant, in physical form this time. I cannot forget the amused pouting of my companions, knowing that we were literally in the midst of a sea of olive trees: "Okay, you won't kill yourself on this one!" Jeff threw at me with a falsely reproving tone.

So off we went into the surrounding fields, and obviously, I didn't have to look long to retrieve an olive tree branch. My second discovery was most troubling, though. I stumbled upon a plant strongly resembling this chandelier tipped with small bells. I would later identify it as Conyza, a widespread species in Europe. However, I never managed to find the exact same variety I had seen in Spain, and which was surprisingly similar to my original vision.

Of course, some will only see a coincidence here, but when you begin this kind of magical journey, this is just one of the many synchronicities you constantly encounter on your way. Jeff, for example, had the vision of a green oak tree. He had immediately gone in the direction which had, after a pretty long walk, led him right to this tree. Just to be sure, and to challenge his findings, we had looked all around the vast area we had explored, to see if we could find another specimen. Without success. As if the only tree in the vicinity had directly called him to it. After all, this plant was supposed to be his power ally, and this kind of curious detail gave weight to an experience that was becoming more and more intriguing. At least, it was fun!

Night had fallen, and the time arrived for the first ayahuasca ceremony. Some were a little nervous regarding this new adventure —our group was mainly composed of people who had never taken the medicine before—but the atmosphere was generally relaxed. Ross cleansed the room with a short ritual, and explained how the ceremony would unfold. First, he informed us he would not sing during the night: He wasn't going to pretend to be a Peruvian shaman, or a specialist of the "icaros"—these soothing and repetitive songs supposedly taught to the healers by their plant allies, while they are in altered states of consciousness. He would therefore play CDs containing icaros recorded by various "maestros" of the Amazon, collected during his travels in South America. Regarding the always delicate question of the amount to take, he advised to start with a small dose. With a new shaman, and a new brew, even more experienced participants should always be careful. We could always go to the next level during the second ceremony, if necessary.

Ross passed the bottle to each member of the group, who had to blow a puff of smoke, taken from a pure tobacco cigarette—also considered sacred in American traditions. This would clearly not improve the taste, and I carefully kept my tube of toothpaste at hand: It was a tip given to me by Milagros, Diego's wife, in Peru. She also had great difficulty swallowing the medicine, and regularly had to resort to a small amount of toothpaste on the tip of the tongue, to mitigate the disgust she felt every time.

I formulated my intention to strengthen my communication with the entities I had already met, and swallowed the contents of the small bowl Ross handed me. The taste was indeed awful, although the quantity was substantially smaller than the one I had taken a few months ago.

The effects were much gentler and more progressive than during my last experience. Actually, I was more aware than other times, almost doubting the action of the brew. But when I tried to get up, and felt I was not really able to move, I realized I was well under the effects of ayahuasca. This turned out very interesting, by the way. Not being taken into the fireworks of visions and energies allowed me to feel the underlying healing process taking place behind the scenes. I was just watching discreetly beyond the veil, seeing the medicine at work.

However, I had a few strange visions I could not necessarily interpret. I saw several giant figures, like bright and colorful statues resembling Hindu deities. I was a small butterfly flying next to the head of a gigantic goddess. Another spontaneous image, just as surprising, showed me rows of fetuses scrolling before my eyes, as if I was witnessing the assembly line of life itself.

I heard Jeff breathe heavily, and then was certain we were very closely connected. Like slightly different expressions of the same energy, which would explore similar but parallel paths. I was also sure that our current work on ourselves was directly related to the relationship we maintained with our respective fathers, and the education we had received.

All this was pretty subtle, and felt through successive flashes. I then tried to reconnect to my primary intention. In response to my request, I saw again the Inca character I had seen during my last ceremony in the Amazon: a strong warrior, or a shaman, painted face and strange eyes. He was spinning before him a long, decorated staff, then stopped to present it to me in a vertical position. I asked him his name, and received something resembling "Quachahualpa."

I then decided to seize the opportunity, and asked him if he was willing to help me on my way, and support me in my new altruistic activity. He "answered me" bluntly and with a certain authority. "Yes, I will help you, but only if you honestly and seriously dedicate your efforts to support others." On receiving this powerful response, I deeply felt what this statement involved: all the necessary self-discipline, and all potential pitfalls I would have to avoid; the extreme commitment this approach would require; and doubts, weariness and discouragement I may inevitably feel. I was thus earning a precious but demanding ally, who would only put his energy at the service of a respectful and honorable cause.

I was shaken by the strength of this pretty rough and uncompromising—almost severe—message. Today I realize this clarification was necessary, because it focused on the crucial aspects of any approach dedicated to helping others. I had to understand it wasn't just a game to be taken lightly, used simply to rebuild another social mask compatible with the new character I now wanted to be. First, I had to humbly realize the importance of the commitment I was taking, as well as its ultimate purpose, before asking for external assistance in this work.

The effects of ayahuasca, already very gentle, began to dissipate. I had yet again a small series of visions related to entities. For example, I saw a ball of pulsing energy, which came to visit me while expressing a bouncing and jovial personality. For some unexplained reason, it seemed related to an Asian concept. I also saw a circle of childish spirits dancing on the ceiling of the room—unexpected participants who had invited themselves to the ceremony and happily shared this special moment of celebration. These apparitions marked the conclusion of the ceremony, and Ross rekindled the lights.

The night had been quiet, and I hadn't heard anybody vomit. The dose had been probably too small to cause strong physiological reactions. Or maybe this introduction had simply been a gentle and peaceful first contact. We returned to our room, Jeff and I, too tired to talk. We postponed the reporting of our respective experiences till the next morning.

SHAMANIC JOURNEYS

After a night of dreamless sleep—incidentally punctuated by Jeff's resounding snores—we felt pretty rested. I felt my friend was struggling to put his ideas together, and communicate about his experience. I guess its abstract nature, related to the lightness of this first contact, did not help him find the right words.

His first intention was simply to heal. Being overweight caused him joint pain, and his desire was to improve his overall physical condition. He hadn't had visions, and everything had actually happened through various bodily sensations. He had felt heat in his shoulders and knees, the parts that hurt the most. The plant had obviously dedicated this night to purely physiological manipulations and healing, without other purpose than relieving pain and recurring energy blockages. All in all, his experience had not lasted very long, and everything had gone smoothly. We later learned that the rest of the participants had felt more or less the same type of effects.

The same morning, and following the Amazonian tradition, Ross invited us to take a flower bath. He explained to us that after this kind of ceremony, shamans practiced ablutions with a preparation made of petals, which depended on the nature of the work: There was one to increase power, another to promote serenity or to cleanse... A member of the center staff brought a basin, filled with an exquisitely smelling floral liquid. We were all lined up in swimsuits, waiting with apprehension to receive an icy shower, since the morning in the Spanish countryside was particularly cold. Ross had also taken a perverse pleasure in maintaining the suspense, making us believe until the last moment that the ritual was only effective if it caused a freezing shock.

Finally, the person who had prepared the bath obviously had mercy on us, as the water was warm and smelled really good. A real treat. It felt great, and we came back a few times to receive this beneficial purification. We were then covered with flower petals, which we had to keep on our body until they fell naturally.

The afternoon was going to be interesting, since it would be dedicated to an interactive divination experiment. Indeed, we were going to work in pairs, and in turn, go through a shamanic journey for our partner. The goal being to receive information that could be useful, regarding the themes that he or she was exploring. Ideally, it would include getting a vision of a plant suitable for this particular process. As we were an odd number, we formed a trio composed of Jeff, Ron—a friendly Australian fellow—, and myself. Ron was going to journey for Jeff, I was going to do it for Ron, and finally Jeff would do it for me.

We settled comfortably on the grass, in the sun, and Jeff communicated his intention to Ron, which was to seek general advice on how to better manage his life. Ross began beating the drum and Ron went into a light trance, while we were waiting quietly, our eyes closed. At the end of this first session, which lasted about fifteen minutes, Ron admitted he had had no visions of plants. But he had felt very strongly the recurring theme of low self-esteem, and that Jeff should deal with this topic as a priority to feel better in his life. My friend seemed to agree.

Then came my turn to journey. Ron explained to me that he wanted to work on some of his past activities, which he was not necessarily proud of. He did not go into any more detail on the matter, though, and I started the exercise by relaxing as much as possible. The images came quickly: I actually expected a vision of a medicinal plant, but I saw a huge oak tree on the top of a hill. Its branches went in all directions, and I knew it represented the symbol of expansion of consciousness. What I was told, at this time, was that any experience is an opportunity to evolve. Like a solid oak that grows inexorably, Ron's experiences were many stepping stones he could use to mature and expand. Then suddenly came a second image, that of a reed. Here again the message was clear: It called for flexibility and leniency. It was the symbol of true justice—not one that judges blindly and punishes systematically, but instead, one promoting understanding and a fair outcome above all. No self-flagellation, no life sentence, but a verdict which advocates compassion and forgiveness. The remorse Ron felt this day was the best evidence he had changed, and his past actions had allowed him to understand the individual he no longer wanted to be. I shared this message with him, encouraging peace and self-acceptance, as guilt was no longer appropriate.

Finally, it was my turn to receive advice. I expressed my desire to understand how to treat a persistent pain in the knees, which had lasted almost a year, and which I couldn't get rid of. I could not crouch longer than a few seconds, and even sitting with crossed legs quickly became uncomfortable. Jeff returned with an interesting piece of information: He had had a vision of me in the middle of an arena, where the terraces were occupied by dictators yelling at me. I recognized myself completely in this picture, and I had no trouble associating these tyrants with the pressure I could feel in my professional environment, and even in my life in general.

When Jeff shared this thought, I suddenly remembered that a similar message had been given to me the day before by Ayahuasca. I had a real problem with authority, and this pain in my knees was directly related to my refusal to bend in front of others. As if I had set wedges behind my knees to make sure I would always remain standing, even when faced with the more coercive behaviors. Unfortunately, these wedges made me suffer too. Jeff told me he had also received the image of an olive tree, the plant that could help me with this problem. Strangely the first idea that came to me was related to olive oil: Should I symbolically "oil" my joints to become more flexible? It seemed pretty relevant.

Finally, Jeff told me about one last vision, that of a cactus with big flowers. I could not help thinking about the San Pedro cactus, another master plant used in the shamanic tradition of America, and which I had regularly heard about. These repeated references were perhaps a recurring call to experiment with this new medicine. I decided this sign was strong enough to seriously consider the possibility of working with this plant, should the opportunity arise.

When we shared our feedback with the rest of the group, I was amazed by the relevance of the information received overall. From the outside, an observer surely could not help but find this too good to be true: Indeed, that a group of "ordinary" people could suddenly become clairvoyants, with only the help of the throbbing beat of a drum... Difficult not to suspect these people had embellished their experiences, or even invented them so as not to give the impression of falling behind. And yet... Admittedly, those perceptions resonated powerfully with the individuals concerned.

Personally, I think that drinking ayahuasca the day before had been a real game-changer, and had facilitated access to other levels of consciousness. We were not in an urban seminar, with participants coming with their minds still full of daily worries—and which they may struggle to disconnect from. Here we were in the middle of nowhere, in a completely foreign setting. The ceremony of the night had had a significant effect on our ability to perceive subtle energies, and this seemed finally normal, natural. It seemed we felt no obligation to get results during our exercises, just a peaceful detachment and an honest desire to explore our potential, beyond the limits commonly accepted in our logical and rational world...

Evening came, and after a frugal meal—we would definitely not gain weight in Spain—Jeff and I set out to walk in the surrounding countryside. It was very dark, and we sat down in a field to talk. I shared with him the impression I had received at the last ceremony: that our current problems were strongly related to our education, and the relationships we had built with our parents. After talking for a while, we decided to go to bed. Lying on my bed, and just before falling asleep, an unexpected vision came to me. I clearly saw a white wolf looking at me, and then walking away, inviting me to follow it. But I was very tired, and I quickly fell into a welcome sleep.

THE WOLF SPIRIT

The next morning, Ross explained we would repeat the experience of the first day, by performing a shamanic journey to find our ally. The difference was that, this time, it would not be a plant but a power animal. Indeed, shamans work extensively with animal energy, totem symbols whose properties they use to gain strength and protection. They thus call for their specific abilities to overcome certain difficulties, and to find inspiration in their daily practice. We would therefore go into this light trance again, and expect an animal would come to us. We would then meet each other, consciously sealing a pact with this spirit, which was already present in our lives on a subtler level.

I let myself go, trying to relax while focusing on the sound of the drum. The vision which arose suddenly, that of a wolf, surprised me in many ways. First, because of its suddenness and clarity, but also because of the memory of the night before. How had I not made the connection earlier with what I had seen before falling asleep?

So the wolf was there, present in my mind. We were in a snowy landscape, and we began to play together, rolling on the ground. It was a really delicious experience, and I put my face in its thick and soft fur. I had never really been interested in wolves until then, preferring the cats for which I have a real fascination. But right now, in this special moment, I felt a great connection with this animal. And I was also starting to "know" what it meant to me, and the teachings it had for me. The first one being endurance and constancy: I saw it walk for miles in the snow, never giving up or turning back. Another of its intrinsic qualities was undoubtedly its sense of family and loyalty to its clan.

This last point strongly resonated within me, as this theme had recently resurfaced in my life. Indeed, upon my return from Peru, and feeling a little lost regarding the next steps I would make, I had considered all options. Including leaving France to throw myself headlong into this mysterious universe I had literally fallen in love with. Considering a possible departure, I then faced many hesitations. Stéphanie didn't want to go and live in South America. And what to do with our little cat, who had become a real member of the family over the years? Imposing such a trip on her could not be undertaken lightly, especially since one of our friend's pets had been denied entry to Peru because of health restrictions. If this happened to us, Steph would be totally desperate about it—and I would too. I was thus faced with many concerns, which had nipped in the bud any departure for a country I did not know much about. I felt paralyzed, and naturally began to wonder if my loved ones prevented me from realizing my full potential. Were they obstacles to fulfilling my destiny? Should I cut the cord to be free to take risks?

I wasn't proud of these thoughts, especially about those I loved the most, and who gave me essential support in my daily life. But, sometimes, I didn't know if it was still an excuse for not acting, and not taking the path that seemed to call me so strongly. And that's what the wolf expressed: My family was of paramount importance to me, and the idea of abandoning it was completely against my nature. A sense of attachment and belonging filled me, and I knew that all these questions had been a new manifestation of fear of uncertainty. They did not match my values or my desires. Safety and respect for the ones I cherished were my priority, and my own happiness was also dependent on their presence by my side.

I remained in that energy for a moment, enjoying the impact of these soothing certainties. Then the drum rhythm accelerated, indicating the end of the journey. The group shared their experience. Jeff had clearly seen an owl—which, I would learn later, is a symbol associated with wisdom, intellect and sacred science. As he was working as a researcher, this animal definitely suited him perfectly.

The afternoon was dedicated to various creative activities,

aimed at expressing the visions we had seen in our journey, as well as with ayahuasca. We had an artist among us, and she kindly offered to paint tattoos for the second ceremony, which would take place on the same evening. With enthusiasm, I asked her to draw a wolf head on my belly, so that it could be present with me during the night.

When the time came, we met again in the same room, sitting in a circle. This time, Ross didn't blow smoke into the bottle, as the tobacco had been mysteriously swept away by strong gusts of wind a few hours before. My taste buds were not going to complain... So I went with the idea of asking for a higher dose, the last one having been a bit light. On the other hand, I was puzzled about what to ask for. I was not especially inspired, and my mind couldn't come up with new requests. So I decided not to insist, and I humbly asked Ayahuasca to show me what I needed to know.

The effects came again gently and gradually. It seemed other attendees were going through the same mild experience, and some quickly came to take an extra dose from the shaman, apparently determined to not miss out on this second attempt. I would spend the rest of the night as a toothpaste distributor for my companions, attempting to mitigate the taste of these successive shots—which may have been particularly sickening for these brave candidates.

Personally, I preferred to stick to the initial dose, knowing how ayahuasca effects could be delayed. I slowly entered a sweet trance, and I leaned my head against the wall behind me. I had a first vision: I "saw" the spirit of the wall. It was a white serious face, very similar to the heads of the Easter Island statues. I felt its absolute immobility, as if it was meditating in a deep silence, impassive since the dawn of time. I finally understood what shamans said when returning from their journeys: That everything has a consciousness—the tree, the mountain, the rock... I just came into contact with the "soul" of the wall, and I grasped the magnitude of Existence: Everything that surrounds us is only pure consciousness.

I stayed connected to this feeling for a while, then Donna, Ross' assistant, came to take care of each of us. She poured a very pleasant-smelling liquid on our heads and faces, which relieved me a lot. At this moment, my neighbor Mike was out of the room, and had not been able to take advantage of this beneficial treatment.

When he finally came back to sit in the circle, Donna came again, and applied the same care to him. All this was happening in the dark, of course, and in an altered state of consciousness where the sounds were magnified. I had enjoyed the smell of this lotion so much that I craved a second application. But after Mike, Donna went directly out of the room, passing me by.

This sequence of events connected me immediately to a deeply buried emotion, proving to me once again that ayahuasca ceremonies were perfectly orchestrated plays, allowing us to work on our themes in a very meaningful way. In fact, it had made me identify a recurring concern: the fear of being neglected, of being left out. When Donna went out after caring for Mike, thus leaving me waiting for attention I would not get, I realized how this sadness and apprehension were underlying feelings in my everyday life. I had to always be the center of attention, always be the top of the class, and never be the one who is invisible—at the risk of being left on the side of the road. In other words, the syndrome of the ugly duckling who is always afraid of being rejected, and who is obsessed about being accepted by others, and mattering to them. A rather paradoxical feeling, since I had been handicapped in my whole life by a pronounced shyness, which didn't allow me to verbalize this need.

But this realization would soon take another form, even more explicit. Indeed, the next moment, Ross also went out of the room. And Ayahuasca then made me follow this emotional thread, to confirm my fear of abandonment. I was definitely terrified at the idea of being left alone, of people disliking me and rejecting me. Like all those outcasts in our society, who beg on the street and whom nobody talks to any longer. Pariahs we even avoid looking at, and who reflect to us our own fears of exclusion. Yes, I was scared to death of being excluded, professionally, socially, emotionally... And my behaviors compulsively revolved around this threat I had to avoid at all costs. It wasn't obvious at first, and the people who knew me would not have necessarily defined me in this way. And yet, I needed to face it, and be aware of all the ploys I had developed to hide this huge weakness.

As a consequence of this revelation, I had a strange vision about Mike. I knew he had long been suffering from digestive problems and stomach pains. In this vision, I was standing in a tunnel, in what I thought was his intestine. Next to me sat a jaguar, an animal I had already perceived as an ally when it came to explore my fears. Then I saw Mike rushing toward us. His face was distorted by terror, eyes bulging. He was pursued by a giant ball that rolled behind him, like in the famous scene of the Indiana Jones movie. I asked my jaguar companion to help him, and it pulverized the ball with a ray that went out of its eyes... Did I mention it was a strange vision? Mike stopped, out of breath but grateful, and he thanked us.

Suddenly a new ball appeared in the distance, rolling straight to us! Mike screamed when spotting the danger coming, and set off running like crazy. During all this vision, I was told this was the process he had been living for so many years. Each of his fears—symbolized by a giant ball threatening to crush him—rolled in his digestive system. When he managed to neutralize one, a new one arose, as if he had put a coin in a candy vending machine. And there he went again, in an endless attempt at escaping his torment.

Speaking of digestive system, mine was also roughed up by Ayahuasca, which was a first. Stomach aches twisted my bowels, and I finally had to take refuge in the toilets. I saw the connection of all these related events, and the whole process of elimination. Then I came back to my place—in the Amazon, Diego had insisted on the importance of keeping a cohesive circle, and I shared this opinion. We were a group and had to stick together. Especially since Jeff, who had purged a few moments before, kept breathing heavily. He was the only one throwing up, by the way, but I was delighted for him. I was picturing all the negativity he had symbolically expelled, and the relief he would benefit from this.

The effects of the medicine were slowly fading, and the ceremony eventually ended. Jeff and I were half-asleep, and we quickly went to bed. I was still in a severely nauseous state, and I wished I could finally throw up. But I hadn't, so I took a bucket with me in case the purge happened in our room. I sat down on my bed, unable to fall asleep. Ayahuasca obviously continued to work. I closed my eyes, but I was not really reassured. Jeff had probably fallen into some kind of coma, and I was then alone in this big dark room, knowing I was no more in the protected space of the ceremony. I didn't want to think about the possible danger involved with my situation, and I decided to pull myself together.

Despite the fact my eyelids were closed, I continued to see the room. Close to the back wall, I clearly perceived the circle of happy spirits I had seen during the previous session.

Suddenly I "saw" a humanoid luminous being in the middle of the room. He began to move very slowly toward me, as if he was moving in slow motion, like an astronaut walking on the moon. He shone a golden light, which pulsated around him in concentric circles. He had a hood on his head and I could not see his face. This profusion of details made the vision even more realistic and impressive. Eyes still closed, I knew he was now in front of me and my bed, and I was paralyzed by fear. I dared not move.

This presence finally vanished, but fear made me realize I surely had to purge something. I knew I was badly influenced by all the stories of witches, ghosts and bogeymen which had always fascinated me—and which had caused me many night terrors during my childhood. And I understood this conditioning was a hindrance to my exploration, as I probably expected to run into a demon or a malicious spirit one day or another. It was clearly a handicap, and I knew I would have to overcome it to wander further through those alien territories. I had the feeling that there, then, in this context where I felt very vulnerable, I would have to confront something dark and aggressive in order to win a final victory over my fear. But with the spooky things at the edge of my consciousness, I decided I would not be brave enough for tonight. I had the time to mess with this kind of challenge later.

This acceptance seemed to soothe the nausea, and I began to breathe and relax. I rested my head against the wall and had a final vision: I saw the drawing of a face, as we often see in the anatomy manuals, but looking up at the sky. There was a bouncing arrow pointing to the forehead, as if to symbolize the idea that data were directly "downloaded" to the brain, at the level of the pineal gland—also called third eye. Seized by that last picture, my mind was really beginning to get saturated. Tired, I decided I had had enough for tonight, and I laid down to slip into a protecting and peaceful sleep.

TUNING IN

Awakening was a bit difficult. I still needed more sleep, but I forced myself to get up for our morning meeting. I would never have missed out on the adventures of the day before. On the other hand, I was less excited by the prospect of the flower bath...

We met in the usual room, where everyone shared their experience. I was obviously anxious to hear Jeff's report, as we hadn't yet had an opportunity to talk. The effects were significantly stronger than the first time for everybody, and he was no exception. This time, his intention was focused on understanding better what was wrong in his life, and receiving messages to learn how to be happier.

He had been destabilized by the much stronger action of the medicine. For a moment, he had struggled against loss of control. Then, realizing the ineffectiveness of his attempts, he had quickly decided to let go and surrender to the healing process. He had then had the vision of a huge snake coming towards him: It had opened a gaping mouth, and swallowed him completely. According to shamanic tradition, this typical vision is particularly symbolic of total acceptance from the plant.

After this impressive vision, everything went dark. Then came images of purple and yellow spirals, similar to DNA helixes. Jeff then found himself in front of a huge wall, which he followed by sliding on its surface. It was covered with golden leaves and symbols, and its construction was reminiscent of Inca architecture, with its huge, perfectly fitted stone blocks. Jeff had thus kept hovering, to finally be faced with a huge double golden gate, whose handles were also gold circles. He knew his answers were behind that door. According to Ross, it was also a recurring symbol linked to knowledge.

At that time, Jeff vomited. Then came fleeting, but very clear visions of his childhood, which he was literally reliving. He understood he was seeing what was behind the door. He especially reconnected with the age of four or six, when his mother took him to school. He was remembering his despair, his sobbing and the deep sense of abandonment he had experienced at that time. Again, he felt this fear of not being wanted, of being left behind and being abandoned. Obviously, this corresponded to my very own themes, and I could perfectly understand what he was struggling with. My impression that we were exploring parallel paths got even stronger...

Healing came through the reconsideration of these fears: From a new adult perspective, he realized this perception of abandonment was biased, even unfair to his parents. His underlying impression of not having been wanted, of always having been a burden for them, didn't seem believable to him any longer. He then understood the situation from a much higher point of view. Obviously, this had done him much good.

Mike, meanwhile, was in a bit of a state. He had taken at least three successive doses, as he hadn't immediately felt the effects of the medicine. They were only delayed though, and had finally triggered after the ceremony. He had then spent an extremely intense night in his room, tripping like crazy. In the end, the amount he had taken was just huge, and he seemed to have a massive headache. He kept mumbling that he was "totally wasted," and by the looks of him, it was easy to believe. However, he had done an amazing job during all these hours. When I shared with him my vision of the giant ball, he thanked me and said that this was exactly the process he had also identified: the permanent creation of new threats to escape, in a perpetual headlong rush.

We then went for the traditional flower bath, whose delicious smell fortunately compensated for the discomfort of a shower in the morning cold. The rest of the day was devoted to the integration of these experiences, and our reflection on their impact on our daily lives, once we returned to our respective homes. It was the second time I participated in an ayahuasca retreat, but I was already beginning to identify recurring elements: the impression of having shared something exceptional, the testimony of a fast and deep process among the participants, and the feeling of belonging to a new family. The next day, when we set off by car to the airport, I couldn't help but feel sad, deeply moved by the idea of leaving my companions.

Our return to Paris went without incident, and I said goodbye to my dear friend. I knew I had to return to work two days later, and the idea seemed no less surreal than when I came back from Peru. However, I knew I was now in a transitional process, and this perspective greatly softened the shock of returning to my office. I had a few months to go before leaving my job, and I decided to fully assume my role till the end. Even if at that time, my interest was more than ever dedicated to other subjects which had always fascinated me, especially shamanism.

During my research, I stumbled upon a documentary which was not directly classified in this category, and which yet had a major influence on me: *Tuning In*,[1] a movie dealing with the "channeling" phenomenon. This practice consists of going into an altered state of consciousness to retrieve information supposedly sent by various entities, or at least a higher aspect of ourselves. This could be compared to mediumship, even if the latter has often been associated with communication with dead people, or even spiritualism. Here it is more achieved by a light trance, through which very diverse energies can be expressed, in many different ways: verbally, but also through singing, drawing, or any other physical or artistic form.

My old self would have immediately been skeptical about this practice. People who speak in an "automatic" way, supposedly inspired by discarnate entities... I would have quickly thought this process was suspicious regarding its authenticity. Yet two things strongly attracted me in this phenomenon: First the nature of the messages—which showed a surprising consistency—touched me at a deeper level than I would have imagined, and seemed to me both positive and constructive. But above all, this discovery finally allowed me to put a name on what had happened to me during my

---

[1] *"Tuning In, Spirit Channelers in America,"* by David Thomas and Matthew Klinck.

last ayahuasca ceremony in the Amazon. I had started to speak spontaneously, without intellectualizing my words. They had flowed from my mouth, apparently suggested by the benevolent presences I had felt during this memorable night. After having experienced this personally, I was much less inclined to play smart, and dismiss it out of hand, by classifying it as "New Age humbug."

By studying the art of channeling further, I realized the content of those transmissions—which were mostly based on the ability of humans to evolve to a new level of consciousness—found a special resonance within me. A resonance I had not felt since my reading of Castaneda's books, actually. Like a logical continuity in my personal evolution, forming a coherent whole with my previous research and my recent shamanic experiences. Everything seemed to blend harmoniously, thus opening new prospects to explore. By the way, I realize my ayahuasca ceremonies had probably opened my consciousness to a level beyond intellectual comprehension. Many underlying elements had been given to me, allowing me to accept this kind of premise with a more receptive and tolerant spirit.

The topic which fascinated me—and which was also in line with my previous research—was linked to the very nature of reality. Many spiritual and esoteric traditions often define reality as an illusion. But this concept remains vague as long as we do not experience it first hand. The use of plants like Ayahuasca, or any other way to enter altered states of consciousness, then allow us to better understand this idea: We realize this experience, although different from daily "reality," is just as viable and is only one perspective among countless others. Life is not only limited to our usual lucid state of consciousness, forcing us to classify any other kind of perception as "illusory and unreal hallucination." On the contrary, all perceived experience can be considered valid, and there are many points of view under which we can approach our existence.

Even quantum physics today corroborates this more subjective view of things, by defining the universe as an abstract energy whose physical manifestation depends above all on our conscious interpretation. Change this interpretation, and the universe becomes literally something else for you—and not only on a psychological level, but in all the more concrete aspects of your life.

As with all my previous explorations, I decided to digest these concepts, by integrating them in a pragmatic way, and see where it would take me. Actually, putting it immediately into small narrow boxes would prevent me from grasping a subject as vast and open. I would take the measure, step by step, of the infinite possibilities it could open for me. My reality had never seemed so fragile, so uncertain, based ultimately on an arbitrary belief system whose foundations had been shaken beyond any repair. I would have to review it completely, gradually revisiting everything I had been taught through my education, and my social conditioning. This fundamental questioning was going to be as exciting as it would be destabilizing.

A SHAMAN IN PARIS

The date of my professional departure came quickly. During my last weeks at my company, I could not escape the fateful and recurring question from my colleagues on what I was going to do after. I remained evasive, unwilling to reveal the experiences that had caused this upheaval. It was an opportunity to realize how many people I worked with were deeply dissatisfied with their situation. They also felt the need to escape the social shackles in which we all had gradually—and voluntarily—imprisoned ourselves. However, fear of the unknown, of cutting the single rope that supposedly prevented them from falling, represented a decidedly formidable opponent. Some openly admitted it, while others took refuge behind various reasonable-sounding excuses which poorly concealed their frustration...

If I had to acknowledge a major benefit from ayahuasca, it was the temporary relief from feelings of anxiety and insecurity, giving me access to undying optimism and confidence. As if I had unknowingly received the assurance that I was always supported, and that the entire Universe only wished my total success.

My positive approach was constantly challenged by the fatalism around me, though. After all, was I just a little crazy, or totally unrealistic? My grim mind tried to come back and show me the inconsistency of my actions, added to all the risks I faced. Yet it kept bumping into the excitement caused by these new perspectives, and the joy of finally being in tune with myself.

I started thinking about what I wanted to do once my contract was terminated. I had the idea to create an alternative therapy center, or become a spiritual counselor—or "coach," to use a trendier term. I had the urge to quickly put a label on my activity, but all that came to my mind didn't really match my aspirations. I deeply felt the nature of what I wanted to do, without finding an easy way to express it. "What do you do?" I did not imagine a simple answer to this question. What would I put on this damned business card?

Yet, I gradually realized the role I had played all my life, as a confidante, an assistant, a supporter for people who were facing great emotional difficulties. I knew I had the ability to listen, and that I could help people by sharing all the challenges I had myself experienced in a constructive way. And the love revealed in the Amazon could now express itself more freely. That energy was too powerful to be kept locked in a closet! But particularly in France, this kind of activity was, for me, reserved for psychotherapists or psychiatrists: People who had a nice diploma hanging on their wall—irrespective of their innate qualities of empathy or compassion, by the way. Here, one tends to call anyone who did not follow a "serious" curriculum a "quack" or "guru," resorting to cynicism or despise. And if I still had a deep concern, it was the fear of being seen as an impostor.

Hence my idea of a center, which I now realize was just a way of disguising the problem. This business manager status would have allowed me to have a more recognizable and acceptable label. But deep inside, I knew this administrative approach was far from the energy I wanted to express. What interested me most were human relationships, exploring psychology, interacting with others and dedicating myself to the welfare of people I worked with. I did not want to betray and lose myself again in a job I was not passionate about, just because it was more socially accepted.

In short, even if uncertainty didn't scare me any longer, I still had many hesitations to overcome, to feel legitimate in a role I myself had trouble defining.

As an incredible sign of destiny, Stéphanie—who regularly read the women's magazine I was working for—noticed the last issue before my departure contained an unusual article, to say the least. Indeed, a journalist had the idea to write a quirky article about a Peruvian shaman organizing ceremonies in Paris. Needless to say, the regular headlines usually focused more on fashion and love affairs, but certainly not on shamanism! Facing the incongruity of this, I could not help but see a strong sign. After years of loyal service, was it a last nod from the magazine itself, showing me the next step on my path as a nice parting gift?

The article was about Gerardo Pizarro, a shaman whom the journalist had interviewed. The interview included a tarot reading which had greatly impressed her by its accuracy. We even saw a photo of the man in traditional outfit pose alongside the author, further illustrating the contrast between these two worlds. It was too big to be just a coincidence, and I decided to find out more about this man. I then learned he regularly travelled between France and Peru, and was currently in Paris. When calling him to book a card-reading session, his wife, who was French and who managed his schedule, answered the phone: I now understood better why Gerardo often traveled to the capital.

I met him a few days later in his makeshift office, housed in a center dedicated to alternative medicine, near the famous Père-Lachaise cemetery. I was greeted by Gisele, his wife, who led me to a room with very simple furniture. Gerardo was sitting at a table, and welcomed me. He was a chubby little man, with a laughing face. I had just sat in front of him, when he studied the top of my head. "Wow, you are very mental!" he said immediately in Spanish. It was difficult to contradict him, although at the time, it was a little less obvious to me than it is today. He began to draw cards, aligning them in front of me. I had never seen the type of tarot he used before. He nodded several times. He said I had to purify myself, I was in the process of eliminating old energies I didn't need any longer, and which encumbered me. He told me boldly that I would meet a business partner within six months (and it would be precisely the case, as we will see later).

Obviously, I could not ignore my questions regarding the creation of a healing center. I asked him about this, and he made another card draw in two rows. On the first stood a symbol, a kind of big vase or badge. And the second line only included characters, depicted in various poses and situations. He nodded, saying that the central card symbolized my activity as a "therapist," and that all these characters represented patients who were going to use my services. Visually, it was very meaningful to me—and also very encouraging, of course.

We talked for a while, including about my trip to the Amazon and the experiences I had lived there—and which for him were very significant. He said that many people were using ayahuasca for purely therapeutic purposes, as we take a drug. They came to the ceremonies, took advantage of the beneficial effects of the plant, and walked away to go about their business. But the visions I had, and the calling I had felt, were in his opinion much rarer and expressed an obvious shamanic potential. A vocation, in fact.

I could be cynical and say that he just told me what I wanted to hear. Maybe... Although his tone was pretty neutral: From his mouth, it did not sound like flattery, but merely a fact which didn't feel particularly exceptional. It was just "my thing," and he encouraged me to explore further, saying that the big upcoming changes on our planet would require all the help available— particularly to support people in managing their emotions during this intense period of transition.

Before ending our conversation, he told me he had organized a shamanic "table" for the winter solstice, on the same evening. From what I had told him, he thought it would be nice for me to come. I did not know what to think, but I decided to seriously consider it.

Stéphanie had an appointment with Gerardo right after me. I had managed to convince her to go and see him, despite her reluctance. I must admit that, for her, the last six months had not been easy. On our return from Peru, she had felt better, calmer. Then her mind had gradually got back to work, leading to a lot of self-torture and guilt, and low morale. She could not understand how she could have put our relationship in jeopardy. Her brain did not seem to validate things, leaving her in permanent uncertainty. She was suffering from "obsessive compulsive disorder," which required her to check, and recheck again everything she did.

She could, however, count on my unconditional support, as I was convinced that, whatever had happened, it had been beneficial to both of us—to trigger this earthquake which would change everything. Of course, I didn't fondly recall the events we had gone through, but the benefits of this crisis quickly erased the pain experienced at this time. I could see the whole picture, and could not feel anything but gratitude.

I could see she was still in the energy of total doubt, where nothing could be taken for granted. She blamed herself for not feeling more confident about our marriage. I reassured her by saying that when we are in the energy of doubt, when we question anything, it is a state where everything seems biased—and not a lucid intellectual process which allows us to easily separate the wheat from the chaff. I guess my blind faith in the perfect orchestration of this transition helped her, in some way, to stand firm and hold on to something... But the day before her card reading, Steph had received more bad news: Her hyperthyroidism had returned. A big blow to morale, of course. It had taken eighteen months to heal from this problem, and the prospect of having to start a new treatment, with all its implications, was really depressing.

During her meeting with Gerardo, he said she had been close to disaster regarding her health, and that it was imperative for her to rest and take care of herself. He told her she was also meant to help others, and all the experiences she encountered right now were as many lessons she could use to support other people. He assured her that her situation would gradually improve—not immediately, as there would still be some difficult times to go through. But ultimately, everything would be back to normal, and she would end up stronger. At the end of the session, Stéphanie did not seem entirely convinced. However, she accepted the idea of going to the shamanic table, as she had enjoyed this man's friendly personality.

Actually, we didn't know exactly what a "shamanic table" was. We just knew it was a ceremony during which we would take some plants—nothing as powerful as ayahuasca though—and perform a cleansing ritual. We also had to write two letters to the Universe. One containing all the things we did not want any longer in our lives, and which we gave back with gratitude. And the other one listing what we would like to attract into this newly created space. We wrote them dutifully, before going to the meeting place in the early evening.

When we arrived, the room was already almost full. People were sitting along the walls. There had to be around forty people. Stéphanie and I sat in a corner, before seeing the two plastic bags in the middle of the room, obviously supposed to contain the two types of letters that would eventually be burned. We therefore put ours in the corresponding bags, and came back to our place.

A moment later, Steph started to feel intense anxiety at the idea of having picked the wrong bag. What if she had mixed them up? More minutes passed, and her doubts were becoming unbearable. She had to check. So she spent the next fifteen minutes, kneeling in the middle of the room, emptying both bags to find her envelopes. Watching her, I took stock of the never-ending ordeal she was going through. I hoped this night would bring her some answers, or at least some relief...

This type of ceremony is called "shamanic table," as an altar is set up in a corner of the room, where participants come and place personal gifts or items they wish to charge with good energies. We had not thought of bringing anything, not being familiar with this ritual. So we decided to just sit and wait quietly. After a moment, Gerardo arrived and began to explain how the night would unfold. His wife was with him, and acted as a translator. He explained we would first dance a little, to move and boost our energy. Then we would inhale through the nostril a liquid which was supposed to purify our intentions. Then would come the cleansing of our auras, using various shamanic tools manipulated by Gerardo. Finally, we would end by taking the Dragon plant, which would help eliminate stagnant negativity within our body. What a program!

Gerardo also spoke about his experiences in the Amazon, where he witnessed many scenes of desolation after massive deforestation. He recalled the senseless destruction of nature, essential to our survival, and human tragedies he had witnessed—including the relocation of indigenous tribes who had no choice but to flee the bulldozers, or literally risk their lives to defend their territory... Far from ecological clichés, this was a story of destitute men, women and children facing the relentless assault from companies totally indifferent to the humanitarian and environmental consequences of their actions. Great sadness and spite could be felt in his voice, and I was deeply touched by his speech, especially after having myself experienced the beauty and richness of this extraordinary jungle. He invited us to pray during the night to Mother Earth, to honor Her, and create energy for global awareness—for mankind ultimately taking responsibility in the preservation or destruction of the planet.

The lights were switched off, the room being lit only by a small candle. Gerardo launched an Andean music CD of his own, and we stood up to "dance"—even though I was more accustomed to moving to electro music than panpipes, making my choreography rather approximate... Gerardo walked among us, shaking a maraca. This lasted for a little while, then we settled to receive the first treatment. It consisted of small conical seashells, which were filled with a brownish liquid—hard to identify in the dark—that we were supposed to inhale through the nose. The idea was to suck the liquid through one nostril, focusing on the negative energies we wanted to eliminate. Then do the same with the other nostril, focusing this time on the things we would rather attract into our lives. The liquid was very strong and probably contained alcohol, as it really burned my mucous membranes. Each intake, however, seemed a little easier with practice. My neighbor, apparently more familiar with this than I was, was taking each breath slowly and consciously. On my side, I frenetically emptied my seashells one after the other, obviously sticking to the belief it had to be extreme to be effective... After the fifth, I finally decided to stop, my nostrils being well pickled, and my head emptied. It is true that this breathing exercise, combined with the strength of the liquid and the intention going along with every breath, had a strong focusing effect on the present moment.

After a moment's respite, the second phase quickly followed. Participants began to queue to pass one after another before the shaman. Gisele rubbed two stones against each other, passing them on the body of each person. Surprisingly, these stones seemed to produce light. Friction gave the impression of generating electricity, by powering a small imaginary bulb. However, as far as I could see, they were seemingly ordinary stones. Once the aura was cleansed, or rather "reactivated," Gerardo took over. He was equipped with sticks, again of a fairly normal appearance, knocked them together all around the treated person. With this gesture, he seemed to produce small power discharges. These were not sparks, which could have been due to the friction of two pieces of metal, for example. They were white and blue flashes of light, perfectly visible. In the dim light, and thanks to the pretty special atmosphere of the evening, it all seemed a bit unreal.

Stéphanie was ahead of me in the queue. We quickly understood that the more a participant was charged with negative energy or tension, the more powerful the flashes were, as if the explosions were related to the disposal of these unwanted burdens.

I surprised myself trying to foresee the light a particular person would emit. By observing their posture, their attitude, their more or less tense or sad faces, it was not so difficult to assume the emotional charge they had in themselves. And this was generally verified by the light effects their cleaning generated.

When Steph's turn came, and knowing her emotional state, I naturally expected particularly pronounced effects. When she arrived in front of Gerardo, he seemed to pause to look at her, obviously a little puzzled, and wondering how he would handle this case. He put his sticks down, went rummaging in his gear, and pulled two metal swords. Things were beginning to take a strange twist... He pressed a small cushion on her chest, then put one of his swords over it. He then struck it with the second—quite strongly— triggering a bright light explosion. I heard Stéphanie heave a sigh, reflecting the force of the blow she had just received. She had her back turned towards me, and yet I clearly saw the flash. I watched the scene closely, decided to intervene if things got out of control. After all, I did not expect this kind of experience by coming that night...

Apparently, it was not over yet. He made her rotate by ninety degrees, and I could then see her profile. I was about two meters from her, and I could see clearly what was happening. He took one or two flowers—roses, I think—among the bouquets people had brought, and told Steph to hold them tight over her chest. He also took a flower, and began to move it back and forth over her solar plexus. He repeated: "Breathe, breathe, breathe, brea... ZAP!" He had just yanked the flower, as if he had hooked a fish. Moreover, this single gesture had produced a surprisingly intense spray of light. I could attest he didn't hold anything else but this seemingly ordinary flower. Steph let out another big sigh, mixed with a gasp. Gisele took her aside. Gerardo came closer to talk to me, apparently remembering I was her husband. He told me that a spirit, probably that of someone recently deceased, was "hung" to her and caused this state of anxiety and depression. I remained wary, but I had to admit I had witnessed something very unusual, and a charge of energy was released. He also followed with my own aura, which showed more reasonable reactions. Only two discharges manifested at the heart and knee level.

Before moving on to the next person, he quickly explained what

126

he had seen. According to him, Stéphanie had established an energy link between us in order to withstand her suffering. In a sense, I acted as a power generator, which provided her with resources when she was exhausted and needed to hold on. So her situation concerned us both. But he assured me that he had gotten rid of the harmful presence he had detected with her, and that everything would eventually work out.

We went back to our seats. I confess I did not know what to think. I didn't really like all these stories of vampire spirits. They implied again that we really do not have free will, and we can be victims of external entities. It was not what I wanted to believe in any longer. However, it is true that her condition coincided pretty well with the death of her grandmother, with whom she always had a somewhat stormy relationship. Rumors said the woman studied esoteric practices in her lifetime, and what I had heard about her evoked a pretty shady image.

That said, I was ready to admit that even if we were not forced to be slaves of external powers, we could at least be influenced by them. Those negative energies could of course match the vibration generated by our own state, like a moth attracted to a light bulb. In other words, we could not justify our dark thoughts by a "possession" that would have taken control of us. But in an already existing state of fragility, low energies could be momentarily attracted by this negativity—thus possibly creating a vicious circle. At worst, I didn't need to believe in this process as long as it was effective for Stéphanie. I just hoped this meeting would do her good, despite the fact that some may question it. In any case, she seemed quite touched—even a little shocked—by what she had just experienced. The process had an undeniable impact on both of us.

When all participants had benefited from their treatment, we moved to the third and final stage. We would then take the Dragon plant, a dried and crushed carnivorous plant from the Amazon. The ritual involved kneeling in front of Gerardo, who then decided the dose he would prescribe to us. He first put a little snuff in each of our nostrils, which we had to inhale strongly. Then he put in our hand a small quantity of powdered Dragon plant. The feeling, at least for me, was unpleasant. First, the tobacco was strong, and caused a runny nose and a sore throat. It took me a moment to eliminate it. Then the consistency of the dried herb was quite unusual, and its peppery and pungent taste made it a little sickening. As mentioned earlier, this plant was expected to swell in the stomach, thus absorbing the negativity contained in the body. It would then be eliminated by natural means, but vomiting during the night was not excluded.

The ceremony ended at about 4 a.m. We had decided, for a small fee, to spend the rest of the night in the room where it took place. We were a small group having chosen this option, the Parisian public transit not being fully operational at that hour. Stéphanie and I lay on small mats. Finding sleep was not easy, especially because of the energy the shamanic table had activated within us. However, we were calm, relaxed, and the treatment Stéphanie had received seemed to have been beneficial. We heard our neighbor vomit in a plastic bag, and we could not help sharing a chuckle and knowing glances while remembering our adventures in the Amazon. We knew all the good things this kind of cleansing process could lead to...

A few hours passed, and everyone began to slowly wake up. There were about ten people in the room. We naturally started to talk, and shared our feelings about the ceremony, which was obviously a novelty for most people present. I recounted our ayahuasca experiences, in connection with the Dragon plant. With a surprisingly new confidence, I said that we would probably go back to Peru the following year, and if someone was tempted to come, they would be welcome. Two young women reacted immediately by showing their interest. The first one, Sylvie, yet seemed quite shy and reserved. I had noticed her at the beginning of the evening: Her slim body, sweet smile and round glasses gave her a nice and slightly childish look. However, this was obviously only an appearance, for being able to jump at an invitation of this kind... Alexandra, meanwhile, was the person we had heard vomiting a few hours earlier. An original way to establish a first contact. She was pretty, with long curly hair, very friendly, gentle and cheerful. I was struck by the fact she had also caught my attention earlier the previous evening, when she paid her entrance fee. I had ignored the rest of the participants, but these two persons had stood out from the rest, long before I knew the role they would play in my life. I would actually confirm later that this sixth sense was an alarm signal, which would regularly sound with each new important meeting…

We learned that Alexandra lived a fifteen-minute walk from our apartment. We had a little conversation, during which she told me she had had a stroke a few years earlier. She then made a quick recovery, especially with the help of her young students, as she was a teacher. I told her straight out that this accident was a way for her to "reset her hard drive," quickly erasing old patterns to start afresh. It was quite daring for me, especially with a person I did not know a few minutes ago. Yet this intuition seemed like an absolute certainty, and not a mere intellectual deduction. Surely one of the most radical changes generated by ayahuasca experiences: Knowing with unwavering conviction certain things, without having learned or deducted them beforehand, was for me totally unprecedented. Apparently, she was unconcerned by my remark—she thanked me and gave me her business card. It was time to go. We left our new friends, promising to contact each other soon to discuss our future adventures in Peru.

CONNECTING TO SPIRIT

We had decided to go back to Peru in April 2010. Stéphanie was not really that excited about doing another ayahuasca ceremony, but my enthusiasm was strong enough to persuade her. She had decided to ask Diego for a small dose, refusing to fall again into such an intense experience. I kept assuring her that her letting go at the last ceremony proved she had already overcome the obstacle. But she had decided to continue thinking of it as an ordeal rather than a victory. However, she felt a little better after the shamanic table, and this renewed energy helped her consider this perspective with a little more self-confidence. And she wanted to compare the progress she had made in a year, by confronting herself with what she saw as a new challenge.

One of her biggest concerns remained her hyperthyroidism, which was aggravated by very unpleasant interactions with her endocrinologist. I accompanied her to each of her appointments, and even when the results of the analysis were encouraging, we were inevitably demoralized leaving the hospital. Her doctor, in addition to having a generally aggressive and abrupt attitude, apparently had no hope of her recovery. When Steph wanted to be optimistic, noting the progress she had made, he seemed to insist on denying it. Since her relapse, he wanted, at all costs, to remove her thyroid. For my wife, it was out of the question, and she wanted to give another chance to the drug treatment that had already proved beneficial. He then tried to frighten her, telling her that in any case, it was "putting off the inevitable," and that if she had relapsed once, she would again. The only solution was the surgery to remove her thyroid, plain and simple. Faced with his patient's refusal, which seemed to deeply annoy him, he tried to show her at each visit that his diagnosis was correct, and that she was deluding herself.

We had a similar history, Stéphanie and I, regarding paternal submission. This physician was the perfect representation of this dominating male figure. Faced with this power struggle, she was often distraught, especially when the doctor brandished the specter of serious illness before her. Under these conditions, it was difficult for her to remain confident in her choices. I remember many times when Stéphanie cried after a visit or a simple phone call to her endocrinologist, who had bluntly refused to give her further information. He seemed to consider that explaining things to his patients was just a complete waste of time. I found this totally unacceptable, and only the fear of making a big mistake made us maintain this dominating relationship with a "specialist," whom we thought we depended on.

Stéphanie had decided to look for alternatives. We both agreed about the psychosomatic cause of this disease. As with other autoimmune disorders, which I had experienced myself for several years, this problem was related to a dysfunction of the immune system. Her antibodies were excessively stimulating her thyroid to produce more hormones, causing her body to become overactive—causing cravings, weight loss, hot flashes and other symptoms related to her metabolism "overheating."

Of course, it reminded me of my own nephrotic syndrome. For me, this pathology was also directly linked to the overprotection in which Stéphanie maintained herself, whose physical manifestation resulted in an overstimulated immune system. Besides numerous allergies, this defensive mechanism was also impressive in its effectiveness: She sometimes recovered from a flu-like condition in a few hours, as her ability to fight against external "aggressions" was extremely efficient. Of course, those protective responses were sometimes justified. But most of the time, they were only triggered by a terribly hostile perception of her environment. She had to protect herself at all costs, and her walls were still very high.

When we discussed her illness, and I put myself in a receptive state, I perceived the analogy of a "country under the yoke of a totalitarian regime." This image showed me that in her body, the "military forces" had literally taken power, and proclaimed a state of emergency based on fear. The protection from an external threat had become such an obsession that all behavior was justified, even the most extreme.

In addition, we would later learn that hyperthyroidism is often associated with the throat energy center—or throat chakra—and the non-verbalization of internalized emotions. This view of a totalitarian state based on repression made even more sense. In this kind of regime, communication is certainly the first thing to be suppressed. And indeed, Stéphanie had always had difficulty expressing her emotions and desires.

This time, she did not intend to remain a spectator of her convalescence. She promised to prove to her doctor she was able to heal. In that sense, he had done her a favor by reinforcing her determination, even if it was not his prime intention. She therefore decided to give serious consideration to the concept of violence against herself. Obviously, she had to choose between the fear that made her set up such a merciless system, and her self-love which invited her to protect her own body. Like all other autoimmune diseases, the protector turns against its owner: The best way to stop this tendency to paranoia, and to repeal this "martial law" that governs the body, is generally to realize that the cure is worse than the disease.

We often see images of repression and totalitarianism from all around the world. And they can ultimately be compared to the ill-treatment we inflict to ourselves, in the name of our own "national security..." By wanting to protect ourselves and keep control, this control is paradoxically given to someone or something else. Ironically, this power will generally be used to create an even more powerful oppression.

The fact is that by gradually relaxing the pressure on herself, by socializing a little more—especially with the help of Alexandra and her companion, whom we had immediately befriended—and drawing on new unexpected resources she discovered each day, Stéphanie obtained impressive results. She had achieved in four months what had previously taken eighteen. As if this second ordeal was only a means for her to realize the amazing progress she had made in overcoming all these difficulties, and how much stronger she had become. I was hoping our next journey would help her conclude this very stressful period.

I was very excited by this new trip to Peru. My head was filled with questions, and I urgently needed answers. I was passionate about channeling, which I found really fascinating and very positive. I was particularly interested in the innovative perspectives this kind of information could bring. Having had a glimpse of my potential in the Amazon, I really wanted to develop this path. I could see myself opening a practice to offer this kind of therapy, which I found especially profound, thanks to the higher source it seemed inspired by. I could not forget the presences I had felt, who had deeply touched me with their benevolence and love. If I could be the vehicle of such a beautiful consciousness, and thus bring support to people, I would feel blessed.

However, after having returned to my city life, in my western culture, all this didn't seem so easy. Judgments and misunderstandings were inevitable. How to explain this phenomenon without sounding like a looney? And in the face of fear of rejection, I began to doubt: What if I had invented everything? Because the process of channeling is actually very subtle. Some channelers slip into a quasi-unconscious state, to let the entity they channel express itself freely. But it seemed it was neither my desire nor the way it had happened with Ayahuasca. I felt rather like an interpreter who translated the information he received in real time—it is funny to note my studies in high school had already hinted at my predisposition for this role.

Shortly afterwards, I stumbled upon a book describing the life and work of Edgar Cayce, surely one of the most famous mystics of the twentieth century. The man claimed that conscious channeling was the most interesting form, as it allowed the channel's consciousness to participate actively in the process, and thus benefit personally from the information conveyed.

It made sense to me, and allowed me to keep some control without having to completely let go, as I didn't know where this experience could lead me. In a way, I felt responsible for the way things were going during a session, and I did not want them to go "wrong." Obviously, this was not the best approach, as I was also taking responsibility for what was verbalized, which could go against the very nature of this process. Besides, if the information really came from a higher consciousness, it was very arrogant of me to want to control it, and even censor it. But at the time, I felt exposed, and this anxiety prevented me from letting go completely. I had to gain confidence. I now know that the secret of the art of channeling rests on the ability to step aside, and just be a vehicle for direct communication between the questioner and the energy that is expressed.

I realized the sessions were much more powerful if I knew the person well, or at least I had already met them. I had the impression that the consciousness I channeled was "browsing" my inner library, going there to look for the information available, and arranging it in a certain way so that it had maximum impact and relevance for the questioner. As if retrieving information required energy from these guides, and they preferred to get it directly from me if the data were already present. From this point of view, I had to fill my inner library, so that they had as much data as possible— like many puzzle pieces they could then arrange in an optimal way, creating the most suggestive image for those who asked the questions.

I did my best to get familiar with this spiritual domain, of which I did not know much. To make an analogy, it was like having to be an interpreter between two scientists, one Russian, the other American. If the American explained an important concept to his counterpart, and the translator had absolutely no scientific knowledge, there could be translation errors or approximations. If, on the other hand, the interpreter mastered the basic principles of the concepts explained, the dialogue would then be much smoother and more precise. In any case, it is impossible to translate a discourse that is not understood.

There was, however, a counterpart to this approach: The more I grasped these spiritual concepts, the more I wondered if it was not just me repeating them to the people I gave my sessions to. If there was one idea which was unbearable to me, it was that of betraying others by lying to them and lying to myself. My phobia of being an impostor was always present.

And yet, in spite of this constant questioning and vigilance, I felt that the energy passing through—that unique feeling of love I experienced during the channeling session—could not be a purely intellectual construction. At the beginning, my mind was certainly present, and made my life difficult by overwhelming me with doubts and a slight anxiety. I could clearly feel the difference when those thoughts were gradually quieted, giving way to a fundamentally different presence. I began to speak, sometimes hearing the sentences I channeled, saying to myself: "Ha yes! It makes sense!" I became the spectator of my own words, as my everyday consciousness drifted into a soft trance.

I often wondered if there was a way to prove the authenticity of this process, but I realized there was none. And I might lose all my energy trying to persuade people of my good faith. The cynical could always easily accuse me of charlatanism without me being able to do very much about it. I resigned myself to no longer wanting to convince others of my honesty, because in the end, it was me I wanted to convince. I decided to approach it from another angle: As long as the process itself and the information conveyed were useful to people, that was enough for me and justified my perseverance. I knew this letting go would paradoxically reinforce the effectiveness of this practice, because it necessarily involved silencing the mind to the maximum. So I had to get rid of all the negative beliefs which could bother me, interfering with the transmission of this flow of information.

At first, however, I did not have the courage to offer a channeling session to a complete stranger. Besides my fear of a mocking refusal, I did not know exactly the type of dialogue that could be established between the questioner and the guides who spoke through me. So I needed a very open-minded person whom I trusted. She presented herself in the person of our friend Alexandra, with whom I felt a strong connection, and who kindly agreed to be my co-explorer in this unknown territory. The first session went very well, and her companion also agreed to participate to the experiment. The interviews took place in the form of interactive conversations, during which questions and advice could be asked. The answers were then always formulated from a benevolent angle that offered a new, wider perspective.

As I practiced, I realized I really loved it. This reconnected me to a very pleasant state of compassion and serenity, certainly as efficient as the best antianxiety drugs. When the expressed concepts passed through me, I understood them fundamentally. Sometimes I felt I was receiving instantly an "all-in-one" answer, in a package I had then to unpack, to share its contents in a logical order. Moreover, seeing the support this information could bring to others was worth all the gold in the world to me. I felt useful again.

In short, I was wandering in an unknown land, everything was new, and my exploration would certainly require time to feel perfectly at ease with this idea. Yet deep inside, I did not doubt that, in the long run, I would open a practice allowing me to make a living on this activity. My trip to Peru would surely bring me answers, and I was anxious to know what I was going to discover there.

THE GHOST PLANE

The month of April arrived. I was very excited, Stéphanie a little less... As the deadline approached, her apprehension grew a bit more every day. She kept recalling her last experience, and expected the next one to be an upcoming exhausting struggle.

We were going to go with just one other person, Alexandra having decided not to come this time. Indeed, following her stroke, she had suffered from post-traumatic depression. She was therefore treated with antidepressants, which are highly incompatible with ayahuasca. It is always necessary to stop using these drugs several weeks before the first ceremony. Although she had actually stopped taking these medications on time, she preferred not to take any risks. It was indeed wiser to have this kind of experience with full confidence and without second thought. Only Sylvie would come along with us.

We hadn't had much contact with her before the trip. She seemed rather shy, and I was all the more surprised at the confidence she placed in us, since we knew very little about each other. I expected her to change her mind at some point, but she seemed determined to accompany us on this adventure.

Two or three days before our departure, we saw on the news that an Icelandic volcano with an unpronounceable name—the Eyjafjallajokul—had erupted, creating an enormous ash cloud. Nothing alarming yet. But on the eve of our departure, the news came: The cloud was coming to Paris, and it was not yet certain whether the airports were going to have to close.

I remember this moment very well. I looked at myself in the bathroom mirror, and I could not help smiling: "You... You really like Hollywood-type scenarios, right? A volcano threatening your journey… This time, you went clearly over the top!" As the news bulletins progressed, the development of the situation did not seem encouraging. On the date of our departure, all Paris airports had been closed for the day. People were talking about a potential reopening at 8 p.m.—our plane was supposed to take off at 8:20 p.m.—but nothing was guaranteed.

To top it all, we had decided to take advantage of our absence to have our apartment renovated. Workmen were supposed to come three days later, and replace a wooden floor heavily damaged by water. There was almost a week's work. So we had piled the majority of our furniture in two rooms, including our bedroom, making our home almost uninhabitable.

A bit concerned, we left for the airport with our backpacks: This year, we did not want to lose our suitcase again. We had decided to travel lightly, and to have our stuff at hand—after all, we had realized in the Amazon we could survive with very few things. We arrived at Orly airport, where we had arranged to meet Sylvie. She was already waiting for us. As we had booked our tickets online, we had to pick them up at the airline's counter. As we approached the counter, we saw an endless line of people waiting in front of the desk. It was not going well.

A hostess walked through the ranks, answering questions from worried passengers. I asked her if the flight to Madrid would be continued that evening. "Oh! No! Flights will not resume until Tuesday!" Which meant in five days... Needless to say our trip would go down the drain, if that was the case.

We decided to wait in line and see what we could get at the desk. We were not particularly anxious to go home, to a messy apartment, and disappointed to cancel a superb trip. At the same time, facing a volcanic eruption, it was useless to complain. It was way beyond the limits of what we could control, and ranting would have been ridiculous. We preferred to joke. Arriving at the counter, just before speaking to the hostess, a staff member approached me to ask if my final destination was Madrid. I told him no. He asked the same question to the other people around me. I thought it was odd, but didn't really mind it.

I gave my reservation to the young woman behind the desk, who examined it for a moment. She disappeared and came back with a printout, containing our reservation. Then she explained:

- "In fact these tickets were not issued by the correct company. Look at the number at the beginning of the reference: Your ticket is a LAN Peru ticket, while we are Iberia."
- "Yet I bought them on the web, and the first flight is actually operated by Iberia to go to Madrid, right? I even called the customer service of the site on which I ordered them, and it was confirmed that you would deliver the tickets to me."
- "Yes, but I can't do anything, you have to go to LAN."
- "Uh... But there is no LAN counter in Orly!"
- "Wait... I'll give you their phone number."

Oh dear... The volcano had become almost secondary, since we did not even have our tickets. All I had was the file printed by the hostess. But I could see it contained the electronic ticket numbers of our flights, which is normally the only thing necessary to be able to board. I called LAN, and a friendly young woman answered. She told me that all the flights were canceled, and that my tickets were non-refundable. The only thing she could offer me was a later flight, within three days. Then, looking at her schedule, she regretfully told me there was actually no more room available anywhere. In short, she was telling me that we could not leave and that, in addition, we would not be able to recover the cost of the tickets.

I was strangely calm, even joking about this absurd situation with the person I had on the phone. I had confirmation, however, that the numbers printed on my paper were the references of our electronic tickets. It was better than nothing.

As I continued to talk with LAN to try to find a solution, I noticed increased activity at the baggage check-in stations. Very strange, as all the planes were stuck on the ground. There were also some security guards who had created a cordon in front of the counters.

Without thinking, I stood up. With an empty mind, I told my companions to come with me, and made my way to these agents, the telephone still stuck to one ear. Arriving in front of them, I greeted them with a smile and told them that we were going to Madrid. They then asked me again if it was our final destination, and if we had luggage to check in. This time I replied with confidence that Madrid was our destination, and that we only had one piece of hand-luggage each. I suspected that a flight was being chartered, but that the company did not guarantee the transfer of baggage or any correspondence. By chance, we did not need any of those services. Once we were in Spain, the ash cloud would no longer be a problem, and we could leave for Peru.

When the agents let us through, we could not believe it. We looked at each other, speechless. We hastily pushed our way to the check-in counter, leaving without a murmur and praying for it to work. The LAN representative, still on the phone, did not understand anything at all when I told her that we had passed through and that we were obtaining our tickets. I did not understand everything myself. I thanked her and hung up.

We waited for several interminable minutes, hoping the paper I handed to the hostess would be enough to get the magic pass. It was surreal to see a completely empty and silent airport, knowing the threat of the volcano, and the fact our tickets were still unavailable a few minutes before. Finally, after a moment of anxious silence and perplexed looks, we were handed our boarding passes. A unique flight was going to leave in the late afternoon.

Up to the last moment we were not sure what to expect, even though our passage through security controls, and the display on the monitors confirmed that this plane, coming out of nowhere, was really going to take off. Finally, we embarked, hardly believing how lucky we were. We found ourselves in the very back of the cabin, meaning we had obtained our seats at the last minute. As the aircraft left the Parisian ground, the captain made an announcement. According to him, only three flights were going to take off that day from Orly, and we were one of them—but we should not worry because we were going to bypass the cloud. He added that they had filled up with fuel, and the flight to Madrid would even take less time than expected.

We looked at each other, incredulous, both stunned and smiling. I felt like James Bond getting out of a desperate situation, with his legendary British reserve. We would later learn that not only was this take-off totally exceptional, but the airport had been blocked for at least another five days before the air activity resumed. We had gone through a mouse hole, calmly and fluently. I suspected it would be a Hollywood scenario, and it was! If I still had doubts about the beneficial effects of letting go and positive thinking, they would have definitely vanished. Everything seemed possible, and I thanked the Medicine for Her protection.

Later, I would identify a repeating pattern in these kinds of events. This is how Ayahuasca often works: She puts you in a scary or even seemingly desperate situation. You go through those events as best as you can, until you reach a point of surrender, because there is nothing else left to do. Once the lesson is learned and the obstacle overcome, everything ends perfectly well, against all odds. It is a very efficient and powerful—yet dramatic—way of learning how to let go of control. Ultimately, you just have to acknowledge you were safe during the whole process...

CHAOS AND PERFECTION

The rest of the journey was uneventful. Anyway, with what we had just gone through, we felt invincible: Except an attack from Godzilla itself, we didn't see anything that might compromise our trip!

We finally landed in Cuzco, our destination. This year, we were going to spend the week in Pisac, in the Sacred Valley of the Incas, at Diego Palma's house. As in the Amazon, several tourist activities were planned during the day, and we would attend three nocturnal ayahuasca ceremonies. Also, before leaving France, I had asked Diego if he knew a shaman offering San Pedro cactus ceremonies, and if he could recommend one to me. He informed me he actually did some on a regular basis, and that if I so desired, we could organize one at the end of the retreat. I had absolute confidence in the man, and I could not hope for a better opportunity.

This time, I had organized nothing at all, preferring to leave room for improvisation. Another testimony of the great changes that had occurred in me. We had planned to stay a few more days in Peru, with the vague idea of visiting the Machu Picchu—even though the latter was hardly accessible because of the torrential rains that had happened a few weeks before.

Diego was waiting for us at the airport, still as tall and smiling as I remembered him. I hugged him. I was over the moon, happy to see him again and to be back in this country where I felt so good. We then took a taxi to Pisac. After the rainy season, the land was really beautiful, almost fluorescent under the April sun. We arrived at Melissa Wasi, the guesthouse managed by Diego's parents. It was actually a small and nice closed property made up of several bungalows, where the ayahuasquero had his own house, as well as a maloca dedicated to the ceremonies. Milagros welcomed us, accompanied by a big black dog named Simba, whose excitement she could hardly repress. She warned us that despite her height, she was still a puppy, and that she could be a little crazy.

Steph and I were allotted a pretty room in the main house, and Sylvie had a similar room on the upper floor. As usual, the first ceremony would take place that evening, and we found ourselves in the same situation as last year: We knew it would be better to rest, and at the same time, it was impossible to sleep a wink. The excitement was too great. I was impatient, Stéphanie was apprehensive, and Sylvie, if she was anxious, hid it rather well behind a certain impassivity.

The rest of the group had arrived in the meantime, and I noticed we were slightly more than last year. People of all ages and all backgrounds, some speaking Spanish and some English. Everybody looked very friendly, smiling and warm, and I already felt with family. Diego and Milagros gathered us to explain the organization of the stay. It was obvious they were complementary: Milagros, always dynamic, was responsible for logistics, while her husband focused more on the spiritual work.

A little later, we found ourselves in the maloca, where Diego explained to us, like the previous time, how the first ceremony was going to take place, with the usual recommendations. The most important thing was always not to talk during the night, so as not to disturb the other participants. We also took turns to introduce ourselves, explaining briefly our background and the reasons that led us to come and take ayahuasca in Peru. I used to be a translator for Stéphanie and Sylvie. It was more and more obvious Sylvie was not really prone to express herself in public, let alone in a language she was not very comfortable with.

I liked this group very much. It was always impressive and touching to see other human beings sharing with emotion their sorrows, their trials and their search for a better life through the exploration of their potentials. It required courage, not only to recognize one's weaknesses, but above all to undertake to overcome them—especially by using means as impressive as ayahuasca, which is known to be a powerful but sometimes frightening medicine.

Night came, it was time to get ready. Stéphanie was lying on the bed, feeling a growing apprehension. She was hesitant about the quantity she would take, as she still wanted to test herself and measure the progress made in a year. I tried to comfort her as well as I could, even though some of my energy was already dedicated to my own encouragement. Because if I were fundamentally curious and enthusiastic, the building pressure which precedes a ceremony is always daunting. I also had to focus on my own motivations, especially by reflecting upon the intention I wanted to address to the plant before taking it.

This year, I wanted to replicate the same pattern we had already experienced in the Amazon, starting with a rather general subject, and focusing first on an inner cleansing. In my perspective of working with many people—through, for example, the opening of a practice or any other activity involving recurring human interactions—I felt it was essential to explore this purification process further. To be a good supporter, I knew I needed to be able to connect with people, not with my brain, but with my heart. This in order to establish a direct connection, without intellect or judgment, and thus feel the energy of the person through a contact free of any mental interference.

We all sat down in the maloca. Diego began with the usual ritual, thanking Mother Earth, Ayahuasca, and all the benevolent forces that would assist us in our work. Then each of us passed by the ayahuasquero to drink the brew. Stéphanie was first, and opted courageously for a normal dose. As for me, it was very hard to swallow the liquid, which provoked retching. I had to control the spasms of my stomach by breathing strongly so as not to vomit.

The lights were switched off, and silence settled. After only a few minutes, I began to hear Sylvie, sitting on my right, breathing more and more strongly. She seemed to react very quickly to the medicine, and began to speak out loud. In great sighs, testifying to the pressure she felt, she wondered what was happening to her. "But what is this? Oh dear! What am I supposed to do?!" She seemed literally crushed by this wave of energy, and her anguished and agitated reaction worried me. Still perfectly lucid, I tried to calm her down, stroking her arm, and whispering words in her ear.

She moved in all directions, grabbing my hands, and continuing to speak louder and louder. The situation became somewhat uncontrollable, and I saw Milagros stand up and come to kneel before her. Diego's wife tried to appease her, but it was a dialogue of the deaf: Milagros spoke to her in English and Sylvie answered her in French, making any exchange impossible. Milagros turned to me to be an interpreter. She told me that if she did not calm down, she would have to get her out.

At that moment, like a big weight falling on me, Ayahuasca took command. The verbal dialogue was useless, and it was time to resort to more energetic communication. I asked Milagros, as best I could, to give me a moment to try to appease Sylvie, and instill more serenity into her before resorting to this solution. She probably felt that, through my very slow diction, I was under the effects of the plant. She accepted, and came back to sit down next to Diego.

The minutes that followed were very intense. I was literally blending with Sylvie. I had visions of a violet and black light, ebbing and flowing, which made me think of blood circulation in biology documentaries. At a level incomprehensible to my intellect, we were connected to the same circulatory system. This allowed us to connect our two beings, thus forming a greater one. I had actually used the word "instill" to explain to Milagros my intention to send her reassuring energy, and it was perfectly appropriate. I felt that by concentrating, I could calm the waves of anguish Sylvie was sending me. And her physical attitude immediately changed accordingly. But as soon as I released this intention, a cloud of black visions populated with morbid figures rushed at me—and Sylvie got even more agitated.

Milagros came back to kneel before me. I opened my eyes: She had white fluorescent paintings on her face, like a shaman warrior. I knew it was a vision, and was struck by her energy. Clearly, she looked impressive. She told me something had to be done, and that Sylvie had to go out. Yet I knew intuitively my companion was trying to heal her deep issues linked to her fear of annoying people by speaking her mind out loud. If she was expelled while she was overcoming this blockage, she would take it as a punishment, reinforcing her sense of being an "ugly little duck" that the group didn't want. I tried to explain this to Milagros, in probably confused English, considering my psychic state at that moment. Suddenly Sylvie threw herself forward on the ground, knocking over her empty bucket. It was chaos.

Besides, I had difficulty remaining fully conscious, overwhelmed by my visions, until I heard Milagros say to me with authority: "Stop talking!" It felt like a cold shower, and I realized that I had been speaking automatically for a while. I apologized briefly to her. She asked if I could help her get Sylvie out, but I could not even get up. She then asked for help from another participant, who was obviously still lucid, and who helped her bring the young woman outside the maloca. I was frustrated. I was sure it was a bad experience for Sylvie, which would reinforce her fear of expressing her personality to others.

Yet, hardly had the wooden door of the maloca closed again, I was suddenly invaded by total serenity. Everything was just perfect. I was experiencing the beauty of the Universe in its flawless choreography. Ayahuasca explained to me that I did not have to worry, that every moment was absolutely perfect, and that there was no possible flaw in existence. Only man labeled a situation as "good" or "bad," but for Creation, these concepts were completely arbitrary. She told me that what I had lived had not only allowed me to explore my first intention—direct connection to another human being—but that the expulsion of Sylvie was what allowed me now to realize the perfection of things. If I had not experienced this particular scenario, I would not be at that level of understanding. Sylvie, on her side, would also receive her own teachings.

The rest of the night revolved around this theme: the acceptance that even the most unpleasant or seemingly unfortunate events are in fact an impeccable manifestation of a larger and more intelligent vision. This intelligence could even be described as "Divine" by the beauty of its orchestration. I was also told that life, far from being an already-written story, is an infinite succession of choices. Those choices reorient the course of things every second, constantly recreating a new equally harmonious path. And as such, the first rule to follow when one wants to "help" people is to respect their choices and their personal path—without pretending to believe one knows what they really need to live. Otherwise, it comes down to thinking that our human mind can intellectually understand all the mechanics and forces involved, which is totally ridiculous and arrogant, to say the least.

I bathed in this awareness for an indeterminate time. My hearing, sharpened by Ayahuasca, perceived someone vomiting outside. I was sure it was Stéphanie. She had gone out to support Sylvie in her experience. When I heard Steph purge, I immediately connected with her. I viscerally felt her altruistic nature and her sense of sacrifice. The crisis in our relationship had been hard on both of us. But while I had done my best to move on, by realizing all the benefits it had brought to us, Steph was still eaten by guilt. At that moment, I felt how distorted her perception of things was. I understood the difficult choice she had had to make, at a higher level, to get us out of the shifting sands in which we were stuck a few years earlier. I owed her big time, and I found it unfair she suffered for having worked on our rescue.

If she had seen herself through the perspective I was experiencing, she would surely have forgiven herself by feeling the love, courage and sense of responsibility which had led to such an extreme solution. I had to share this view of things with her at all costs—I had done so before, but in this state of absolute certainty, I received an unquestionable confirmation of her deep affection for me: A love so strong she had risked losing it, and losing her self-love at the same time. She was really my soul mate, an irreplaceable partner.

I also felt her strength. She had always seen herself as a fragile person, with emotional turmoil she sometimes considered as insurmountable. In reality, she had to have an incredible resilience and boldness to go through such extreme experiences. As a complement to this realization, I had the vision of a sitting brown bear, radiating a green light. I knew I was shown Stéphanie's totem animal, and how she healed the world.

Her core energy, her presence, her ability to take care of a person and stay with her when she feels bad: That was the gift she had. Not necessarily a spectacular way of supporting people, but yet infinitely precious—rather like the warmth of a good fire, the light of a lamp in the dark night, a hug when you feel downcast, and all these comforting things in times of trouble. She who felt so vulnerable was actually an unshakeable pillar, and I was definitely very lucky to have her at my side.

She finally returned to the maloca, accompanied by Diego who had gone out for a moment. When he had seen her sitting outside, he had told her how impressed he was by the way she had changed within a single year. She came back and sat down beside me, visibly exhausted. Diego lit the lights shortly afterwards, and I could see her condition—she could barely move, totally empty of energy. I did not dare to get up, to go and talk with other people in the group: I kept her huddled up against me, wondering how we would go back to our room. Finally, after a moment's respite, she found the strength to stand up, and we went back to bed.

Sleeping did us good, even though our mind was still foggy. It was market day in Pisac, and several members of the group had decided to go there to have a walk in the morning. It was beyond my strength, and even more so beyond Stéphanie's. We met Sylvie at breakfast, who remained very evasive about her experience of the day before. She seemed embarrassed by her reaction at the beginning of the ceremony, and wondered if the next session would be so agitated. She did not really tell us about her night in detail, and simply referred to strange creatures in her visions, resembling monkeys and other animals. I did not want to rush her and I did not insist. Words are sometimes limited in describing such perceptions, especially just after the ceremonies.

The day was quiet. We did a little tour of the market in the afternoon, before going to the maloca for the integration session. By sharing my feelings with the group, especially regarding the constant choices we make, and which we can change at any time, I realized what the symbol of purge represented. As I understood it now, this act was not the simple release of negative energy or the expression of physical discomfort, but rather the refusal of a choice, a definition, a belief that no longer served us. We vomited all these choices that we no longer wanted to make, literally expelling them from our behaviors.

Stéphanie, for her part, was far from those intellectual considerations. She was suffering from a terrible migraine, and wondered if her adventure with Ayahuasca was not definitively over: She was really fed up with going through such intense experiences...

JOURNEY INTO
THE UNKNOWN

The following day, we visited beautiful Inca ruins, near Pisac. Very well preserved, they were perched on the slopes of a mountain in the Sacred Valley, which we then descended on foot. We had to climb down an incalculable number of stone steps, which did not particularly please my sore knees. The people who once lived in that area certainly had rock-hard thighs!

After a good lunch, we decided to have some rest. A new ceremony awaited us that evening, and we needed some calm and contemplation to approach it in the best condition. Stéphanie asked me to go and see Diego, to tell him she wished to considerably reduce her dose of medicine. She had finally decided to come, if only to support me. When I saw Diego, the ayahuasquero nodded with a smile, saying he would give her a "contact dose," very light but sufficient to establish a connection with the rest of the group. Then we waited for a while at Diego's parents' house, where we were lodged. Sitting comfortably in a leather sofa, next to a stove located in the middle of the main room, we were relaxed. Henry, a member of the group, came to join us, and we began to talk.

He explained to me the delicate situation in which he found himself: By a chain of complicated circumstances, he was now the father of two children, each of a different mother. He found himself torn between these two families, for which he felt responsible, knowing that the time he devoted to one made the other suffer from his absence. He loved them both, however, and did not want to abandon them. This dilemma seemed to be reflected by his physical appearance: He suffered a partial unnatural baldness, causing holes everywhere in his thick brown hair. If the expression "pulling one's hair out" had had a symbolic representation, it would have looked like this.

This discussion touched me, and I sympathized with his dismay. After our conversation, I took a few moments to refocus on my own intention. Tonight was the evening when I was going to further explore the themes related to channeling.

To explain my purpose, I must first come back to an important point: As I said before, from all the discoveries that had transformed me during my experiences in the Amazon, one was accepting it is possible to know something with certainty, without having been taught beforehand. Before this awareness, I started from the principle—very implanted in our Western culture—that all knowledge must be transmitted by an individual who "knows," and who has learned it before from another teacher. Our whole education system relies on the idea that there are students and teachers, and that the former are the receptacles of the latter's knowledge.

Yet in my previous ceremonies, and even when I was back in Paris, I had experienced certainties that went beyond mere deduction. I did not understand why I knew such or such a thing, as I hadn't followed any intellectual path to come to this conclusion, and yet I was certain of its veracity, as undeniable evidence. Carlos Castaneda evoked in his books the concept of "silent knowledge," and I was finally touching what he was alluding to.

From this perspective, and to push further what I had lived in the Amazon, I wanted to learn to connect more with this knowledge—in order to be able to extract it and transmit it. Many esoteric traditions are based on the idea that everything already exists in the Universe, and that it is possible to visit this infinite library in order to extract the information we look for. This source is often known as the "Akashic Records."

This may seem rather exotic to the uninitiated, but it was an attempt on my part to rationalize the states I was experiencing. And then it put a semblance of explanation, even partial, on all the phenomena of clairvoyance, precognition and other visionary dreams that we regularly all hear about... If it were really possible to search in an inexhaustible mine of information, and if what I was experiencing was the expression of this process, then I had only one desire: explore this potential thoroughly, for I found the idea absolutely fascinating.

We settled in the maloca, nestling under our blankets. Sylvie, on my right, remained silent, trying to find every bit of courage within herself... Stéphanie, seated to my left, seemed more confident, especially thanks to the prospect of taking only a minimal dose. As for me, I decided to take a larger quantity of Ayahuasca, as I had already done in the Amazon.

Sylvie was visibly better prepared this time, as she managed the rising effects of the plant much more calmly. Moreover, she probably did not need to relive the teaching she had already received during the previous ceremony, and a new scenario was now being played out.

I was vigilantly waiting for the slightest explanation about accessing silent knowledge. But nothing came in those terms, probably as they were again too intellectual. I had the impression of swimming in midwater, in a slight torpor, but still very present. I was told this was the necessary state to connect with Creation, and that there was no need to be in a deep trance to extract the information. As usual, I had imagined a complex and convoluted process, punctuated by fireworks, where there was only simplicity and sobriety. I kept floating in this gentle energy.

Henry's story came back to my mind. I then received the idea his situation was much more positive than he wished to admit. Above all, it allowed him to live his absolute happiness of having a family and children, so much so he had two! And through this duality, he could explore even more widely the different aspects related to this experience. At that moment, I was impressed to hear him thank me aloud, on the other side of the room—not respecting the rule of remaining silent. This spontaneous "Gracias Frédéric" echoed my own visions so synchronously that I could no longer doubt the magical connection between the participants in a ceremony of this kind.

This connection was actually stronger than ever. I felt that through my breath, I could communicate with the rest of the group, bringing calm and comfort. I put my left hand on Stéphanie's leg, which she held immediately. I did the same with my right hand, placing it on Sylvie's knee, who started to massage it slowly. On a visceral level, I knew we all three were forming a larger entity: a clan, a trio of healers, a pyramid of which I was the point, and whose women were the unshakeable and nourishing basis. In my masculine principle, I was an antenna, a transmitter, or even a distributor of soothing energy, fed by all the sweetness and strength of the partners sitting next to me.

I began to receive a great deal of information about the feminine principle, whose beauty overwhelmed me. I was told this principle, so harmonious and rich, could be expressed in many different ways: as with Sylvie, by calmness and delicacy. As with Stéphanie, by unconditional love and unwavering support. As with Milagros, by passion and fire. In this last image, I realized I had not completely digested the fact that Diego's wife had ordered me to be quiet at the previous ceremony. Generally, I hated to be prevented from speaking, but I realized that when it came from a woman, I had even more difficulty accepting it. I was shown that in my upbringing, women never had the last word. I gladly purged all this macho vision, which had prevented me from seeing all the power and nobility of those women around me.

As a logical follow-up to this demonstration, I came to the feminine figure that is essential to all of us: the mother, whose image just formed before me.

I was then overwhelmed by one of the most terrifying visions I ever had to endure under Ayahuasca. I began to relive my birth. I saw my mother's image literally dissolve into me, and a cloud of nightmarish and grimacing faces rushing in my direction. To sustain this vision, filled with anguish and creepy creatures, I had to cling more strongly to Stéphanie and Sylvie, who provided me with the necessary foundation to handle the assault. I knew what it meant, without a shadow of a doubt: I was told that at birth—and even during gestation—the child inherited her belief system from her parents, especially her mother. In fact, since the newborn had no "user manual" to evolve in a world where she had no reference, she adopted the only one she had access to, and in which she had bathed for nine months. My mother was filled with fears: fear of violence, fear of domination, fear of judgment of others... Once I had adopted these basic rules at my birth, they had been reinforced daily by my father's authority and my mother's submission. And what I knew above all else, was that my soul had chosen this precise context to incarnate itself, in full knowledge of the facts!

One of the themes of my life was precisely to get out of this victim and perpetrator system, to regain my self-esteem and my personal power. I was shown a very fast recapitulation of my life: my early childhood, my adolescence, my twenties, the present moment... How I had gradually gone from shadow to light, how I had started from a hostile and violent vision of the world, to arrive at the discovery of love for myself and others. Such was my path: to live this polarity, this contrast, the intent of which was precisely to know both sides of it, and then to make my choices in full awareness. Everything I had lived in my life had a meaning, every minute of it. The plan was perfect, implacable, of formidable efficacy and absolute benevolence. I could only feel gratitude for this intelligence, and for all those who participated in it. For I was convinced that at a higher level of consciousness, we all knew the part we played for each other, such as actors who make each other grow through the characters they incarnate. I was the witness of this fantastic story, played on a cosmic scale.

After this incredible realization, I floated in a state where space and time no longer had any real meaning. Then Diego began to speak in a long litany, thanking the Earth, Ayahuasca, the Mountains, the Sky, San Pedro... At this last evocation, I felt the spirit of this plant connect to me. I had the prospect of meeting it in a few days, but this temporal projection no longer really made sense. As if everything existed there, now: I could have jumped directly to this day, as one goes immediately to the next chapter of a DVD, without transition. I had the feeling San Pedro made me this proposal, to experiment the non-linearity of existence. "Do you want us to meet now?" He seemed to propose. I felt like a time traveler who would have the ability to move instantly into the future. This idea was both exciting and intimidating, and I felt on the edge of the precipice, ready to jump. Another part of me, however, refused to take the plunge, for—I realize it now—the main purpose of this proposal was to make me understand the immense range of possibilities.

I realized all the point of the experience on Earth was precisely related to its linear structure. The events are linked together, making it possible to experience a process, a progression, a transformation. I felt it was not the way the Universe was fundamentally structured—it was actually possible to perceive it immediately in all directions, through all its potentials—but time was a useful limitation towards growth and the discovery of ourselves. One step after another. I thanked San Pedro, by giving him an appointment in four "days."

The ceremony came to an end shortly after, even though my condition made it difficult to measure the minutes or the hours that had elapsed. After a moment of regaining my senses, I stood up, staggering a little, and we went back to our room. I collapsed on the bed.

I woke up the next morning, surprisingly rested, but in a somewhat gloomy mood. It was always strange to see how certain ceremonies could be so energizing that they compensated for the lack of sleep. Stéphanie seemed more fit than usual, and was finally satisfied with her experience, which had proved much smoother than the others. She had spent the evening in a half-sleep filled with dreams and visions, but never too intense to make these feelings overwhelming.

We prepared for the visit of the day. Diego had announced the day before that we were going to visit the site of Moray. He explained that this particular place was a huge hole dug in the ground, literally symbolizing the womb of the Earth. He advised us, when we were at the bottom, to feel this peculiar feminine energy. The Feminine was definitely a very present theme.

So we left by bus for this atypical Inca site. Despite the magnificent landscapes we were passing through, and the splendid weather, the atmosphere in the group was rather grim. Everyone was digesting and integrating what they had experienced the day before. Apparently, the program had been intense... As usual, Sylvie had remained very evasive about her experience, and I was careful not to insist.

After a couple of hours on the road, we arrived at our destination. The amazing view justified the travel! Moray is actually made up of concentric terraces that gradually sink into the ground. It is assumed that the site has served as a laboratory for agricultural research, notably because of the great temperature difference between its summit and its lowest point in the center. Evidently the shamans relate to it more as a connection to Mother

Earth, and through the love those ancient people could have for Her, rather than a clinical explanation. And it is true that after having descended to the bottom, the atmosphere is very pleasant and peaceful.

I must admit I did not feel any particular sensations, I was simply relaxed. But some people had pretty intense releasing processes by laying on the ground, and offering their suffering back to our loving Mother Earth. After having spent a good time meditating in silence, and feeling the energy of the place, we rose to begin our return. It proved a bit challenging though: At an altitude of 11,500 feet—and despite coca-based infusions and candies—this climb is very physical and the heart beats hard. I had to make several pauses before arriving painfully at the top.

After a restorative lunch in the nearby town of Urubamba, we returned to Melissa Wasi. During the integration session, I shared the happiness I had felt while connecting to members of the group. This time Sylvie refrained from sharing her experience—speaking is not essential anyway, especially if the themes explored are too personal. Stéphanie had also strongly felt the bond that binds us all together. In this quasi-dreamlike state, she had "visited" the other participants, perceiving the processes they were going through. She had felt their joy, hardship, difficulty with communicating, and even the barriers they had set up to protect themselves from their environment.

She had also seen a strange vision she later shared with me. She had seen me sitting on a throne, she was standing to my left, and one of the group members was kneeling before me. It was Nicola, a man in his fifties, nice and calm, who seemed to have known Diego for a while, and who played guitar during our ceremonies. Behind him stood an assembly, apparently composed of Inca warriors. They were getting closer to us, little by little, and the vision became so impressive that Steph preferred to open her eyes. I was clearly intrigued, and my ego, decidedly hopeless, did not find the image unpleasant... I wondered what it meant, if it meant anything.

DOORS OPENING

The day of the last ceremony passed quietly, filled with beautiful visits and encounters. When evening came, I had no precise intention in mind. As I knew Stéphanie had found a formula that suited her, the atmosphere was more relaxed. I decided that, as last year, I was just going to ask the plant to advise me on how best to apply Her teachings on a daily basis, once back in Paris. I did not know what waited for me...

When my turn came to take the medicine, I opted for a "regular" dose. Our group had been joined by a young couple, increasing the number of participants. There was thus a significant delay between the first and last person being served. The lights were not off yet, but I began to sink into a light trance. Eventually, Diego blew out the candles, and everyone could completely dive into their experience.

My concerns always revolved around the same theme: If I were considering a new professional activity, based on channeling and the opening of a practice, would it be really viable? Would I be able to earn a living, and support my family through such an unusual job? And above all, would I be good enough to meet the expectations of the people coming to consult me, and to make it work through word-of-mouth? All these questions were not necessarily the right ones, but at the time, I could not really escape them when I tried in vain to project myself into the future, and to devise a semblance of strategy.

Of course, that's what the plant allowed me to purge a few minutes later. She made me abandon these doubts and anxious considerations about a future I could not clearly see through my limited intellect and experience. I cannot remember exactly all the details, but it was simply a global cleansing process that would precede a fundamental revelation.

I then had a first clear vision: A lynx suddenly appeared in front of me, leaping in my direction. I would learn later the lynx is the symbol of secrets, of which it is the guardian. As a totem animal, it favors clairaudience, clairvoyance, and everything related to the perception of subtle and hidden energies. I began to feel something coming, the imminence of a meeting. I was filled with a growing reverence, convinced that I was in the presence of something extremely wise and noble. I even bowed, so great was this feeling of respect.

I then had a second vision, just as clear: I saw a humanoid being, very thin, very long, sitting with the knees rising under the chin, in the typical position of some mummies. He looked at me. He had large, completely black and vertical eyes, as well as a sort of small stem planted on his head. He was clearly of vegetal nature—like a pictorial representation of a Nature spirit. What followed is quite difficult to account, as the events all seemed to unfold at the same time, in a non-linear way.

I found myself in front of a circle, some kind of council whose members had inspired me with this immense respect a few moments before. They welcomed me. At a very deep level, I *knew* these beings were entities dedicated to healing, and that by being so welcoming, they meant I was also a healer. I felt like I was joining again a familiar brotherhood, which I had left behind for my incarnation on this Earth. I then began to receive an uninterrupted flow of information, so fast that my intellect could not grasp it all. I was told not to worry, that I did not need to understand everything right away, and that all these teachings were as many seeds that would blossom at the right time. In this benevolent atmosphere, I felt like I was in front of some sort of biblical Wise Men, each of them welcoming me with a personal gift. Everything was very fast, filled with fleeting visions of these beings—who clearly did not all have a human aspect.

This process seemed to last an eternity, even if at that moment, time absolutely meant nothing. I was surprised when Diego lit the candles. I would have never suspected the ceremony was already over, and I could barely open my eyes. Milagros rose and stood in the center of the maloca. She held veils in each hand. Then the music began, and Milagros danced to the dynamic sound of the guitars, spinning around the room. She handled these veils in fluid, graceful and incredibly energetic gestures. I was totally hypnotized by this striking performance, admiring this woman who—after drinking Ayahuasca and spending the night taking care of the group—still had such a strong energy.

When she finished this incredible dance, the ceremony seemed to be officially over. Yet I didn't feel like I was done, still completely seized by the effects of the plant. A voice in my head seemed to tell me that after the theory, I had to go to practical work. My intellect was totally off, and I did not really understand what this idea implied.

Then in a completely automatic way, I turned to Sylvie on my right, and laid my hands on her belly and her throat. I could feel her embarrassment, even though apparently no one was paying attention to us. I knew these two points required an energy adjustment. André, a tall Canadian fellow, came to stand in front of me, and took me in his arms. He began to growl like a bear, in an amusing and joyful demonstration of affection. I put my hands on his chest. He told me they were very hot, which I was not aware of myself.

I was sitting there, unable to move, but the people in the group started to come to me spontaneously. As they approached, my gaze literally clung to a part of their body, apparently perceiving the place that could benefit from a "treatment." Nobody was telling me anything verbally, but someone or something focused my attention on the issue to treat. For some people, I knew their problem was more mental, as if they had a "can of worms" in their head, and I put my hand on their forehead to appease them and "put things back in order." In others, I felt a stagnation of energy, and I even shook them vigorously, knowing it was what they needed most at that time.

It could sound crazy, but I showed a very unusual boldness, bathed in an unshakeable conviction and a knowledge of which I did not know the origin—and I was actually totally uninterested in those technical questions. I was just doing what I had to do, with no other consideration than my love for the man or woman who was before me.

As these interactions continued, things became more and more fluid and automatic. I waved to the young couple who had joined us for the third ceremony, and to whom I had not even spoken before. As they approached, I immediately detected a problem on the boy's shoulder. I asked him if this was the case, which he confirmed to me by explaining that he was a waiter, and that holding a tray all day was causing him pain. I asked him to bend over, and I put my hands on his shoulder. "Wow, it's hot!" He exclaimed, laughing. When I had finished, I asked his girlfriend to sit in front of me, and to turn her back on me, without even knowing why. I began to put my fingers on her spine. I could see a sort of reddish gleam, which seemed to dissipate as I made the passes with my hand.

I was the spectator of my own actions, apparently inhabited by forces guiding me, and showing me how to take care of people. Then the young woman stretched, visibly attentive to the sensations in her back. She explained to me that she had had spine surgery a few years earlier, and that she had since struggled to make the pain disappear. She said she was feeling good now, and if I had not been in that state of pure certainty, I would have been the first to be skeptical.

Of course, I ended with Stéphanie, focusing on her chest. By making the corresponding symbolic gesture, I literally tore the envelope which, it seemed to me, compressed her rib cage. She later told me that this treatment had relieved her by lightening the weight she had felt for months.

I could say I was surprised, perplexed, excited or full of doubts. But I did not experience any emotion of this kind. Just satisfaction and profound joy. I had the impression that I had always been able to do it. My confidence was that of someone who has been doing an activity for so long that he is not even surprised anymore.

In this state of plenitude but still dizzy, I finally went back to our room, with Stéphanie's kind help.

COMING OUT

How do you wake up from such a crazy night? Actually, pretty gently. This is the marvelous thing about this medicine: We find ourselves in such new worlds, going through experiences so unprecedented, that not much can ultimately surprise us. Everything seems to flow, even the most unexpected discoveries. It had just happened. Doubts and uncertainties would be for later. Anyway, like the first time in the Amazon, it was a fact I would not be able to easily deny afterwards, labeling it as mere hallucination or misinterpretation of my visions.

The day was calm. In the afternoon, we decided to put a blanket on the grass, and enjoy the sun. Kevin, a member of the group, came to sit under the porch of Diego's parents' house, a few meters from us. Surprisingly, he was the only person who had not felt anything with Ayahuasca during the three ceremonies. He had tried to take stronger and stronger doses, with no obvious effects. He actually joked about it during our integration sessions. But behind his rather casual attitude, one felt a deeper wound and the desire to mask a likely disappointment behind a cool smile.

Sylvie observed him for a while, and remarked Kevin looked deeply sad. She was definitely very intuitive. I gently approached him, and laid my hands on his chest, again without questioning anything. Then I began to speak, with a voice almost from beyond the grave: very serious, very slow. What was expressing through me was saying San Pedro could help him, but from now on, he had to stop joking, take things seriously and get involved. He nodded, and told me my hands were really warm. After remaining silent for a moment, I returned to sit on the lawn without further ado.

When we all gathered for the integration session, in the late afternoon, I was particularly happy to share my experience with the group. I admitted I had never defined myself as a "healer," mainly because I considered it such a noble role. I would have felt like I was putting myself on a pedestal. But after that night, I had to admit something had happened, even if I could not explain everything. It seemed there was a potential in me which I had never acknowledged—and I realized it still bothered me a little, as if it jeopardized my humility or my security. In any case, I was deeply grateful to the members of the group, this family, who had agreed to play this scene with me. I hoped they would derive from it a benefit as great as the gift I had received.

After my testimony, I was surprised to see Kevin make a statement, and tell me he also believed I was a healer. According to him, after the brief meeting we had had together during the afternoon, he had felt much better. To the point of renting a scooter from Diego's mother, and going for a ride. He admitted he had fallen on the bumpy road, and I then realized it was his entire problem: not engaging, not getting too much involved, for fear of falling. And Ayahuasca had finally reflected his reticence to him, which was surely a big teaching. I hoped this mini-event would be a symbolic trigger for him, showing him that one could stumble and get up unharmed. Without it being a drama or a failure, but simply a natural learning process.

Another testimony troubled me. Linas, a man with whom I had had little interaction, seemed to echo Kevin's remarks. He explained during his speech that he had had a very difficult ceremony: He was kneeling on the ground, as in prayer, swinging rapidly back and forth, and overwhelmed by very intense and painful visions. I did not remember, but during the night, I had bent over and had blown air on him. He was sitting next to Stéphanie, and I had made this gesture without even thinking about it. Besides, I realize I was blowing air on the group very regularly, which was a way for me to send energy and support. He explained that, at that moment, his black visions had literally flown away. My breath had been like a powerful wind, dissipating dark clouds. I was surprised but also very interested in such concrete feedback, about an act I had done in a totally spontaneous way.

After this sharing, the young boy whose shoulder I had taken care of approached, to tell me he also practiced energy healing. What had happened the day before appeared clearly similar to him. I thanked him, grateful for any form of confirmation that could help me accept this new idea. Another young woman came to see me, and asked me if we could do a healing session together before she left. It was totally surreal, but I gladly accepted.

The week had been full of surprises, and I was over the moon. Not out of pride, but because I felt I had done some kind of coming out. In addition, I had the prospect of the San Pedro ceremony the next day, which excited me very much.

We had befriended Ron and Ann, a lovely couple in their fifties, and then planned to go to Titicaca Lake together. Farewell then Machu Picchu for this time, our timing being too tight to visit everything. I did not care. Things had been organized spontaneously and smoothly, and that suited me perfectly. I had definitely changed since last year, and I saw my progress on the delicate question of letting go.

We had an appointment with Diego the following day, at 8 a.m., for our meeting with San Pedro—whose traditional name is "Huachuma." I decided to go to bed early, and get some rest in anticipation of this new experience.

THE SON OF THE SUN

The next day, on an empty stomach, we found ourselves in Diego's kitchen. The taking of San Pedro was going to take place in a very informal way, around a desperately empty breakfast table. There were three of us, besides the master of ceremony: André—my new bear-like Canadian friend—Sylvie and me. Stéphanie had decided she had enough, and would be our official guardian.

Diego explained how the ceremony would be conducted: The effects of Huachuma would be felt as a single, very long wave, lasting between eight to ten hours—unlike ayahuasca, which is a succession of peaks and lows during the journey. He reassured us by saying that this medicine, associated with the masculine principle, the grandfather, was much softer, calmer and progressive. The ayahuasquero suggested we choose a dose, ranging from one to four teaspoons. Four being, in his opinion, a bit extreme, even unreasonable.

I opted for three. Despite our departure the same evening for Cuzco, I did not want to miss out on the experience. Even if it meant being half awake in the taxi taking us to the hotel.

We still received some basic recommendations: Huachuma is a very contemplative medicine, but can sometimes give the sudden urge to wander in all directions. The lawn in front of Diego's house would be our headquarters, and we would have to notify him if we wished to leave. Finally, he warned us that the taste was horrible, and for him, it was even harder to swallow than ayahuasca. That said it all…

André chose also three spoons, and Sylvie took two. Diego diluted them each time in a glass of water, creating a not-soappetizing greenish liquid, covered with thin foam. I tried to swallow it in one gulp, with a single intention: the respectful desire to meet the spirit of the plant—letting Him pick any theme or work that would be relevant for me. The taste was certainly not pleasant, somewhat similar to mild liquid pepper and earth, but I expected worse. That said, the first take of this kind of beverage is always the least difficult. When the brain has associated a smell with unpleasant physical sensations, the apprehension can then become greater, creating even certain disgust for the ingested substance. So we went to sit in front of the house, facing the mountains of the Sacred Valley. With beautiful sunny weather, the day looked promising.

I am aware I am going to have some difficulty in recounting the experience I had on that day. It is very challenging to describe the sensations, the power of the emotions and the state of perception in which one can be with this plant. I will simply share what I felt with maximum objectivity, in the most factual way possible, leaving it to everyone to interpret it.

After a moment spent looking around me, sitting on the grass, I began to feel strange sensations. I had the impression that faces were appearing gently on the mountainside. It was not really a vision, for the view remained the same. But it seemed that certain details of stone and vegetation had taken on a new meaning, and the faces of the Ancients were there, looking at me. After a while, I realized I had the ability to focus on the elements around me, and just look at them for hours without losing interest. Every flower, every tree I could watch was simply fascinating, so much so that their sole observation could have filled a whole life. It was a very pleasant feeling, despite the fact that San Pedro was not very gentle with my stomach at that time—Diego had told us that some people even purged with this medicine.

Then I felt the wave became even more intense, plunging me into a slight trance. I had the curious feeling of vaguely remembering something, without being able to put my finger on its exact nature. It was quite subtle, since I had no strong visual distortions or other reactions of this kind: just the sensation that I gently unveiled a part of my previously untapped consciousness. Then things took an increasingly strange turn. I had the impression I remembered events I had not experienced in my current life, and that seemed to be directly related to the Inca Empire—and more precisely, to the last Inca.

At that moment, I was lying on my stomach, my face sunk in the cool grass, and my arms stretched out in front of me. Imagine Superman flying and you'll get a picture of the scene... Diego came and sat right next to me.

- "Do you know anything about the last Inca?" I asked him.
- "Well, yes... His name was Atahualpa, he was considered the son of the Sun. When the Spaniards captured him, his people were lying on the ground, in a posture of veneration, as you are at this moment. The Spaniards then decided to kill everyone present: Everybody was taken by surprise and it was a real massacre. Then Atahualpa was imprisoned and Pizarro asked for a ransom, which consisted of filling a room with gold, up to the level of his raised hand. But although the ransom was paid, he did not respect his word and killed the Inca."
- I heard myself say, "You know what? I think I was that man..."

Yes, I suppose it sounds totally insane, but that was exactly what I was feeling at the time. I "remembered" I had been Atahualpa. Then an avalanche of memories literally fell on me. I was told about the role of the Inca, why I was killed—since I lived this as a first-person experience—and all the companions who were currently with me were actually people I knew at that time. Diego was then a high priest, and Milagros was already his wife. Stéphanie was my own wife, or at least someone I had deeply loved. Sylvie was my oracle. André was in charge of my personal guard and was a military figure. Ann was a lady of my court, while Ron was a sort of diplomat or chamberlain who was responsible for organizing the routine business for me.

Most of these people were then sitting on the porch of Diego's house, and as I watched this scene, I had the impression that another image was superimposed, revealing the characters of ancient times. I was looking at a live painting representing a scene from another age, based however on the characters I knew today. Again, it is a very difficult feeling to describe, because things were no longer quite linear, and several layers of existence seemed to blend together.

A silent voice was telling me what the Inca really was: a being benefiting from a specific energy configuration, which allowed him to remain connected with the spiritual worlds. He was not a god, but just a symbol to remind human beings that they all come from the Source, and that our incarnation on this Earth is simply a temporary choice to learn from each experience. The Inca was a lighthouse whose light said: "Hold on, my dear companions. Learn and never forget you are eternal souls, actors coming to Earth to play a role. This role will teach you who you really are, and will contribute to the expansion of your being. So be strong and never remain completely in the illusion of the character you are playing. Live your life to the fullest, while honoring your true nature and connection to the Source."

I was told that, over time, the people of the Empire had forgotten the true function of the Inca and his primary role. Instead of using him as a source of inspiration and personal power—and above all as a permanent reminder of their own divinity—people began to venerate and idolize him. And rather than take care of their own expansion, they had put all their power back into his hands.

Huachuma then showed me the global plan: the fact that the fall of the Inca Empire was a collective agreement among those millions of souls, who had recognized that the present situation was a dead end. These people had forgotten the light within them, and only focused on the one the Inca represented. Atahualpa's death, the culmination of a literally co-written history, was thus deliberately chosen.

Blowing out a candle when another thousand burn has no major impact. But blowing out the only one that is still lit up plunges the world into the dark. The challenge was: Now that people are in complete darkness, they will have no choice but to find the light within themselves. True, it will be a very difficult path, filled with violence, misery and oppression, but it is the only way to help these individuals rediscover who they really are.

The information, which came to me in the form of allegorical thoughts, was very clear. If at that time these human beings had consciously preserved the idea of their own divinity, killing the

Inca would not have made a big difference. But as they had placed all their power and faith in his hands, the disappearance of one man had caused the fall of an entire empire. Such was the lesson to be learned... "Now you are alone, so become your own guides."

So you can picture me sitting on the grass, lost in all these thoughts, trying to make sense of these teachings. Their nature was very disturbing, as this story was not whispered in my ear, but was experienced as a personal memory. I tried to focus on my breathing in order to stay centered, while watching those people around me, whom I felt I had known before at a very deep level. I had the intuitive insight that this day was a celebration. All these souls had been close to each other during the fall of the Inca Empire, and they finally met again to see if the plan had worked: If people had begun to find their inner light, not relying on idols, gurus, gods or any other external figure one can imagine...

Even if these persons did not remember, I knew they were there for an appointment we had all agreed on. And a part of them helped me fetch the information and remember it—and then be able to share it with them in return, on a more conscious level. For example, André had difficulty breathing, and I remembered he had been tortured and drowned. Sylvie was a powerful oracle who hardly ever spoke, but every phrase uttered was considered sacred. She had predicted my death and the fall of the Inca Empire. I also remembered Diego, my old friend, crying when he knew I was going to be executed, knowing that it meant the end of a world.

But I believe that the most crushing memory was connected with Stéphanie: I relived the moment when she had been killed before me, her throat cut, in a cruel and barbarous act. In doing this, the Spaniards' goal was to break me through sorrow, and turn me into a puppet they could easily control. I really relived the horror, the incomprehension and the deep despair I had felt at the time, when she had been murdered before my eyes. I began to cry, shaken by uncontrollable sobs. Stéphanie, seated beside me, was handing me handkerchiefs to wipe away what seemed to be an endless flow of tears.

Here is a very strange emotion: You have lived more than twenty years with a person, and suddenly you feel a deep sense of losing her. And at the same time, you are overwhelmed with immense relief by realizing that you are back with her, celebrating this reunion after an endless absence. I'm not sure I'll ever be able to really explain the intensity of this experience, and its extremely destabilizing power.

I felt deep within my being that we were all actors, choosing to create our reality as we would act in a play. At the time, I had the intuition that Stéphanie's thyroid problem was in some way the symbol of her former death. And that she had chosen this throat-related disease, in connection with those tragic events. I understood that I had decided, not without mischievousness, to return in the guise of those who had killed me: white skin, black beard, married to a woman of Spanish origin... All the irony of the situation hit me hard!

It is important to say that what I am describing here is a summary of my experience. But it actually lasted twelve hours without interruption. And having these thoughts of remembrance for twelve intense hours can't be easily dismissed out of hand.

Of course, I was excited to tell Diego and others what I had perceived. I was convinced that, at one level or another, they were only waiting for that! Yet I don't think I managed to share my "revelation" with them, obtaining at best a polite interest. Later, I was almost ashamed of being carried away by my enthusiasm, at the risk of passing for a perfectly wacky guy. Yet, on the instant, I could not doubt for a second the validity of my perception, especially when this information had been rehashed in my mind over such a long time. But in the face of the apparent lack of interest of my companions, and in spite of my slight frustration at not fulfilling my part of the contract—at least that is how it felt to me—I secretly wished this might later awaken a possible insight in them.

At the end of the day, I then felt a little downcast, tired by so many emotions and the integration of all this information. Diego advised me to eat sugar to stop the effects of San Pedro, which didn't prove to be very efficient. I had the impression of bothering all my entourage with the account of my day, always hoping to trigger something in the person with whom I shared it. But resignation soon followed my initial enthusiasm, and I decided to give up.

Actually, I later had difficulty deciding what to think about this experience. Was all this the fruit of my imagination, and had I only succeeded in ridiculing myself? In any case, I first had to be pragmatic, and see what I could do about this incredible day. What was San Pedro's goal, by focusing on this theme? I was sufficiently aware of the wisdom of these medicines to know that these teachings contained a real treasure. I would have been stupid to consider this gift lightly, simply classifying it in the "oddities" category. I had to put everything back into perspective.

If I were to describe the wonderful blessings received during this ceremony, I would first say that it matters little whether I was actually Atahualpa in a previous life. Or if I was simply shown what his life and his role were by living them firsthand—which is what I believe now, by the way. Anyway, I would never expect someone to follow me if I had the naivete to say, "Hey, you know what? I am Atahualpa's reincarnation!" I can only imagine they would slap a straightjacket on me, and throw me in a padded room.

But my goal in coming to Peru was to understand what a perfect "channel" of energy might be. And feeling who Atahualpa was taught me a lot about this subject: his connection to the Source, his sense of harmony and balance, this elevated expression of love, nobility and power... I can still reconnect to this state, which brings me real inspiration.

Moreover, when we want to help others in one way or another, it is very important to integrate this fundamental lesson: We can be a reflection for someone, but never a "master" or a "guru," trying to impose our views on this person. We all must now find our own inner light, be our own guides. And the best way to assist people is to respectfully remind them it is not only possible, but even essential. Everything is there, within reach. And of course, as far as I'm concerned, it begins by living myself according to these principles.

Finally, when we go through such an experience, with the absolute feeling that everything is a marvelous play, and that we are all actors with full control of our existence, we can no longer take things so seriously. The concept of identification shatters. And when we remember other lives, fictitious or real, as if they were part of a single, continuous existence, we can no longer cling so hard to our identity.

I think that day, Frédéric became more of a character to me. Eventually, I would begin to become aware of the larger, eternal actor behind. After this experience, nothing would feel as "real" as before. I would be able to examine the elements of my life with more distance, understanding better the purpose and value of all things—even the most unpleasant ones...

Of course, I would regularly dive back into this role, but it would be easier to get out of it in the most overwhelming moments.

After saying goodbye to our hosts, we left that same evening, and took a taxi to Cuzco. I was still a bit nauseous, but lucid enough to exchange a few words with our driver during the ride. The effects of San Pedro were stubborn, and even when we got to our hotel room, my mind kept wandering. I had had enough of this sensation, and I only aspired to go to bed, to put an end to the experience. After a while, I finally managed to fall asleep, welcoming that rest with gratitude.

REINVENTING MYSELF

So the next day we left with Ron and Ann for our trip on Lake Titicaca. I felt better, but still unable at that time to give any meaning to my previous day's experience. I was torn between the embarrassment of ridiculing myself with the people I respected, and the magic of a day that had allowed me to explore unknown territories of my consciousness.

I did not regret our choice: The beauty of the lake, the energy of the place, and the kindness of the inhabitants touched me deeply—and still are a fond memory. We returned three days later to Cuzco to begin our trip back to France.

When we returned home, we went to spend a few days with my parents, who were the first to hear about our adventures. Once again, I was surprised by their open-mindedness to the intriguing story of what we had experienced in Peru. I even offered them a healing session, which they accepted with curiosity. My father suffers from numerous joint and muscular pains. I was wondering if I could relieve him...

After a long moment of laying my hands on him, during which he felt an undeniable warmth, he seemed to feel better. His body seemed to have been "showered" with energy, and made more flexible. He could even perform movements the stiffness caused by his pain prevented him from doing until now. I was hesitant: On the one hand, I showed total acceptance, as if it were just natural. And on the other hand, I felt disbelief for a practice that was still totally foreign to my intellect. Yet my father told me that if he hadn't felt any benefit, he would have told me clearly, in my own interest and so that I wouldn't delude myself. This was a sincere opinion that I could not ignore.

I was stunned by the evolution of my relationship with him. Since our trip to the Amazon, there had been a relaxation on my part that had changed everything between us. I had finally been able to tell him openly that I loved him, and this simple statement had been the beginning of an unexpected rapprochement. This love was now expressed without embarrassment, and I felt much freer in what I could exchange with him. Our relationship had become more frank, more loving, more demonstrative as well. We regularly hugged each other, fully enjoying our mutual affection. A new confidence had developed, where honesty and outspokenness seemed to have replaced the permanent fear of offending each other.

Back in Paris, I had to integrate everything into my life. A task that wasn't going to prove so simple. For my mind, always anxious, put before me the logical question: "What now? What are you going to do?" A vast subject, of which I really did not see the global plan. I had discovered a potential I didn't know anything about. Should I reinforce my learning? The old demon of diplomas was surfacing again. How could I be seen as legitimate in a role of healer, if my only training was: "You know how to do it, then do it!" And at the same time, Ayahuasca had made me practice by showing me I was capable of it, and that everything was already there within me. I had the impression that a training, no matter how good it was, would have confined me to a modality that would be too specific.

I decided to meet some healers, to introduce myself to this world I didn't really know. I wanted to break the image I had of the countryside bonesetter, who receives people in his kitchen, and who is paid with a warm handshake or a chicken. At least that was the stupid caricature I had in my mind at that time. And I have to be perfectly honest: Among my concerns, of course, was my financial viability. How would I be able to support my family, while following this path that represented both the Unknown and my greatest joy? The spirit of the pack was very much present through my wolf nature, and ensuring the well-being of my loved ones was definitely as important as my own desires.

One of my next meetings was particularly significant. I had made an appointment with a well-known healer in Paris. I was burning to ask him my questions, one of them being whether he felt I had a potential similar to his. This shows the meagre confidence I had in my abilities at that time: I desperately needed a concrete validation. He didn't really proceed with an energetic healing, but our conversation was just as beneficial. Although he did not comment on the presence of a possible healing power within me, he explained that if I had this "gift," it was already there. So he strongly advised not to follow any training. He admitted it had taken him a very long time to get rid of the principles that had been taught to him, at the beginning of his practice. He had to gradually relearn how to work according to his own methods and sensitivity.

Moreover, he cited the case of one of his friends, who organized seminars to learn how to become a healer. According to this friend, only a small percentage of the participants were ready to express a healing gift at that time. When he asked him why he was still giving his students a diploma at the end of the seminar, he shrugged: "Well, you know... they paid for it..."

This anecdote had a powerful effect on me. Not that I want to debate about the real capacity of all these people to heal, because I sincerely believe we all have this potential within us. And I am sure the simple willingness to start this process proves they fundamentally have the will and the predispositions necessary to develop it. But I realized that going through this kind of seminar would be also an indirect way to buy me a certification, regardless of the actual nature of the work done and the results obtained during the training. Did that really make sense to me?

Later, I would be surprised to see many other practitioners suffer, like me, from this legitimacy syndrome. Their business cards or bios often contained rather pompous, even extravagant names: "great masters," leaders of obscure associations, PhDs of all kinds, even the most improbable... Would our society be so skeptical and suspicious that it must be constantly reassured with titles and certificates? Even though I understood this could be part of the game, it no longer seemed justified for my personal development. While I wanted to reassure others, I wanted above all to reassure myself. So if I were to make a name for myself, it would be by word of mouth. It didn't necessarily seem the most comfortable way, but it was more in line with my convictions—

even if it meant putting me under another kind of pressure, and having to obtain concrete positive results with my clients.

Moreover, this book idea had been in my head for a while. I sincerely wanted to share these experiences with others, and I realized they aroused real interest among those to whom I told them. After all, I had really experienced them, and they were full of positive lessons and energy. They had totally transformed my life, and it would have been a shame to keep all those benefits just for myself. So I decided to start writing this book. And my hard-working mind—definitely hopeless—thought that, in addition, it would represent an interesting reference for my future resume as a healer...

I spent the next six months discovering this universe, through interesting meetings and readings. People who practiced healing, professionally or not, often told me the same thing: This kind of exploration requires time, not through master-student learning, but by letting this potential express itself freely and naturally. We are usually our biggest obstacle, and we just have to let go, and risk presenting ourselves to the world in a different light.

During this period, I was bombarded with micro-events that would be too many to list here. Whether it was in the form of conversations, synchronicities or even dreams, it looked like I received messages constantly. The channeling sessions I did with my friends or Stéphanie were also very enriching sources of information. When I retransmitted an idea that my "guides" expressed, it literally passed through me. I thus deeply understood the meaning of these teachings, which I received in the form of thoughts and concepts. Even if I didn't realize their impact at the time, I was sometimes surprised later by their natural integration into my daily life.

The discourse of my guides often dealt with the malleable nature of "reality" as we perceive it, and our ability to create the circumstances of our lives. The intention was above all to give people back their power, and I realize how central this theme has been in this learning. Whether through master plants or channeling, the teachings I had always received revolved around this idea, in an almost obsessive way.

It would be difficult for me to relate this process step by step, which allowed me every day to observe my internal patterns, and to put the pieces of the puzzle in place. It wasn't always pleasant—I would say the challenges were even richer, because they put in contrast certain beliefs and definitions I had acquired since my childhood and that were deeply rooted in me.

For example, the concept of courage and cowardice. Was it cowardice not to open a practice right now? Or was I really not ready? I realized that this fear of being a coward had been with me all my life, and that it obviously went back to my adolescence and the bullying I had experienced. But even long before that, in my relationship with my father. I realized I was prey to contradictory definitions: On the one hand I secretly admired him, because he had never let anyone walk all over him—even if it meant going into extremely violent reactions. And on the other hand, this same person who embodied absolute insubordination would never have tolerated a similar behavior on my part. He would have immediately nipped in the bud all my attempts at rebellion. I realized this kind of insoluble paradox was at the origin of many sufferings. And that in reality, all these dissonances in our thought system are linked to these principles we are taught from an early age, and that are often in opposition.

A boy had been bothering me on the playground in kindergarten, and I couldn't understand why: "Bah, let them say! They are idiots, they don't even deserve attention," my mother replied. And the next day, if I told her something that made her sad, she would fall into victimization: "I am so kind to you, and that's how you thank me? Aren't you ashamed to do that?" As a result, it's hard to believe others' behavior doesn't matter.

Or as said above, my father would regularly tell how he had taught a lesson to someone who had disrespected him or openly contradicted him. And then he led the family with an iron fist, never offering us the freedom of speech or consideration he expected from others.

Of course I don't blame them, as I know they were acting by their own psychological conditioning. My purpose is simply to explain that these influences are omnipresent during our whole life. And that the contradiction between those definitions can even induce a kind of schizophrenia. By trying to make sense of those principles, and apply them in our daily lives, we can simply get lost, and alternate regularly between extreme behaviors:

aggressiveness / passivity, love / hatred, domination / submission...

Of course, parents are far from being the only source of these beliefs, which come from all our interactions with our environment in general. For example, we are told that work is healthy and a source of fulfillment, to the point of considering idleness as a vice. Yet, it's extremely common to hear someone complain about an unrewarding job, an upstart colleague, or a tyrannical boss... Money is another thorny subject: "That's all there is to it. And you have to pursue studies to be able one day to succeed and to gain plenty of it!" said my parents. And the next minute, during a lively family discussion: "Another big money story! As long as there's money at stake, it corrupts everything!"

The question is then simple, especially when you are still a child: What should I choose? Become rich and possibly corrupt? Or poor, but at least stay a good person, even if it means giving up on my happiness? And if I choose poverty, then why do I have to study, since I have always been encouraged to do so only to become richer?

There is sometimes enough to make you go crazy, tossed between diametrically opposed strategies that no longer make any sense. Because what might sound like mundane thoughts, actually reveals a global and implicit programming that we constantly use for the most fundamental and automatic acts of our life. Each time I spoke with various people, it was obvious that their deep conditionings were at the origin of their fear of losing their job, of engaging in a loving relationship, or even of embarking on a new professional activity... To deny those conditionings was then equivalent to endless suffering, without hope of correcting them.

Some will say there is nothing new here: All human sciences are based on this principle. Indeed. But then what can we do about them, in a pragmatic and concrete way? First of all, to become aware of those beliefs. To dig and reveal them in the open, without shame and with the greatest honesty, which then makes it possible to own them and change them. This can be an absolutely fascinating job of observation and investigation, and does not necessarily require the services of a qualified specialist in human thought. We are in the driver's seat, and have privileged access to this information. Everything is available to us without someone from outside necessarily having to come to probe the depths of our head. This can, of course, help to take a step back and confide in a benevolent ear. The challenge, however, is not to put our fate entirely in someone else's hands.

For my part, I knew some of these issues were intractable without throwing everything away, and starting from scratch. I had to tear up my page, and completely revise my copy. I decided to examine and question all my definitions. I knew I was able to rearrange all this junk and clean it up. I wanted to reshape my life and mind in a simpler, purer and more harmonious form. And in reality, I was the only one who could do it. Taking responsibility for it was a crucial step in creating a happier life. Blaming the whole world for my condition would have quickly ended up in a dead end anyway. Because in the end, I was the one who had decided to adopt a specific belief, so it was now up to me to decide if I continued to give it credit. And no one else could do it for me. In other words, I no longer had to find a user manual for my life: I had to rewrite every word myself.

THE PROPOSAL

The following months were very pleasant. I was integrating the lessons I had learned, I worked on fulfilling personal projects that matched my passions, my goal was to go back to Peru the next year... In short, I was simply happy. I thought I had reached a kind of enlightenment, or at least come closer to perfect happiness, which finally seemed accessible and concrete to me.

I woke up every morning with a smile on my face. I was constantly struck by jolts of joy and love, and I felt divinely well. My nights were particularly rich, filled with dreams and messages. It looked like a kind of dreamlike initiation, in which I was shown my mental schemes, and even sometimes how to heal. I had never realized how much dreams can be an absolutely magical tool for self-discovery. Once one is attentive to the messages they contain, they get more and more meaningful and detailed. It is all about going to bed with a real desire for discovery and exploration.

We all constantly receive a multitude of information every night, but we have been educated to relegate all this to fantasy of the mind. "It's just a dream," we were taught as a child. Others say they never dream, but that simply means they don't remember it when they wake up. When we fall asleep with the intention of remembering our dreams and understanding their meaning, such as praying to higher forces or to our own subconscious, we can be surprised by the intensity of the information received.

I had even placed a small notebook next to my bed, determined to note down a few words allowing me to recall the different dreams of the night. The mere fact of having done this had in itself greatly improved my dreaming activity, and the fact of noting a few details was more than enough to bring back whole parts of my dream journeys, which I would never have remembered otherwise.

One very memorable dream struck me in particular. I was in my beloved maternal grandmother's dining room, a recurring setting for my experiences. I sat in a chair and started talking with Stéphanie, who was in front of me. I began to see images, old black and white photos. In one of them, I clearly saw a young woman cycling along a canal. I then suddenly received one of these "packets" of information which are then unraveled as they are examined. I was told that, in a previous life, I had been a German officer during World War II, and that I was shown Stéphanie, the young woman on the bicycle, who was Jewish. I was in love with her and we were having an affair. I saw my face, in close-up, with incredible clarity: my very fine blond hair combed on the side, an acne scar on my chin... Every detail seemed to be examined through a looking glass. It was very strange to identify myself with this man, who did not share any of my current physical traits, and towards whom I felt no particular familiarity.

I was then told a story: Stéphanie was a nurse, or at least a student in this field. We had fallen in love, necessarily having a high-risk affair. Love implied constant danger. I felt Steph's fascination for this officer, who attracted her like a flame attracts a moth—even if it meant burning her wings. There was also a lot of dependency in this relationship. I held her fate in my hands, and for her, our union had to last at all costs, as much out of desire as out of necessity. I felt viscerally, and very intensely, the contradictory nature of these feelings.

But one day, she finally saw the German soldiers coming to her home, understanding I had abandoned her. I had sacrificed the love of my life—of my lives—on the altar of obedience to my hierarchy, condemning her to the horrible fate of deportation. I felt I had not survived the guilt of this terrible act for long, perhaps even committing suicide.

When I woke up, the incredible strength of this dream was still there, and I knew it had very personal meaning. Despite my experience under San Pedro, and the sobriety lesson it taught me about how to respond to this type of perception, I had little doubt: This time, I could take the message literally. It echoed so much of who we were, Stéphanie and I, that it was hard to ignore it. Steph's constant fear of lacking, her hostile view of her environment, and the vital importance she placed on our relationship. And on my side, the permanent fear of being seen as a traitor by others, the visceral need not to disappoint, and the constant theme related to submission to a higher authority. Not to mention the visions I had had under Ayahuasca, which had clearly shown me that my life had been a path to freedom, to dissent from a system into which I had surrendered my power. What a striking parallel with the story of this officer, who had committed the irreversible for failing to say no to an overwhelming authority!

Had I explored this theme in another life in such an extreme, total way that I now had the goal of learning how to regain this freedom? Was it why my visions, the messages I received, and the story of my life were imbued with this central theme? I no longer count the number of events in my life corroborating this hypothesis.

One could also say more coldly that this dream was an allegory representing an entirely fictional portrait, describing my current life through a parable invented by my subconscious. Why not? An important detail however makes me want to consider this from a more literal angle. Indeed, at our last return from Peru, I had made an appointment with a young woman whose psychic talents had acquired an impressive reputation in the area: The waiting list for an appointment with her was spread over more than a year! When I finally met this person, in a marathon interview lasting over seven hours in a row, she clearly felt the same energies. Without telling her anything, she had immediately captured this past existence in Nazi Germany, loaded with a very heavy emotion. Even more surprising, she had felt that I myself was Jewish. The moment she shared her feelings and her vision—symbolized by the image of a shop front into which a paving stone was violently thrown—it seized me. I could not say why, but I knew on an unconscious level, without a shadow of a doubt, that she was right and that this implied even deeper considerations.

Through a synchronicity I was more and more used to, a few days later, I came across a documentary about Hitler's Jewish soldiers. It told the little-known story of these young Jews, some of whom had Aryan traits, who had grown up in Hitler's youth, like many other German kids. Some had managed to hide their origins, and had even served in the army, fearing discovery at all times. It was surely the ultimate framework for anyone wishing to explore the theme of submission and rejection: an environment where one has the power of life and death over you, the need to keep a secret at all costs, the difficult choice of betraying family and friends, or embracing a cause that becomes more and more overwhelming and impossible to leave... The scope of all this made me dizzy. Did I condemn the one I loved, but also betrayed everything I was, by denying even my origins, torn between two worlds?

One might assume that with such a realization, other mixed feelings—such as sadness or guilt—might arise. In truth, this was not the case, at least not consciously. For either I remained in the concreteness of everyday life, focusing on my present existence without bearing the weight of any previous incarnations. Or I embraced the global idea of an eternal soul and multiple lives, and this perspective greatly tempered the judgment I could apply to each of my acts: It was then a question of explorations, of themes, of teachings, in a context so vast and enriching that it went beyond all moral considerations. It was an endless learning on a cosmic scale.

I was surprised the concept of reincarnation was suddenly so present in my life, whereas I had not paid particular attention to it before. At best, it had been a vague idea I wasn't even sure I wanted to believe in. But since my experiences in Peru, this vision had become simply obvious to me, finally making each step of my journey much more meaningful, and part of a broader plan with unquestionable coherence.

All in all, this period was well-filled. I felt like I was reconnecting to a completely buried part of myself, gradually digging up unsuspected parts of my personality. It was striking to realize I had been able to live all this time without realizing it, only touching the surface. I now accepted the fact that my exploration would probably never end, regularly revealing new aspects of the greatly underestimated human mystery.

December arrived, and with it an event which was going to make me come down violently from my little cloud. One evening, I received a message from one of my former colleagues, whom I had briefly met during my short time spent in the video games industry. This medium had always fascinated me with its innovative, fun and extremely creative side. But my professional experience in this field turned out to be much more austere and boring than the idealized image I had imagined. So I had quickly changed path, but I had kept in touch with Matthieu—who had arrived the same day as me in the company where I had temporarily worked, and with whom I had immediately sympathized.

He had left me a message on my phone at 18:18. Very mindful of the signs, I was now in the habit of spotting all these little details relating to numbers. I no longer counted the "coincidences" that manifested every day through these kinds of singularities. They were so many and insistent that I could not have ignored them, even if I wanted to. So I decided to take it seriously, and I called him back.

His call was indeed a serious one. We hadn't spoken for several months, and I learned the video game studio he was working for had shut down. Like me, he was unemployed, and wanted to start his own development studio. He was looking for a partner to found his company and create his first product.

It was a shock. In a few minutes, I found myself immersed in my old universe. His proposal was tempting, because it involved a very creative activity and would allow me to finally design a game corresponding to a more personal vision. Being able to express myself, through a passion that had never left me, was very appealing. The objective was to create our studio during our period of unemployment, taking advantage of our allowances to finance our project. I would later learn that four out of five companies are created this way in France, the government encouraging this type of initiative to generate wealth and jobs.

But it was absolutely putting all my plans into question. For me, my future was now clear: writing my book, becoming a "healer" in one way or another, and dedicating my life to expressing that part of me that had revealed itself in Peru. I was out of my hell, and I had no desire to go back. That said, several points slowed my enthusiasm about this...

First of all, at the time, I hadn't practiced my healing skills on many people, and it was still relatively uncharted territory for me. I didn't have the necessary confidence to be sure I could make a living from it, or even to know if it deserved to be made a professional activity. So I had a global desire, but nothing well defined as for its concrete realization. Moreover, Matthieu's offer touched on a domain I had always loved, and he offered me on a platter what I would have described as the job of my dreams a few years earlier.

Finally, and perhaps most importantly, I felt intuitively that there was interesting potential, beyond the apprehension I felt about returning to an environment I didn't like. Whether it was in the messages I received constantly, or in what my own guides expressed, a recurring idea prevailed: "Follow your joy." And thus trust this emotion as a guidance system, which always points in the right direction.

In our western culture, however, we have been taught to do exactly the opposite, encouraging us not to take our desires for realities. A principle that is adopted and maintained for fear of failure, or as a means of protection. Pessimism has a reassuring aspect. We have the impression that if we see things in black, we are "realistic," we prepare for the worst, and we are not likely to be disappointed. I am now obviously convinced this is the best way to shoot ourselves in the foot, and that joy and enthusiasm are not just inconsistent emotions that we must quickly get rid of, to get back to Earth. On the contrary, it is a fundamental energy that clearly indicates whether we are in tune with our profound aspirations. And above all, like an internal GPS, it guides us towards our most beneficial achievements.

Of course, I regularly hear a whole bunch of objections to this point of view, the idea visibly offending the sensitivity of people who do not want to let go of their way of functioning. But none of them convinced me of the contrary: Systematically following our joy, I am sure today, is the best thing we can do in our life—and also the safest in the end!

Regarding Matthieu's proposal, I must admit, this joy was not obvious at first sight. The fear at the thought of returning to a world that seemed hostile and aggressive, was the first emotion I felt. Yet, beyond this immediate veil, I felt our partnership could have many positive consequences. It was a subtle but persistent intuition.

I also had the feeling that I still had to explore the healer's path at my own pace, without pressure linked to a profitability objective. To have a parallel activity ensuring me an income in an interesting professional framework, would allow me to progress step by step in the field of energetic healing. I mean, that's what my reason told me... Another part of me was screaming to run away without looking back! Sometimes I had the impression of betraying myself, of not having understood anything, and of willingly returning to a prison from which I had managed painfully to escape. Was I doomed, to the point of applying this sentence to myself, entering my own cage and closing the door behind me?

All this was very disturbing to me. I felt I was inexorably overtaken by my old patterns, and I wasn't sure how to react to this proposal. If I decided to give it a chance, it would be reluctantly. I also had the prospect of leaving three months later for Peru, for a new exploration that would surely have its share of surprises. And what if I made a commitment to Matthieu, to finally realize with Ayahuasca that my path was elsewhere? My first two trips had been so full of unexpected revelations, that anything was possible. In short, I was in the middle of a dilemma, and my anxiety was beginning to grow. Either I stayed on my track, diving into the unknown without really knowing how to give shape to my desires; or I made a 180 degree turn, and set off again in a direction that was certainly more familiar, but also much more stressful for me.

I was, however, driven by Matthieu's enthusiasm and latent impression that this partnership would be constructive in many ways. During our first meetings, I vaguely explained to him I wanted to give a new meaning to my life, and in particular in helping others. Matthieu had interpreted this as a desire to participate in humanitarian works, and I had deliberately left this question unclear—openly talking about Ayahuasca might have sounded really strange to anyone outside this universe. However, after a few weeks, I decided to speak frankly to my potential partner, telling him about my recent experiences. If he was going to think I was crazy, it might as well be before we officially signed on together.

So we met again at a restaurant, where after a slight hesitation, I explained to him the profound transformations I had undergone in recent years. Once again, I was surprised by his reaction: Even if he was inevitably confused by this information, his first reflex was finally to wonder if his proposal was up to my expectations. Given the opportunities I wanted to explore, creating a video game studio seemed dull in comparison.

Not being myself sure of my intentions, I suggested a three-month "trial period" to see if our collaboration would work. On my return from Peru, we would then take the final decision to seal—or not—our association.

BACK TO LIFE

The following weeks were painful in more than one way. First of all, I had lost that state of grace which had characterized me in the previous months, and anxiety was eating away at me again. I felt like the magician who lost his magic wand, and all his powers at the same time. In order to realize our project with Matthieu, which was to create a game on a well-known Internet social network, we needed to partner with a company specialized in this field. As part of this partnership, they offered to welcome us—including offices and interns—in a corner of their open space.

I immediately reconnected to the atmosphere I had so deeply hated during my last years of work in a company: an austere environment, political wars and egos to deal with in boring meetings, rather sad lunches around a canteen table in the middle of the building, interminable public transport... In short, I realized this no longer suited me at all, and explained to Matthieu I had paid too much for my freedom to endure this again. So I offered him to work from home, coming to these offices one or two days a week to debrief. He was very understanding, and agreed.

There was actually something else that made me want to maintain some distance: Matthieu's own personality. He could be very friendly most of the time, and all of a sudden, could hit you with a very harsh and unexpected remark. This moody behavior, which he himself readily admitted, was coupled with a rather overwhelming and peremptory personality which I found pretty aggressive. I never knew, when I voiced my opinion, if a verbal slap would come out. I saw the effect this had on some of our less assertive trainees, who in the end had lost all sense of initiative, waiting for Matthieu to simply decide for them.

This was actually the reason for our first argument, when I expressed to him—as diplomatically as possible—my disapproval of his attitude towards trainees. I found his public comments humiliating, and his reactions excessive to the "fault" they had committed. For him, any wrongdoing had to be punished, and he reproached me for giving lessons easily, me who remained hidden at home three quarters of the time, not being confronted with the reality of the office.

I couldn't blame him for looking at it that way. Yet I had had to fight so hard in my previous position to keep a human approach to management, faced with a hierarchy that pushed me more and more to treat my team like cattle. I had explored this theme at length, and I could no longer adhere to this vision consisting in "hitting hard immediately to discourage people from doing it again." For me it sounds more like domination-based management, where the employees' desire to do well gradually turns into a fear of punishment.

I felt that Matthieu didn't really want to be mean, but he had this violence and anger in him, of which he didn't really seem to be aware—or at least a clumsiness that could easily turn a joke into a derogatory remark. At least, that's how it felt to me. I must say I had been sensitized to this subject during my discussions in Peru, where several people spoke to me about "Non Violent Communication," a practice that tries to revisit verbal communication from a much less aggressive angle. Today, words have replaced physical blows, and yet can do much more harm. To become aware of their power, and not to use them indiscriminately, seems to have become an essential issue in improving our communication and our community life, especially with the omnipresence of social networks.

In painting this rather dark picture, one might wonder what still motivated me to pursue this adventure. I am well aware this situation brought me back to my relationship with my father: a permanent relationship with someone fundamentally kind, but authoritarian and tense, who could easily hurt me in an unpredictable way. Especially after my experiences in Peru, I had the impression that all my shells had shattered, leaving me extremely sensitive to the energies that surrounded me. So much so that since this unexpected change of plans, I began to regularly have hives on my face, like an oversensitive reaction towards my return to work.

Fortunately, I had acquired in return tools to help me deal with these circumstances and challenges: strong intuitions, a great receptivity, a hindsight allowing me to consider the deep meaning of the events I was going through... Also at that time, I had already studied the Marseille Tarot for a long time, whose archetypes inspired me a lot. I regularly made readings for myself, whose relevance was always striking. By looking at the cards for a few moments, and by stopping the flow of my thoughts, messages and directions came to me spontaneously—like a mirror helping me to see myself better. But every time I made a reading about my association with Matthieu, I inevitably came across the same theme: undeniable success and constructive partnership. I felt deep inside that this relationship would be rich and fertile on many levels, and that it would make us both grow and evolve.

So I did my best to handle all these concerns while waiting for our trip to Peru, which I hoped would shed a new light on all these events. In fact, just before we left, I had already made my decision to pursue our association. In a way, I didn't want to bet everything on what I was going to explore with Ayahuasca, and I wanted to make a choice based on my free will. After all, I would not systematically use visionary plants at each new stage of my life... I announced to Matthieu my intention to extend our partnership, and that he could prepare the administrative formalities we would sign upon my return.

THE WHITE WOLF
AND THE BLACK WOLF

This year, we would go to Peru as a larger group, forming a five-person team. Besides Sylvie, who would come back for a second trip, we would be joined by Jean-Marc—my only other long-time friend besides Jeff—and Alexandra. The French delegation was on its way!

The journey went smoothly. No lost luggage, no erupting volcano... It was almost suspicious. Jean-Marc and Sylvie immediately seemed to appreciate each other. Alexandra, for her part, had left a week before us to visit Lake Titicaca, and was waiting for us at the airport in Cuzco. Once again, I was excited to share this kind of experience with people I really appreciated, curious about the positive transformations they would surely undergo—at least that was all I wished for them.

We arrived at Diego's house, where we met part of the group we would share this adventure with. I was surprised at the number of French-speaking people there. Besides the five of us, there were Alicia and Dave, a very nice couple from Quebec; Jean and Claire, who worked with Diego and were going to participate in the ceremonies as singers and musicians; Doug, an American who had spent several years in Africa and spoke French... We had the impression of being in a very familiar environment. Sometimes it was necessary to remember to speak English to make sure the other members of the group were not excluded from the conversations.

As usual, the first ceremony was to take place that evening. This time I had no trouble finding the theme I wanted to explore. My relationship with Matthieu had made me aware of many wounds that I thought were closed—and yet still proved to be as painful. I felt that something inside me, deeply buried, needed to be dug up and brought to the surface for treatment. I suspected this would lead to a painful ceremony, as the work involved seemed very significant, going back to my childhood and touching very heavy emotions.

Around 6 p.m., the presentation meeting took place, with Diego's traditional recommendations: remain silent, hold the space, be aware of the plant's benevolent intention even if the visions were painful. I still acted as translator for Steph and Sylvie. When it was Jean-Marc's turn to introduce himself, I was struck to see him having difficulty expressing himself in front of the group.

We had met in high school, over twenty years ago. At the time, his life was far from simple. His father had died during his childhood, and his relationships with the rest of his family were chaotic to say the least, as he visibly shared little in common with his mother and brothers. He had a personality I immediately liked. Almost introverted at times, exuberant at others, he had an excellent sense of humor and showed great sensitivity. Over the years, we had followed different paths, but still had regular contact. I had seen him evolve, developing his confidence as well as an athletic body, and getting ever more important professional responsibilities. He held consulting positions within his company, involving regular international business relations.

However, during this meeting, I was seeing again the Jean-Marc from high school: head down, having difficulties to verbalize his emotions, obviously very uncomfortable. It must be said that, in this kind of moment, social masks fall. People put their guts on the table, and openly evoke the trials and sufferings which pushed them to undertake this process. It's hard to joke and stay light in such an emotionally charged time. I understood why he and Sylvie seemed so compatible. They shared the same anxiety about speaking up, where shyness and the feeling of not being legitimate, even unwelcome, were very present.

Evening arrived. In turn we came to position ourselves in front of Diego, to take the earth-colored brew. Stéphanie, still rather reluctant towards this medicine, had previously asked the ayahuasquero to give her again a "contact dose." He had been a little surprised by the term, even though he had suggested it to us the year before. Obviously, he did not remember it, but he had of course agreed to give her the minimum dose. However, by seeing Steph's upset face when she came back to sit down next to me, it seems his concept of "minimum dose" was not shared by my wife, who had felt forced to swallow a little too much for her taste.

I tried to settle comfortably, preparing myself for a difficult night. I really wanted to know why my relationships were so regularly painful. The effects came gradually, but were far from the emotional outburst I expected. My thoughts were floating around the theme I had set for myself. At one point, I got almost puzzled by the sweetness of this experience. Then I heard a "voice" say to me: "Your relational difficulties are linked to the low respect you have for yourself. If I came and shook you up and down, imposing my views on you and telling you what to do, I would only go further in that direction. To teach you self-respect, I must already show you with compassion the one I have for you." I realized how I always expected others to treat me violently, because I had the same attitude towards me. If I had to learn something, it always had to be "the tough way."

I began to grasp the scope of what I was about to receive. If I never respected myself, how could I also respect others? And above all, how could I expect them to respect me? This question did touch on all aspects of my life involving interaction with others.

I brought back memories of my relationship with Matthieu into my consciousness. Ayahuasca sent me precise thoughts, such as instructions I could apply concretely, if I wished. She explained to me that contrary to what I seemed to think, Matthieu did not need a servant who would execute every whim he had. He needed the opposite, a solid partner, with his own personality, and confident enough to support him in this ambitious project. I thought I should always keep a low profile in front of someone else's authority, in order not to upset anyone. But I was shown that rebellion and difference of opinion could sometimes be the best service I could do Matthieu. Otherwise he would end up alone in his decisions, accompanied simply by a slave who would provide only limited help.

From this point of view, Ayahuasca told me I too was

legitimate. I belonged to this world, I had my place in it and I did not need to fade away. Only a real devaluation of myself, totally illusory and unfair, could lead me to think the opposite. Apparently, the feelings I had perceived in Jean-Marc and Sylvie were only a reflection of what I also felt deep inside me. That was probably why I had identified them so easily.

The plant seemed to explain these concepts even further to me, using the image of a white wolf and a black wolf. She told me that sometimes, the white wolf aspect, calmer, more loving, could be seen in me. But there was also the black wolf, more action-oriented, but potentially more violent, even angry. And that I could also let it express itself. At the time, I did not understand how Ayahuasca could encourage me to release a darker, more aggressive side of myself. For me, I had to tend towards the light, to show only a positive aspect and a luminous facet of my being. I had difficulty reconciling this with the idea of sometimes being more extreme and more violent in my positions. In other words, I was told, "If you ever want to throw a punch, and let your black wolf express itself, go ahead!" I was not very comfortable with this idea, but I would explore it in detail later.

Still in this perspective of learning to be happier in my relationships, Ayahuasca showed me some of my behavioral patterns. She insisted, for example, on the fact that I almost systematically expected recognition for everything I did. I did give, but not unconditionally. I was always waiting for a "minimum of gratitude." If the latter was not expressed, then I felt cheated or exploited. I thought that I and my kindness were being abused in this way.

I also had an unfortunate tendency of wanting to control others. I sometimes insisted on convincing people of what I thought was beneficial to them. But the respect I learned for myself that evening was directly linked to the respect I could have for the choices of others. I received a beautiful lesson of humility, purging each of the facets the plant showed me. No wonder these aspects, perfectly insidious and often hidden under a mask of righteousness, had constantly perverted my relationship with others.

I had received a lot. One last piece of information came to me, however, echoing that idea of the wolf. I was told that each animal species was like an "energy model," a particular configuration, each representing a specific archetype. By connecting myself to a symbolic animal, I could then immerse myself in its energy and call upon its particular skills. This was of course in line with the concept of "totem animals" in shamanic traditions. To illustrate this point, I saw in front of me a series of small icons, resembling a computer interface. Each of them represented the symbol of an animal: the owl, the wolf, the bear, the snake... One after the other, they were highlighted, as if to express the fact I could connect to one or the other, according to my needs and the characteristics I wanted to call upon. I thus had an inexhaustible source of inspiration from which I just had to draw.

The teachings seemed to fade, and I opened my eyes, not knowing if the end of the ceremony was near. Sylvie had disappeared, having likely gone by herself, probably out of fear of annoying the group with potentially excessive reactions. To my left, Steph was throwing up her guts. I looked at her and felt compassion for her, not knowing what to do to mitigate her difficult experience.

I heard Ayahuasca, gently mocking: "Well, well, what do we have here... We really have to tell her to stop putting herself in such a mess, she has nothing more to vomit." Like when a little child stumbles and falls, and begins to cry loudly: We know her reaction is disproportionate, and that it aims at attracting her parents' attention, even if the pain is not really serious. We want to take her in our arms and say, "Sshh... Come on, come on, don't scream like that, it's over."

Through this intuition, I understood that for Stéphanie, having such unpleasant experiences with Ayahuasca was a way to tell me: "Look how I suffer for you! See how much I love you? I did not want to come here, but for you I am ready for this sacrifice, so see all the efforts it requires."

I then received an incongruous but familiar image: that of a soccer match, where a player, in the heat of the action, commits a totally inexcusable tackle on his opponent. Realizing the extent of his fault, and wanting to mitigate the referee's penalty, he often rolls himself on the ground, as if the shock had hurt him as much as his opponent. The idea was clear: It is sometimes preferable to join the victims' side than to remain in the perpetrators' side. Some responsibilities may seem too difficult to bear. Of course, I knew I was being shown an unconscious process, a kind of emergency procedure used when the situation becomes unmanageable. And I knew that Stéphanie, following the crisis of our relationship, had not adopted this depressive posture to openly manipulate me. But I understood the reasons why we sometimes prefer to go to rock bottom, rather than assume an untenable position of guilt. And I, for my part, immediately placed myself as an understanding savior, thus sealing our respective positions. I was as responsible as she was.

I was shown a dungeon in which she had locked herself, and it was now necessary to invalidate the sentence she had imposed on herself. No need to continue this unhealthy game of self-punishment, there was no one to judge her, except herself. I decided to bring her all this information, hoping to help her put an end to her recurrent depressive states.

Later, when the ceremony was over, I asked her how she was. She was obviously very angry, blaming Diego, and his too strong dose, for her very difficult night. I preferred to save the explanations and visions I had received about her for the next day, letting her fulminate while we returned to our room.

THE INDIAN TALE

The next morning, I shared with Steph my visions of the previous night. I tried to explain to her, with the greatest gentleness, that her suffering had become useless, obsolete. It solved nothing, healed nothing, and was only the result of self-inflicted punishment. I did not want to give her the impression I believed she was faking it, by pretending to suffer so she could side with the victims. As I expected, at first she thought I was accusing her of being manipulative. By carefully choosing my words, I assured her this was not what I had seen: I knew that her depressive state was very real in her life experience. But she had to understand how it had served her until now, and why she was attached to it, giving it a purpose. When you realize that something is no longer useful to you, you naturally drop it. I am now convinced that if a situation persists in our lives, it is because we still consider it the best possible option, even if it causes a feeling of fear, sadness or frustration.

She finally seemed to welcome this information with some relief, or at least with enough interest to give it more thought.

My other companions had trouble putting words to their experience. Sylvie, as usual, remained discreet about what she had been through. When the effects of the plant had begun to increase, she had preferred to leave the maloca and isolate herself. Jean-Marc seemed to have had an interesting night. He had felt a deep inner work, whose transformative potential had obviously encouraged him to continue this exploration.

As for Alexandra, she had had visions she still couldn't put a very clear meaning on. She had spent a long time exploring a building with garish colors, resembling a doll's house, with a very polished appearance—but looking actually extremely ugly. Add to this the recurrent fear of suffering the effects of dysentery caused by Ayahuasca, and all this brought her back to her deep issues: the realization that always playing good girl, in a nice and polite manner like a perfect little princess, was actually a real nightmare. She felt she needed to go beyond this self-righteousness attitude, especially thanks to artistic expression—which is surely one of the best ways to explore any form of rebellion. She seemed a little disappointed, however, and did not show overwhelming enthusiasm. I wondered if during the last two years, I had not sold her Ayahuasca as the ultimate solution to happiness. I was confident, however, that the work had taken place, and that this experience would make sense later.

In the evening, we met in the maloca to share the results of this first ceremony. Our group consisted of twenty-five members, and I was always amazed at how familiar some of them seemed to me. I especially noticed a young girl about twenty-two years old, with long brown hair and a pretty face. Her name was Vicky, and she was from Venezuela. She seemed to have had a rough night, and her voice was full of emotion. Another young woman, Kathy, had surprisingly felt nothing at all.

When Steph spoke, she gave Diego a falsely angry look, saying she had asked for a small dose, and that she had received much more than she wanted. Diego feigned to hide his face behind his hand, pretending to be ashamed. Claire, who works regularly with him, and who sang at the ceremony, could not help exclaiming: "He does that all the time!"

When my turn came, I recounted my visions and the duality I had felt between the white and black wolves, the plant having told me I could express both aspects. It seemed sensible to me, but at the same time, I was surprised that Ayahuasca suggested to me, for example, a more aggressive or combative attitude—I who only wanted to be peace and love.

In a beautiful moment of synchronicity, at the end of the session, Diego spoke up and said he had a story to share. It was a Cherokee Indian tale:

"It's the story of an old Indian sage, sitting with his grandson on top of a mountain. After meditating for a moment as he looked down the valley, the old Indian finally began to speak:

'You know, my boy, we all have two wolves fighting inside us all the time. A white wolf, representing love, compassion, trust, serenity. And a black wolf that embodies fear, anger, envy, suffering. So they fight constantly, there, in our chest, in an endless struggle.

'And who wins, Grandpa?

'The one you feed...' "

Diego also suggested we embrace our two aspects, light and dark, instead of trying to reinforce the segregation between the two. All this made a lot of sense to me, especially thanks to the experiences I had already had in the Amazon—and it shed a new light on my visions from the day before. The plant simply encouraged me not to deny any part of myself, but on the contrary, to integrate them all in a balanced way. I thanked Diego for this sharing.

SPIRITS AND ALIENS

The next day passed quickly, with a variety of pleasant tourist activities. I really loved this country. Stéphanie, out of irritation, had initially decided not to take Ayahuasca again, but finally changed her mind: She considered we were partners and that we should go through this experience together, and share everything. She thought this medicine was not for her, but she wanted to support me in my approach, and be with me that night. Of course, I found that very courageous, and I realized once again how exceptional my companion really was. Moreover, I was convinced of Ayahuasca's efficiency and benevolence, and I secretly hoped she would also benefit from it. Not necessarily in the same form as my own experiences. But I was sure that at one level or another, these ceremonies could inevitably contribute to her own healing—even if she didn't admit it.

Personally, I didn't know what to focus on for this ceremony. Moreover, I was a bit tired of this attitude, and I had the impression of always asking for more from the plant, which had already helped me so much. I decided that tonight, as proof of my gratitude and blind confidence in Ayahuasca, I would not only take a strong dose, but also leave her free to decide the program. In short, offer myself to her, and abandon myself to the experience, in a total letting go. I wasn't going to be disappointed with the ride.

In fact, it will be quite difficult for me to relate this journey in a perfectly coherent way, as the visions were so strange and sometimes quite abstract. I will simply try to tell what I have experienced, without necessarily trying to add a rational explanation to it—I would be unable to do so anyway.

When evening arrived, I then came in front of Diego and asked him for a bigger dose. I declared to the plant my love for Her, and my complete trust. Steph, for her part, finally seemed satisfied with her dose, which this time had been really minimal. Kathy, the woman who hadn't felt the effects of the medicine, had decided to take an absolutely incredible amount. The ceremonial glass Diego used was full to the brim, almost preventing him from performing his usual ritual gestures—like raising the glass over his head for a few seconds—under risk of spilling the drink. It must have been at least a dozen sips, and I watched in amazement as the young woman swallowed this impressive dose. Some of us looked away, others made faces of disgust. When she had finished drinking everything, by making small regular pauses, we were almost relieved for her. I wondered what made people tolerant of such extreme doses. Was the body's ability to eliminate DMT stronger in some people? As far as I was concerned, I was convinced that if I had taken such a quantity, I would have remained glued to the ceiling of the maloca for several days. It wouldn't have made any sense anyway.

The journey began. Diego started to play a first song, very calm, very deep. I was perfectly still. Shortly afterwards, I heard Jean-Marc begin to speak aloud. His words were muddled, he was already under the effects of the plant. He was trying to say something to the group, as if he was making a public statement, but his state was not really compatible with the practice of English. At the other end of the room, I heard Milagros whisper: "Shhh... Don't speak, Frédéric." The French accent must have misled her. I then heard myself answer her, with a very slow voice from beyond the grave: "That was not Frédéric. That was Jean-Marc." I was the first to be surprised by the sound of my voice. It was very deep, strong, almost authoritative, yet I felt no aggressiveness or irritation. Simply an unshakable inner power, which had made me pronounce these words with exceptional assertiveness and strength, at least for me. Some of the people in the group giggled at this bass voice. Milagros apologized, obviously as surprised as I was. Jean-Marc, on his side, seemed to have calmed down.

Then came the first visions: I saw a kind of red horizon, with black motifs in the foreground. Then the image began to scroll vertically, giving me the impression of gaining altitude. I had the intuition that I was on my way to visit "higher," more elevated realms. But, as an improvised reaction to this idea, the upward movement began to slow down, stopped and suddenly reversed. I fell in free fall. I prepared for the worst.

I suddenly found myself in a very strange "place." I was inside a huge multicolored sphere. In the middle of this sphere, I distinguished an entity, which was, however, at a good distance from my point of view. It was there, motionless. I knew it was very ancient, beyond what the intellect can imagine. I was told it was one of the "Lords of the Earth"—at least that is how my mind tried to translate the meaning of this message. I bowed, crushed by the reverence inspired by this solemn figure. I felt both tiny in front of such nobility, and incredibly honored to be in its presence. Thus I was told that not all elevated spiritual forms were necessarily found in the higher planes, and that there were also magnificent entities associated with the Earth and the concrete aspect of our physical world.

I remained there for a few moments, in front of this indescribable vision, grateful for this priceless gift. Then I returned to the feeling of ascension that I had experienced a few moments earlier. As if Ayahuasca had first made a detour to show me that my conceptions of spiritual elevation were quite simplistic. The content of my visions then took an even stranger turn—that's an understatement.

I found myself propelled into the Cosmos, where I immediately met other entities. I did not distinguish them very well, but I rather understood them in the form of concepts: diversity, plurality, union, love, association... That is what came to me in their presence. For some reason, I "knew" without a shadow of a doubt that these beings were not from our planet. I had already heard stories of people taking Ayahuasca and interacting with extraterrestrial beings, but I hadn't paid much attention to them. Perhaps I should have. I was convinced the visions I had with this medicine were never to be taken lightly. I didn't know why I perceived these things, but those experiences always had a deep meaning and relevance for me. Last night, I had asked Ayahuasca for a ticket to the Unknown, and that was what she was offering me.

So there I was, chatting with aliens... Right. It felt like I was in the presence of a very diverse set of races, a sort of association of civilizations. Confronted with what seemed to be an immense organization on a cosmic scale, I could not help but smile: We still keep wondering, stuck in our arrogance, if God bothered to create life on another planet. But by what I was seeing at that moment, this question seemed totally preposterous.

These beings explained to me that humans had now to change their definitions and their attitude about them, without fear or denial. Because in our current culture, especially through our media and the film industry, they were almost always portrayed as a threat, predators seen through the filter of fear or conspiracy. Today things were changing, interactions were multiplying, and it was time to review the way this topic was being addressed, so that things could move forward. In this explanation, there was also an implicit demand: Speak about it around you, spread this message.

I slammed on the brakes.

Becoming an official spokesman for alien races... Well, I'm really sorry, but I'll have to pass. Even under Ayahuasca, I knew the potential ridicule I was exposing myself to. I respectfully expressed my reluctance, explaining to them I was not brave enough to endure the mocking of my peers, and to become the leader of a whole bunch of UFO enthusiasts. I had, however, begun writing this book, and promised to mention this interaction in it: I would recount it in a factual way, as part of an experience in a modified state of consciousness. Then everyone would be free to believe it or not. I couldn't do better.

They seemed to agree. I was a little ashamed of my cowardice, especially knowing the credit I gave to all these explorations. Even as weird as they could seem, I was sure they were absolutely relevant and precious. But imagining the sniggering and cynicism of those around me, my former co-workers and even my family, it was too much to bear. I realize that in our culture, talking about spirits and entities is one thing, but the issue of extraterrestrial life, despite increasingly recurring phenomena, observations and witnesses, is still a strangely taboo subject.

This seemed to close the "conversation," and the figures faded away. This would be my last meeting of the night, the rest of my visions returning to a more intimate work. It is very challenging for me to relate the sequence of events in a linear order. My experience was so intense that the notion of time had totally disappeared.

I suddenly saw a kind of flaming eye coming towards me, leaving a trail of fire in its wake. I immediately understood it was a kind of "power" that was presented to me: the power to "see." Even though I didn't know exactly what it was, my greedy mind was racing. I was called to order: I should never forget that these gifts were not made to satisfy my ego, but on the contrary, to be put at the service of all. If I misused them, for a purely personal purpose, they would be taken away from me.

The effects of the plant were very powerful. I started connecting with other people in the maloca. The first was Pam, an American woman in her fifties. During our last group sharing, she had told of her inability to open her heart. She struggled a lot with that idea. I was told that her difficulties did not come from her inability to "open her heart"—which she did constantly—but from the definitions and labels she put on it. She was so critical of herself that it prevented her from seeing just how constantly she gave to others. She was in search of a kind of intellectualized ideal, totally arbitrary, and particularly unfair in view of her generous nature. She had to stop constantly denigrating herself in this way, and if she had to open her heart, it was to herself first.

Then a picture of Vicky, the young woman I had noticed earlier, came to me. She appeared to me as a high priestess, draped in a long white and blue robe, her long black hair resting on her shoulders. She was standing on the steps of what seemed to be the staircase of a temple or pyramid. She looked great, to say the least. Above all, she radiated impressive strength, confidence and majesty. I knew I had to share this image with her, even if I didn't know what it really meant.

Then came a much less pleasant vision. I was focused on Alicia and Dave, the young couple from Quebec. I was shown a series of events, like an accelerated projection of a possible future: They had had a little girl. When she was about eleven years old, a fire had started in their home during their absence, linked to a defective electrical appliance—I had the image of Christmas lights. The little girl, who stayed at home, had perished in the flames. I was then shown the deep sorrow of her parents, bitterness and resentment settling in their relationship. The suffering was too great, the guilt too overwhelming, leading to an inevitable rupture. I had received all this in a split second, almost as a memory. At this time, I was looking at this information in a very detached way, like a totally neutral observer. I could not say why, but I knew this vision was communicated to me by the soul—not yet incarnated—of the little girl herself, as a kind of warning message to prevent these terrible events from happening. "Tell my parents, so this doesn't happen to me," she seemed to tell me...

Time had vanished. I had the feeling this concept itself was no longer relevant: the past, the present, the future... everything was accessible. The linearity of time, as we know it, had been replaced by a wheel running in all directions, allowing all potentials to be explored. My ego was gone. I free-fell.

I regained a certain coherence after an indefinite "time." I remember one last interaction, one last gift that Ayahuasca gave me that night. She had put on her temptress costume, similar to the one I had already experienced in the Amazon. She praised the benefits of all this power, and the aura it could give me—while at the same time showing me the attraction it could potentially exert on women. "Flirt, seduction, pleasure of the senses, it feels so good, don't you think?" she seemed to tell me. I was divided: A part of me, inexorably attracted, actually wanted to dive into this exacerbated sensuality. The other part, on the contrary, expressed a real rejection, plugging its ears to the echo of the siren's song. Finally, this second aspect took over. Despite the attraction of the almost erotic sensations that Ayahuasca sent me, I swore to always remain faithful to Stéphanie. The visions immediately ceased, and I felt like the hero of an initiatory tale, who has successfully passed the test of temptation. Apparently, it had been necessary, and I was pleased with this clarification. Not only had I solemnly made a commitment, but the setting in which I had made that promise only made it more sacred to me.

The ceremony ended. Stéphanie had remained very calm next to me. She would later tell me the small dose had allowed her to spend the night quietly, in a semi-wakeful dream. I preferred to postpone any further exchanges with my other companions until the next day.

THE SHADOW

The next day, the five of us shared our experiences of the night in our bungalow. Alexandra finally had a fairly calm ceremony, visibly oriented towards inner silence. No fanciful visions or theoretical teachings, just training for reaching deep and perfect silence. She also had a strong analytical mind, so I thought it was probably a nice gift.

Jean-Marc explained why he spoke out loud during the ceremony. The plant had actually urged him to do so. At first he refused, but at Ayahuasca's insistence, he finally resigned himself to speak to the group. After he did, She told him, "See? You spoke at a totally inappropriate moment, in approximate English, nobody understood anything... and it didn't kill you!"

I then described to them the visions I had, especially the one about Dave and Alicia's little girl. I didn't know what to do, and asked my companions for their advice. Some were cautious, others downright reluctant to share this with the couple. The risk being obviously to create a permanent fear of such a drama. I might condemn them to years of anguish.

I understood their arguments, and it was a difficult choice indeed. But something pushed me to do it, like a voice constantly repeating to me, "Tell them, tell them, tell them." Admittedly, given the seriousness of the matter involved, it was a big responsibility. But who was I to decide what someone was supposed to know or not? If I had received this message, it might have been for a very good reason, and censoring it might be irresponsible. I finally decided to share my visions, starting from the principle that it was a benevolent approach. Nothing to do with a prophecy intended to scare them, but on the contrary, a protection to make this future potential impossible.

I thought Dave and Alicia might as well come across a documentary on television about the dangers of domestic accidents, and receive the same information. But it had happened in a more exotic setting, in Peru, during an Ayahuasca ceremony. It was not for me to judge the relevance of this—I imagined, however, that those circumstances would necessarily have a greater impact on the people involved.

Later in the day, I went to see Dave, telling him I had received a message for them, and if they wanted, we could discuss it later. He immediately said "Alicia is pregnant, right?" I was surprised by this spontaneous reaction, especially considering the theme of what I had perceived. Apparently, the question of becoming parents was very present, making the subject even more relevant—and sensitive. I smiled and said it wasn't quite that, and it would be better to talk about it together. I didn't want to sound alarming. He agreed, and we met in our bungalow in the evening.

Then we joined the rest of the group in the maloca, to exchange our experiences of the previous night. I could hardly see what I was going to say. After my visions of energy parasites in the Amazon, and the mixed reactions they had provoked, I decided to remain sensible. How do you really share that with someone who hasn't experienced it, anyway? So I was evasive, simply speaking of an encounter with ethereal beings who seemed to want to strengthen their bonds with mankind, and gave us an appointment a little further on the path of our spiritual evolution. Which was another way of expressing what I had felt during that interaction.

As we left this meeting, we went to our bungalow with Dave and Alicia. We sat down comfortably, and I took every precaution possible to express what I had seen. I insisted especially on the fact that it was not a prediction, but on the contrary, a precautionary protection which would prevent the event from happening. Barely had these words been spoken, the curse would thus be dispelled for good, leaving it no chance of being fulfilled. The couple seemed receptive and open-minded enough to listen to what I had to share with them. After all, they also had strange experiences with Ayahuasca, and knew that, in this context, an overly analytical mind was not necessarily the best approach. I feared anger or worry on their part, but they were intelligent enough to understand the meaning of this initiative. For my part, I felt better. The insistence to share this message had disappeared from my mind, and I felt I had been relieved of a burden that did not belong to me. This allowed me to understand once again that the future was in perpetual rewriting, and that a prediction—especially a grim one—was only offering an opportunity to change the course of things.

The next day passed quickly, and I found myself confronted with the recurring question regarding my intention for this last ceremony. Not being especially inspired, I decided not to change a winning formula. I would ask the plant for advice on the application of Her teachings once back in Paris.

As far as I am concerned, the atmosphere of this stay was significantly different from previous years. I felt more in the role of an assistant, thus offering my friends support in this opportunity for transformation. So I wasn't sure I had myself received all the answers to the personal questions I had in mind when I started this trip. As they mainly dealt with the management of my relationships in my professional projects, I assumed this night's session would be able to enlighten me even more on that topic.

Night arrived, and the ceremony began. Stéphanie got up to take her minimal dose, which she had been very satisfied with the previous time. I saw Diego pour the brew, then Stéphanie started to talk to him, not taking the glass in her hands. They were talking quietly and I didn't really understand their exchange, but I assumed it still had to do with the quantity given. Finally, Diego gave her an answer that seemed to satisfy her, and Stéphanie took a sip.

I would later learn she had simply refused to take the dose she had received from the ayahuasquero, telling him there was too much. After a mini-negotiation, Diego finally told her to drink what she wanted, and leave the rest. I was next in order, so I was going to complete my own dose with what she would have left. When I returned to my seat, she explained what had happened. She seemed very happy to have finally been able to say no to something she didn't want to do—despite the solemn setting of the ceremony, and the fact that refusing Ayahuasca might appear as a sign of disrespect. This rebellion was a huge step forward for her: She would never have dared to do so before, even if it meant doing things she didn't agree with.

We were many in the maloca, and as I had been among the first to drink, the effects of the plant appeared almost before the end of the distribution. To my great relief, the lights were finally turned off.

The mood at the beginning of the ceremony was not very light. The visions were confusing, restless, almost violent. I was in a reddish atmosphere, and a smell of blood and raw meat began to overwhelm me. It was pretty disgusting. I had the impression of being bombarded with a message whose meaning I knew fundamentally, but which my mind could not intellectualize, for lack of rational reference points. The concepts that came to me were "worn out," "exhausted," "faded," always associated with these visions of raw flesh, these red walls that reminded me of a uterus. If I had to find an analogy to these ideas, I would evoke the image of an old prostitute, who at the end of her career, after having spent years practicing cold and insipid sexual acts, expresses an image of extreme tiredness and an extinguished look.

I then received one of these "packets" of information, which arrive simultaneously in various forms—thought, image, concept—and which make sense once examined in a linear way.

In a split second, I saw the image of a greyish creature, set in the lower left corner of my field of vision, lying down. She had the appearance that is generally described when we speak of extraterrestrial beings: a big head, big opaque black eyes, an almost non-existent mouth and nose... She turned her head towards me, smiling—she was not smiling physically, and yet her eyes were still smiling, in a loving and indescribable way—just as a woman could look at her husband after giving birth, exhausted but proud of having given him a child. At least that's the exact concept I was getting.

Following this thread, I knew that I was being shown a whole process of mass reproduction. As if I were shown beings participating in a large-scale biological experiment, aimed at preserving a species from extinction. In a spirit of sacrifice and self-denial, they seemed to put their own bodies at the service of this project, even if it meant consuming all their vital energy.

I didn't really understand why I saw these images, even though a part of me seemed to accept this information without blinking. However, I would later find a surprising similarity in the work of psychiatrist John E. Mack, who was interested in the phenomenon of "abductions." Although obviously controversial, this theme deals with the many testimonies of people who experience "abduction by extraterrestrial beings." Mack, a respected psychiatrist and professor at Harvard, was one of the few to give credit to this subject, even if it meant committing what many would consider a professional suicide. But it was based on the pragmatic premise that if people were going through these experiences—most of them extremely traumatic and anxiety-provoking, far from the stories of a simple liar trying to attract attention—it was worth studying them from a psychological point of view. His purpose was therefore not to prove the veracity of the events possibly experienced by these people, but at least to analyze their sincerity and psychiatric symptoms related to the belief that they had actually experienced them. Was it madness, paranoia, a form of psychosis, or a process for which we do not yet have a satisfactory definition?

In his first book[1], he describes a psychiatric study spread over more than a decade, involving two hundred men and women who report experiences of recurrent abductions. While reading this book, I realized the elements mentioned during these testimonies—most under hypnosis—often evoked the theme of my visions under Ayahuasca, notably those related to reproduction. In any case, these experiences, very coherent as a whole, seemed quite terrifying for the people who relived them in modified states of consciousness with their therapist. It sounded far from a bad taste joke, and Mack was absolutely certain that these individuals were not crazy in the clinical sense of the word.

Honestly, as I write these lines, I still don't know what to do about this, or why I received these images in Peru that day. All this still seems very strange to me, with feelings mixed with familiarity and rejection. It is all the more frustrating to talk about it, as it is an experience that is difficult to describe, and therefore to share. Maybe it will make sense later for me or others reading this book, and that's why I decided to mention it anyway. In doubt, I prefer to

---

[1] "Abduction, Human Encounters with Aliens," John E. Mack, Simon & Schuster 1994.

208

deliver the elements as I experienced them, in a raw way, leaving it up to everyone to interpret them.

In any case, unlike Mack's patients, these images did not cause any emotional discomfort afterwards—apart from showing me something that would be impossible to share with my entourage, thus creating doubts and isolation feelings sometimes heavy to bear. After a while, they finally faded, and the ceremony changed themes.

Then I suddenly saw a wolf, or rather a werewolf. It had brown, shaggy, dirty hair. It came yelling its anger at me. The images left and returned, in violent assaults. I saw a wolf greedily eating bloody flesh, and so I understood that eating meat, which I had always been fond of, somehow brought me back to that bestial aspect of myself. I knew this hyper aggressive werewolf was a part of my personality, and I didn't like it at all. It was ugly, stinking, mad with rage. I even physically recoiled in front of its repeated attacks. I was put in front of my anger, and it was not pretty.

Then I saw myself sitting on a trunk, smiling tensely—almost a grin. The werewolf was locked up in the trunk, beating like a madman against the lid to get out. And I sat on this lid, impassive, wanting to look good and trying to ignore the ever stronger tremors of my anger. That's obviously what I had been doing all my life: pretending to smile all the time, even when the behavior of others made me boil inside.

This vision put in front of me what I had tried to ignore all these years. I could no longer bury my head in the sand, and I knew that I would now have to deal with that part of myself. Finally take care of this black wolf, pay it attention, brush its hair from time to time so that it does not end up in this pitiful state. The idea was not to feed my anger, but simply to listen to it, instead of immediately smothering it by saying "No no, everything is fine, no big deal." From now on, when my anger would manifest itself, I would no longer be in denial. I would converse with it, to find a solution and appease it, finally showing it some consideration.

This theme would last a good part of the night. I was immersed in this understanding which, I guess, needed to take root deep within me. Ayahuasca showed me more. For example, how omnipresent the fear of mockery was in my relationships. That my anxiety about being introduced to someone, my hands suddenly sweating, was linked to my fear of being immediately mocked or rejected by that person. Which, through my adult eyes, was absurd, because I hadn't been laughed at openly for a long time. But this program was always running in my mind, automatically, and without me even being aware of it. The plant helped me clean up all those bad reflexes that no longer had any reason to be.

I was particularly sensitive to the songs of one of the members of the group, Antonio, who had come spontaneously to discuss with me a few days earlier. The group was relatively large, and I hadn't had the opportunity to speak with him before that moment. He was very friendly and spoke excellent French, having grown up near the French-Spanish border. He was already versed in healing through teacher plants, especially San Pedro. He knew healing songs, which he had shared with us during the two previous ceremonies, and whose effects were extremely powerful. When he sang that haunting melody again, during that third ceremony, I was taken by violent abdominal contractions. I felt we were closely connected. His voice and the sound of his little rattle seemed to emanate directly from the center of my skull. I purged all I could, in an exhausting physical effort.

At the end of the ceremony, I had the feeling I had experienced one of the biggest healings related to Ayahuasca. Beyond what my intellect could imagine, I suppose. When Diego lit the candles again, I was still very connected. I knew that I was ready to share a healing session with my companions, like the previous year. I was struck by energy discharges, which regularly shook my head to the right, like nervous tics. I knew these movements were linked to an influx of energy which passed massively through me.

This time, however, I was not given any particular indication of the physical or emotional problems that people might have. It was a simple and direct communion between them and me. My hands, which felt like they were literally burning, automatically moved to the right place. The receptivity of my companions was total, in perfect harmony, and we simply stayed there, enjoying this contact in a state of mutual love and profound serenity.

I went to thank Antonio for his songs, which had healed me that night. He told me he had a vision about me, and that one day I would work with groups. We were all there, sharing this timeless moment, and nobody seemed to want to go to bed. We played the guitar, sang, shared experiences... A real family, again.

I AM A MAN

Everyone seemed satisfied with this last ceremony, which had visibly represented a significant inner work. During our group sharing, Stéphanie joked that the dose of Ayahuasca really didn't matter: Her greatest healing had taken place even before taking it, finally daring to say "no" to Diego—which made him laugh. She had then worked on the respect she could have for herself, in a very personal way.

I did not want this journey to end, and I was delighted by the prospect of participating in a San Pedro ceremony two days later. My previous experience with this teacher plant had been so intense and confusing... I wondered if this was going to be the case again. This time, the ceremony was not to be conducted by Diego, but by a young woman named Andrea. I had seen her briefly a few times during our stay: blonde, long hair, blue eyes and a very direct look, a strong voice. Despite a welcoming attitude, she expressed a rather intimidating strength and personality.

After a day of tourism and rest, where we had time to comfortably discuss all our experiences, the day of the ceremony arrived. We had an appointment at 11 a.m. with Andrea. We obviously had an empty stomach, and I was suffering from gastric cramps. Our group was going to be composed of about ten people, most of them from the Ayahuasca seminar. Besides our French group, there were Vicky and Pam, but also Yossi and Jimmy, two very nice guys. The only person I didn't know was called Shiva. She was obviously from South America, with long, straight, very dark hair. She radiated a beautiful energy, calm and deep, which gave her an almost mystical aspect. I would have easily seen her as an Incan priestess. Stéphanie felt she had taken enough teacher plants for that time, and asked to simply stay with the group during the ceremony.

Andrea had prepared a fireplace around which we would sit in a circle, at least for a moment. The fire would burn all day long and would be our "headquarters." Despite the early hour, it was already very hot, and I began to worry about having to stay in full sun. I knew that once I ingested the plant, I wouldn't worry so much about possible burns, so I decided to be careful. Andrea asked us to verbalize our intention, one after the other, and aloud. When it was my turn, I simply expressed my will to grow, to be the best human being possible, and like a tree, to spread my branches to the sky while sinking my roots deeply into the ground. I really wanted to find a stability, a confidence and a foundation I had been lacking in recent months, or even my whole life.

Andrea then gave the medicine to each of us. She used a technique I had never seen before. She took a large tablespoon of San Pedro powder, and poured it down each participant's throat. Then we had to drink water quickly to swallow it. This had the advantage of not putting the substance in contact with the taste buds, and thus avoiding its so "distinctive" taste. When giving me my dose, she seemed to realize she had generously filled her spoon. When she slipped it into my mouth, she asked me if I was ready to take a good quantity. Surprised, already with my head back, I could only agree by nodding.

We sat around the fire for a moment. Then the mistress of ceremony proposed we go to another place, located nearby. I welcomed this suggestion with gratitude, for I was melting in the sunlight. Moreover, the smoke had obviously decided to target me, and I had trouble keeping my eyes open without crying.

So we began our walk on the dirt road. I was already feeling the subtle effects of the medicine. My mind was emptied of all thought and things around me seemed to take on a new interest that was capturing all my attention. I observed the flowers, the plants, the trees, the sky... I could have devoted hours to it. After about twenty minutes of walking, we arrived in a small isolated clearing, at the edge of a rapid river. The place was ideal, and everyone settled in as they pleased. I could feel my body vibrating, and my hands were getting warm. I sat next to Andrea, and gently laid my hands on her back, telling her that I could simply share energy with her, if she wished. She closed her eyes, and feeling the heat, told me it was very pleasant.

So we were all there, sitting or walking, each in his or her own integration process. I had the odd feeling we were in a kind of "healers' convention," and that all the individuals present had a certain potential in this field. We spontaneously went towards each other to provide support and healing, accompanying some of us in sometimes intense emotional states...

I spent a moment with Andrea, who took care of me by singing me healing songs in a soft and bewitching voice. Then I went to see Vicky. I gently took her face in my hands, my eyes riveted in hers, and tried to express to her the beauty I saw in her. I felt it was very important for her to see herself from a new angle, more flattering than the image she had had until now. I did not really know her, and my approach might have seemed daring. But in this state of direct connection, words came to me spontaneously, and I tried to imprint deeply in her the love and consideration I genuinely felt for her.

Finally, I sat down in front of Shiva. She asked me if I spoke English or Spanish. When she understood that I was French, she began to speak to me in my native language, to my surprise. When I told her my first name, she answered with a charming accent:

- " Frédéric... Frédéric the funny one."
- "The funny one?"
- "Yes, the happy one!"

She touched my hands, took them in hers, and said, "Oh what do we have here... Healer's hands!" I instinctively moved them towards her stomach, but she gently pushed them away, telling me she was very sensitive to external energies. She seemed to get messages for me, which she then passed on to me. I took good note and thanked her.

I went to join Stéphanie at the edge of the river. She was still with us, knowing how to remain discreet. I appreciated her presence and support, and I was grateful she was always there with me, even when she wasn't attracted to this kind of experience. I had heard that an Ayahuasca ceremony was being held the next day, and I wondered if I should attend. The San Pedro answered me clearly that I no longer needed plants to progress, at least not immediately, and that I had all the necessary resources within me.

Andrea finally told us it was time to come back around the fire. Everyone seemed to react strongly to the medicine. My body was vibrating like never before. Alexandra also seemed to walk with difficulty. A few moments before, she was lying on the grass, seized with slight convulsions. I had sat beside her, and like a midwife, I had assisted her in giving birth to something I was not intellectually aware of. I had just made various gestures on her belly in a totally automatic way, and she then told me I had helped her in this symbolic act of childbirth. I often had the impression my body was the channel of something that was totally beyond me...

We were now walking on the way back. I gave Alexandra my hand to support her. Immediately I felt much more stable, inspired by the idea of having closed a circuit so far incomplete. I let go of her hand, and again I felt this floating sensation. I took it back, and everything stabilized. This feeling of two pieces coming together to form a whole was surprisingly present. It had nothing to do with my personal relationship with Alexandra; rather, I had the impression that we were experiencing the complementarity of male and female principles.

We passed a shepherdess who was guiding a small herd of cows along the narrow path. Alexandra huddled behind me, telling me she was scared, in a frightened little voice. At that moment I had the image of the knight who protects his lady. Through a process that I would find difficult to explain, I was reconciling myself with my male nature. I realized that in general, I did not like men, whom I found violent, brutal, insensitive. I was always much more comfortable in the company of women, whose delicacy and sensitivity I appreciated. Yet, at that precise moment, I realized my perception of men was totally biased, and that this force I found so aggressive and dominating could actually be expressed with gentleness and protection. I was making peace with myself, and I realized it was directly related to the intention I had formulated: If I wanted to grow up and gain confidence, I would have to reconnect with my male nature. Strangely, the chorus of a French song by Michel Polnareff, which I had heard only once or twice in my life, suddenly came to my mind: "I am a man, I am a man, what could be actually more natural," said the lyrics...

Alexandra, on the other hand, seemed to mirror the same process. She passed her hand through her hair with a sigh, and really expressed the very quintessence of feminine energy and sensuality. So we went on, Stéphanie walking about sixty feet ahead of us. I think my friend and I were both a little embarrassed because we didn't want Steph to get the wrong idea about the experience we were having. It had nothing to do with flirting or seduction, we were simply understanding these fundamental principles by literally embodying them.

Suddenly Alexandra stopped and stared at me with a troubled look in her eyes. "It's downright biblical," she whispered. I understood what she meant. If someone had asked me then which characters we were, I would probably have said "Adam and Eve." And I knew that Stéphanie also played a key role in this trio. Through this scene and these fundamental archetypes, I received an explanation almost impossible to transcribe. I had the impression that I was being told the story of the universe, and words seem very limited to express what I was receiving.

It was as if the Garden of Eden and the original couple were an allegory of the perfection of Creation in its original, unique and inseparable state. But the Universe, having no way of knowing itself, had split and created a new point of view, that of the observer. The serpent was not sin, but the symbol of Knowledge, the one who creates separation with the One, so that the latter can constantly rediscover itself. And the act of biting into the apple was the trigger for this endless exploration, like a Big Bang.

It was far from the moralizing—and incidentally misogynistic—concepts of the Old Testament. Was our existence really a means for the Universe—or God—to explore all facets of Creation, and thus of Itself? That is what I seemed to understand in this moment of almost mystical ecstasy.

We finally arrived at our gathering point, and settled around the fire. Stéphanie was warmly welcomed into our circle, Andrea considering she had been our companion all day, and that it was natural for her to join us. The effects of the medicine seemed to fade slowly. We talked, some played the guitar, and the atmosphere was sweet and calm. The night had fallen, and the end of the ceremony was punctuated by a distribution of fruits which seemed absolutely delicious to me. Under the moon and the stars, it was time to say goodbye and return to our hotel. Two days later, we were ready to return to Paris.

THE MIRROR

I had received much care and clarification during this trip. But that didn't make my bad reflexes go away with a magic wand. Now I had to put that theory into practice. Moreover, the effects of the teacher plants, as I realized again this time, develop over time according to a process of integration which can continue long after the ceremonies.

One example of this delayed realization can be illustrated by the subsequent exchanges we had with Vicky. During a conversation on the Internet, she asked me what energies I felt about her. I therefore promised to meditate on this question, and to see the information that would come to me. Here is the letter I sent her following this session.

"Dear Vicky,

"The other day you asked me what energies I perceived about you, and I must say that I received many things during the last hours—so much so that it is a little difficult for me to put my thoughts in order. So I decided to just sit in front of my computer, and see what would come out.

"If I put myself in a state of receptivity, and I ask what theme you are going through right now, I always feel the same concept: self-love and self-esteem. And now I am sure of one thing: We are exploring the same path, leaning on each other to move forward.

"Generally, when I first meet people, I always feel a strong attraction when I am about to work on an important topic with them. And that's what happened when you showed up the first day of the retreat. Now I understand why.

"It all began during the second ceremony, when I had this strong vision of you dressed as a high priestess. You had an incredibly beautiful, noble, imposing personality. And at the same time, I received the message: "You must tell her!" as if you were completely unaware of it. That's why I shared this vision with you at the end of the ceremony. But now I realize this was also part of my own process, and that the hidden elements of this beautiful teaching are coming to light. What Ayahuasca told me was, 'Look at her! Look how beautiful she is, and at the same time, see how she is unaware of it. Feel this contrast, and you will understand how you treat yourself, because you have exactly the same problem: You are not aware of your own value. It is much easier to see beauty in the other, and so difficult to see it in yourself.'

"And this theme manifested itself again during the ceremony of San Pedro, when we were near the river. I held your face in my hands, telling you how beautiful you were, not just physically, but as a person. I saw your perfection so clearly that I wanted to share that vision with you at all costs. I then asked you to look me straight in the eyes. What I really wanted at that moment was to touch your soul, and engrave that vision into you, beyond the mind.

"Now I grasp many things, because I realize that my theme is similar to yours, and that it deals with my tendency to invalidate this love of myself. If I am a good person, if I do beautiful things, I consider that normal. But if what I do doesn't live up to my expectations, I immediately become very critical of myself. In other words, I am much harder on myself than I ever will be on anyone. I am my only true tormentor, and I do so all the time, constantly judging my performance.

"I had already accepted this idea on an intellectual level, but I had never experienced it in such a personal way before Peru. You reflected to me in an impeccable way what I was undergoing. And I, in turn, am able to reflect it to you in the form of this letter.

"I just realized the strength of this pattern of devaluation. Am I good? Well, that's the least I can do! If I am 'bad' (at least by my particularly demanding standards), then I judge myself violently, get ashamed, and put pressure on myself immediately. I have honestly questioned the reasons for this behavior. After all, when I do a good deed, when I accomplish a difficult task in an elegant way, when someone compliments me, why do I feel compelled to deny it? I see now that this attitude has become a simple reflex, aiming to invalidate all this automatically: 'Oh they say that to be nice, but they don't really mean it.' Or: 'Hmm, they say I'm good at this, but they haven't seen all the times I've failed.'

"Looking carefully at this behavior, I think it clearly comes from my upbringing, during which I was constantly told that it was wrong to brag or to put myself forward. This idea became implicit: If I want to be a good person, I have to devalue everything I am. Otherwise I'll be a despicable and pretentious man, full of pride and arrogance. And people will hate me for that. Yet, in the light of this realization, I then received the most beautiful message I could hope for: 'Only those who love themselves the most can also be the most humble.'

"I just deeply understood the fact that boasting, pride, arrogance were not the result of a high opinion of ourselves, but on the contrary, the consequence of a real devaluation of our person. When people constantly try to convince the world they are brilliant, that is what reveals their total lack of love for themselves. And on the other hand, those who love, respect and value themselves are those who have nothing more to prove, and who can then embrace the most total humility. I lived my whole life on this misunderstanding, which forced me to deny all my qualities and my power. But now I know that if I want to be truly humble, then I must love myself and recognize my worth first. Otherwise I will be condemned to beg in secret the praises of my entourage, in an illusion of false modesty, and this for the rest of my life!

"When I spoke to you by the river, and my words literally flowed from my mouth, I know that I was playing the role of a mirror reflecting this concept. Accept your beauty, accept your priceless worth as a human being. The simple fact that the Universe created you is the best proof of your perfection, for the Universe never makes mistakes. To think that we are an exception to the perfection of the Universe is actually quite arrogant! We are flawless beings playing a role here on earth, diving into the illusion of devaluation and denigration, to then rediscover our true nature better. Our true value is just infinite, like All That Is.

"And it is also for this reason—I now know—that I explored this 'Black Wolf / White Wolf' polarity throughout my stay. Because recognizing my dark side, embracing it, is also a good way to understand that I am a good person. Yes, I could be horrible. Yes, I could hurt people. But I don't do it. To realize I have the choice and power to hurt or harm, and not to do so, is another proof of my integrity and inner beauty. Walking side by side with my dark side, while choosing not to feed it, is a great way to reconnect with a more positive image of myself.

"If I had a little suggestion for you, it would be to think about that every time you look in the mirror. Stop judging yourself for a moment. Focus on all the good things you do regularly, not just the 'bad' things. Feel the love you have for others, and give it to yourself too. For me, there is no process more powerful, more fundamental to transcend ourselves. It is truly the heart of all dramatic change, within us and for the world."

I accompanied this message with a card reading and its interpretation. Vicky seemed very receptive to its content, which confirmed my feelings.

I was always fascinated by these sudden realizations, which often led me to reconsider a fundamental point of my existence from a totally different angle—and sometimes even the opposite definition I had always had. In the months that followed, I would continue to receive new inspirations on the central themes of my life. I understood more and more how the teacher plants acted in their healing power during shamanic ceremonies. They led us to review from a higher point of view all the definitions that made us suffer or prevented us from progressing. In these moments of wisdom, they allowed us to transform beliefs that were no longer in agreement with ourselves. Then we could adopt them—or not— and put them into practice. When a belief is changed so profoundly, it no longer possesses the same strength and power. It is then easier to eliminate the bad reflexes it may have generated throughout our lives. Like a weed whose root has been killed, and which is then easier to pull up.

THE FOUR ELEMENTS

My life was definitely very contrasted. Among these moments of bliss, I also had to face fears I still had not healed. I went once a week to our company's offices, the rest of the time I communicated with Matthieu by instant messenger. He seemed a little more tense every time I saw him. He had spent a lot of time drafting a partnership contract with the company which was hosting us, trying to foresee all possible cases of break-up to protect us. Looking back, I think that clearly had not helped to build a climate of trust, and had stiffened our relationship with our partners from the outset. Moreover, we really needed their technical teams to make progress on our project, and they always seemed to be allocated to other internal priorities. In short, the tension was rising.

Week after week, the situation seemed more and more critical, and dissatisfaction grew between Matthieu and our associates. I tried to calm things down, taking advantage of my outsider position to make the discussions less passionate and sometimes act as a mediator. But things seemed to have reached a point of no return, and after a long consultation between Matthieu and me, we decided to break our association with our host. It was not an easy decision, because in addition to providing us with offices and human resources, they were supposed to become investors in our company, and thus bring in fresh money. But it would have meant a definitive association, and given the relationships we had at the time, it seemed like a long-term commitment to failure.

So we were going to move into Matthieu's house, which had enough room to accommodate us. It is rather ironic that we did not invoke any clause of the tedious contract that was signed between us and our partner, as the separation was completely improvised. I noted for myself that the business world was, above all, a question of human relations, and no contract could replace trust and respect between two partners.

My relationship with Matthieu still made me uneasy, bringing me back to that position of submission I had had all my life. We each were obsessed with being free in our creative processes, and this situation of constant discussion to design a common work put us in an uncomfortable position. We both clearly needed to relax, and this relationship had enormous potential to teach us how to let go and accept consensus. I no longer knew which posture to adopt: either keep expressing my opinions, even if it meant risking annoying Matthieu tremendously; or remain in a passive role of acceptance, and wonder if my partner did not consider me as a dead weight with no constructive views. Depending on the day, one or the other of these postures seemed more conducive to the harmony of our collaboration, and I spent my time switching between them. This kind of behavior was of course totally exhausting, creating a permanent tension in me, and being motivated only by my visceral fear of conflict.

Obviously, all this reconnected me with the lessons Ayahuasca had given me, regarding the value I gave myself, my legitimacy, and my right to express who I was. Matthieu was a wonderful coach for this theme, and during my moments of inspiration, I realized the great work we were doing together—as I saw that our relationship had an impact on him as well. I was more convinced than ever of one thing: We constantly attract the people best able to reflect our weaknesses and our dissonant beliefs, thus offering us a precious opportunity to correct them. We are all mirrors, and perpetual sources of inspiration for each other.

In parallel to all these professional adventures, I had kept in touch with Antonio, the nice guy I had met in Peru and who lived in Spain. He regularly organized San Pedro ceremonies, and he had invited me to attend. I had politely declined the invitation, not feeling ready for a new experience. I already had a lot to digest, and from what I had felt in Peru, I didn't need more to move forward. However Antonio finally made me an offer that I could not refuse. He was doing one last ceremony alone before taking a break of several months, and he offered to share it with me. I was touched by this very personal offer, and gladly accepted. Moreover, I always suffered from unpleasant physical manifestations: chronic hives, burning sensations in the chest, recurrent stress. I needed a break, to get my mind and body in order.

So I went by train to a small town in northern Spain, where Antonio was waiting for me at the station. The ceremony was going to take place on a beach at night. I also learned that it was a nudist beach, Antonio being himself a practitioner. But at that time, the place would probably be deserted—at least that's what I was hoping. When we arrived at our destination, it was almost dark. The place was quiet and had good energy. We settled at the end of the beach, at the foot of a cliff. An extension of the rock wall formed a sort of small circular enclosure, within which we could sit, hidden from view. We were a few steps from the sea. A little further, in the water, lay an enormous sixty-foot high rock, which the gulls flew over. I felt comfortable in this beautiful natural setting.

We prepared a small altar. Antonio explained the ceremony would celebrate the four fundamental elements—fire, earth, air and water, in that order. He gave me a bottle of water, of which I would be the "guardian" during the night, infusing it with positive energy and intention. He put a big candle between us and said: "You'll probably think I am crazy, but as a fire for the ceremony, I brought a mosquito candle. The advantage is it'll burn all night." I thought the idea was original, and was worth a try. Then he took out a jar of San Pedro powder. He told me to reach out, and poured a dose into my palm. All I had to do was swallow it.

I wasn't sure how to proceed, and decided to gobble the powder, like with Andrea. The difference was that in Peru, the young woman had put medicine at the bottom of my throat with a spoon, so I could swallow it with water. I tried the same gesture with the powder in my hand, to regret it immediately. Not only was the cactus, with its horrible taste, all over my mouth, but I was choking. It was very hard not to vomit, the substance sticking to my tongue and teeth. Plus, part of the dose was still stuck on my hand. As I coughed violently and tried to control my spasms, Antonio looked at me, visibly perplexed. I saw how he proceeded himself: He had kept the powder in the palm of his hand, and took small pinches that he swallowed quietly as he went. I had rushed on my own dose like a starving man, and had put medicine everywhere. So classy...

I ended up swallowing all the powder I had been given, sweating and breathing heavily to control my irrepressible urge to vomit. I was a little embarrassed by my attitude, especially with the sacred character I granted to this medicine. A few moments later Antonio began to sing and I gradually calmed down. He used a small instrument made from large dried seeds, attached to a stick, creating percussion noises when he waved it in rhythm. I thought he was singing very loudly, and I was beginning to fear that the occupants of nearby houses would come over to check what happened.

Minutes passed and I felt the first subtle effects of the medicine, my mind becoming clear of thoughts. I focused on my basic intention: understanding what process I was going through, and what imbalances I was experiencing. The huge rock planted in the sea began to attract my attention, to the point that I could no longer take my eyes off it.

The themes I was dealing with began to appear more clearly to me. In my interactions with Matthieu, I relived this fear of rejection, of judgment, of criticism—and which brought me back to the difficulties of my childhood. Suddenly I felt the rock talking to me. It was not an auditory impression, but rather as if the very consciousness of the rock were addressing me. It seemed to say to me: "Look at me. I'm here, massive, imperturbable. I'm stuck in the water, and the waves keep crashing against me. I rise in the air, and the birds spin constantly above my head, screaming and defecating on me. And despite all this agitation, I remain impassive, majestic, indestructible. I AM a rock, quite simply, in perfect harmony with my deep nature. I do not exist according to what is happening around me, I do not define myself according to the vision that others have of me, but only in agreement with my Fundamental Being. And that's what makes me invincible."

I deeply felt this age-old wisdom and strength. In comparison I felt agitated, restless, unstable, always looking outwards instead of focusing on my deep resources. I had to admit, despite my recent realizations, I still lacked confidence and certainty about my intrinsic worth, always defining myself through the other person's eyes... And that was what caused my distress.

Antonio, as the ritual wanted, poured a little water on the wax of the candle, which had an unexpected reaction: The water seemed to create a chemical reaction, and the candle began to burn at full speed, the wax literally dissolving before our eyes. Within minutes, the candle was completely consumed, leaving us in the dark. Antonio was very surprised, but took it as a sign. Tonight we would stay in the dark, just lit by a moon that I finally noticed—it was almost full. This was not to displease me, for the candle, by burning, released heady and slightly unpleasant vapors.

Fire had said goodbye, and the celebration of Earth would follow in the course of the ceremony. Antonio had asked me to bring music on my phone. Not knowing what to choose, I had made a rather eclectic selection. He explained to me that we were going to dance, but not according to a particular choreography. We would simply sink our feet into the sand, and to the rhythm of the music, listen to the energy impulses that the Earth would give us. Pachamama was going to lead the ball, and inspire our movements. Under normal circumstances, I might have been a little uncomfortable with the idea of gesticulating like that, but I was now connected enough to accept that idea most naturally in the world. So I launched the music, my choice being finally an album of shamanic percussions and didgeridoo.

To the sound of these primal rhythms, my consciousness began to drift. I was almost a spectator of this trance, which seemed to envelop me much more quickly than I expected. I thus advanced gradually towards the water, planting my feet heavily in the sand. Suddenly, my body was literally sucked to the ground, and I fell to my knees. I sat down with my legs crossed and my hands on the sand in front of me, facing the waves that almost touched me. There, in this almost animal posture, I was suddenly overwhelmed by the energy of the wolf. Without any restraint, I howled at the moon, thus communicating with the Universe. I *was* the wolf, San Pedro allowing me to live this experience again by literally embodying the principles it showed me. After that scream, I felt my consciousness cut in two: on one side, a shy and scared little voice telling me that I had definitely attracted the attention of the locals, and that they were going to come and get us, to put us in an asylum. And another, stronger one, which had the feeling to be simply part of the world, free to act in total agreement with my very nature.

I thus knew what the wolf was thinking. Actually, it does not think, it IS. It is there, fully present, and does not waste its time wondering whether it is legitimate as a wolf, or whether it deserves to exist. The contrast with my human behavior was stark. From the animal's point of view, everything seemed so right, so natural, simply in the order of things. Next to that, my mind seemed totally out of line, torturing itself over inept and absurd existential questions.

This incarnation experience clearly echoed my perception of the rock a few moments earlier. The wolf seemed to say to me: "You fucking exist! That should be enough for you! Be one with the world that created you, and stop thinking of yourself permanently as a stranger who doesn't belong... Look at me. Do you think I care if my howling woke someone up? Then live, without asking permission!"

I turned around and looked at Antonio. He was lying on his stomach, his arms pointing in front of him and his face buried in the sand, visibly immersed in an equally intense journey. I moved towards him on all fours: The presence of the wolf was still so strong that I could not see how else I could move. I came close to him, and grunting softly, I gave him a gentle head butt. Moments later, the animal seemed to be gone, and I slowly regained my human identity.

We went to sit down by the altar, where we sang again. I began to realize the impact of this experience when I heard myself singing louder and louder, indifferent to the "disturbance" it might cause. At the same time, I had the feeling of reliving the key sensations of my childhood, when I was regularly asked to be quiet: not saying anything at dinner when we had guests, regularly turning down the TV volume so as not to disturb the neighbors... By all means, keep a low profile! My parents themselves had a big self-esteem problem, and had naturally instilled it in their children. I had spent my life making as little noise as possible, so as not to disturb anyone. The whole family had to be irreproachable by its discretion, even to be downright invisible. I often heard my parents say things like, "Oh, they're good people: nice, polite, discreet...

You never hear about them in the neighborhood."

Accompanying this awakening, I sang at the top of my voice. I had the impression that a lock placed at the level of my throat had finally broken. I felt free.

As if pushed by an invisible force, I suddenly got up and knelt before Antonio. I had gone into "healer" mode, and as before, my hands started working on him automatically. I applied my palms on his body, I massaged him, I blew air on him... The medicine was strong, guiding my gestures. I had the feeling that my companion needed a boost of energy and vitality. The session lasted several minutes, then I returned to my seat without saying a word. Words were useless anyway.

The next phase of the ceremony would correspond to the third element: Air. Antonio took a long pipe out of a case. We would take turns smoking it. Not being a smoker myself, I was afraid of choking, but he told me that I could simply hold it in my hands if I wanted to. The idea was to take turns exchanging the pipe, and when it was our turn, to send a positive intention to our loved ones. I ventured to inhale the smoke, which did not turn sour enough to cause discomfort. So I prayed respectfully for my wife, my family, my friends, sending them energy of benevolence and love. I knew that we were all connected all the time, and that they would receive and feel it one way or another.

After we had meditated for a moment, Antonio got up and undressed himself completely. Being a naturist, he obviously had no problem with nudity—which was not my case. He headed for the water and started swimming. He asked me to join him, but a feeling of foolish modesty blocked me. I was starting to feel nauseous. The medicines I had taken—San Pedro and smoked tobacco, which is also considered as very powerful and sacred—seemed to work deep inside me. I had to purge. So I went to throw up a few feet away, and felt a great relief. The feeling of lightness that followed was extremely pleasant. I had the impression I had gotten rid of all the themes I had brought to the surface that night, and that I had thus expelled.

Antonio returned from his swim a few moments later. We reached the last part of the ceremony, precisely dedicated to Water. He asked me to take the bottle he had given me and pour some on the ground. This ritual symbolically returned the water to the

Earth. We sang for a long time. Time passed, and the day began to rise slowly. Antonio undressed again and returned to the sea, encouraging me to do the same. I overcame my reservations and took off my clothes. To my surprise, and despite the very early hour, the water felt good. Bathing like this, naked, after a San Pedro ceremony, had something primordial—a reconnection to the first moments of my life. So we swam for a long time, in a delicious feeling of freedom.

The sun was rising. We went back to the beach, and I dressed again. Antonio preferred to remain naked, the place being, after all, dedicated to that. We talked for a moment. With his plump body, curly hair and pensive look, my companion reminded me of a sad angel. He told me of his desire to engage in shamanic activity, but also of his fear of not being legitimate, of being an impostor. I fully understood his feelings. Listening to him speak, I also noticed he had a negative definition of money, which possibly prevented him from receiving it. For example, Diego's success in Peru—although perfectly deserved and gradually developed over many years—seemed to arouse a certain rejection in him, as if it was not the right way to go.

At that moment, in that state of great mental clarity, I understood how we were always exactly where we wanted to be. Certainly part of Antonio was frustrated by the fact his healer aspect was not fully expressed, and that he had to continue to do ungratifying small jobs to pay the bills. But on the other hand, his fear of corruption from money prevented him from taking the step and become a professional healer. The result was this ultimately unsatisfactory situation, but which represented the best compromise between his conflicting definitions.

This helped me to glimpse my own blockages, especially those related to money. I realized that it was only fluctuating energy, and like any energy, it was basically neutral. Only its use could have a positive or negative aspect. You could do wonderful things with money, such as providing invaluable support to people in need. I decided that this aspect would no longer be an obstacle, and that if I wanted to live fully as a healer, I would have to accept payment in return. It would only constitute a fair return of energy. I shared this perspective with my partner, knowing we had again explored parallel paths, from which we could mutually benefit.

We spent a few hours chatting on the beach, then we left for the station, where I was to take the train back from my express trip.

LEARNING SELF-LOVE

The lessons given by teacher plants can be real gems. At least as long as we want to put them into practice. Theory alone is not enough, and I didn't want to be like an actor who spent his life reading scripts without ever performing them on stage. Even if applying this proved more difficult than expected...

Obviously, the challenge of bad habits is that you must first become aware of them before you can change them. Now I realized the way I related to people inevitably led me to the same result: anxiety, overwork, uneasiness with others. Whenever one of these dissonant emotions manifested itself, I could then identify it and apply another philosophy to it. In that regard, Matthieu helped me prodigiously, constantly confronting me with behaviors I repeated ad nauseam. The further I went, the more I saw that every bad habit revealed was the tree that hid the forest. I hadn't measured the scale of this mess. I really had to reinvent everything, starting from the ground up.

Despite all my efforts to stay on track, this reorganization took a heavy energetic and emotional toll. So much so that, faced with the tensions I experienced every day in my collaboration with Matthieu, I finally cracked. I felt that every decision between us was subject to debate, and I was tired of fighting. It seemed we both had to work on our themes, which were actually very similar: to trust, to let go, not to be constantly in control or in a dominant / dominated relationship—where the acceptance of ideas from others would necessarily be equivalent to a personal sacrifice. The situation had become untenable for me, and I kept wondering why Matthieu had asked me to join him in a co-production, when he obviously wanted to create a very personal work.

After another particularly trying and tense day at work, I decided to send him an e-mail to explain my frustration. The exchanges were heated, and I considered very seriously the idea of putting an end to our collaboration. However, it saddened me to leave a project in which we had already put so much energy. I felt like I was betraying Matthieu, letting him down, and going against my integrity. I felt involved, even a prisoner of my commitment. Moreover, even if certain traits of my partner's character exasperated me, I knew that if they found a resonance in me, it was above all because they were also present in my own personality. Matthieu was just a mirror sending back things I didn't want to see. As Alcoholics Anonymous so rightly say: "When you judge me, you point one finger at me, and three fingers at yourself..."

I spent several days thinking long and hard about the situation, caught between the compelling desire to leave, and the feeling that I had no right to do so. The story of my professional life, in short. One of the things that was obviously a problem for us was probably being both "leaders." There was only one throne, and it was too small for both of us. I had to be clear: If our collaboration was to remain bearable, it would be by accepting it relied on an unrealistic premise. No, we would not be two complementary authors, creating a common work in perfect balance. One of us had to accept the idea that the other would have the final word if we disagreed. Otherwise we would get lost in endless negotiations.

If I put this power in Matthieu's hands, thus giving him the role of decision-maker, it would obviously confront me with all my demons concerning authority. He was already the main shareholder and president of the company we had created. If he also became the one who had the final creative say, I would simply find myself in a boss / subordinate relationship again. In other words, everything I'd been running away from the last few years.

It was during one of my meditation sessions that inspiration came to me. I realized that if I placed myself in the position of a helper, on a vibration of gift and love, everything seemed to me not only acceptable, but even exciting. I knew the nature of the midwife really suited me: That's how I envisioned my healing practice, and my experiences in Peru had convinced me of this. I was someone who helped and supported, and the happiness this idea gave me confirmed how much it was in agreement with my deep nature.

For me, a real healer is not someone who changes the person for the better, like he would repair a car or a device—he doesn't have that power, anyway. He can only accompany the person in a process of self-healing, by emitting himself, like a tuning fork, the perfect energy vibration on which the patient can tune in to heal.

I could apply this notion to all aspects of my life. Yes, I could help Matthieu literally deliver his project. And without finding it derogatory or reductive. When a mother gives birth to her child, the midwife knows her role and does not question its importance. She just fulfills a precise mission, in perfect adequacy with the rest of the medical team, without at any time seeking to occupy the central position and monopolize all the attention.

It was also a humility lesson, and I understood that during all that time, my ego had clearly been involved. I always wanted to be in the spotlight, in the center of the action, surely for fear of being scrapped if I was proven to be useless. By continuing to assist Matthieu in his project, I now accepted a secondary but equally useful role.

Paradoxically, this decision had finally led me to a feeling of peace that I had not felt for months. As a side effect, I began to experience a new energy: a love for myself that refused any kind of ill-treatment. Not a defensive reaction or anger, but the serene feeling that my well-being mattered above all. I still felt that my old patterns resisted, and I alternated between two states: either the usual apprehension of the reaction of the other, or the new conviction to be finally in my absolute right. I was then able to feel a very clear contrast between the two. I knew that I was reconnecting to the quintessence of the self-empowering teachings I had received during my shamanic experiences. I finally had the opportunity to apply them in a concrete way, and I was truly grateful to Matthieu for giving me this possibility, by putting me against the wall. After taking all these blows, I began to grasp this posture of strength, self-respect and self-confidence that had been shown to me by the plants.

With all these realizations, I therefore decided to put things straight with my partner. I did not lose sight of my primary goal, which was to write my book and continue to practice energy healing. But I went on the idea of honoring my commitment until the end, by helping my associate to give birth to his project. I accepted he would be the final decision-maker on the various aspects of our creation. This really allowed me to let go about the future of our collaboration. However, this did not mean condoning everything: One should not confuse "being in service" with "servitude." As long as my role and my help were respected, I would continue. If the situation went wrong again, I would stop, because I was offering to be a support, not a punching bag.

So I made an appointment with Matthieu, with whom I hadn't had an exchange since our argument. I explained my vision of things to him, and offered him my help under the conditions mentioned above. He seemed a little surprised, but accepted my offer. I felt absolutely no triumphalism in his attitude. I realized that these last months had also been trying for him, with a lot of tensions and various pressures. During our open-hearted conversation, I could see that he himself was looking for constant self-improvement—and I had to admit that since the beginning of our association, he had already changed a lot in the way he communicated. We had cleared the air, and could now try to move forward together again.

In parallel with these professional tribulations, I still practiced energetic healing, alternating between two worlds which sometimes seemed totally incompatible. I had started with my close circle, but I was now treating people who were unknown to me, and who had heard of me by word of mouth. I felt more confident, and could let the process go without analyzing it. With an empty mind, I went into a light trance and laid my hands on the patient. They then moved automatically where something guided them. The more I practiced, the more I managed to find this state experienced with Ayahuasca, where I became the catalyst of a presence that went beyond my intellect, and who knew exactly what to do for each patient. Positive feedback encouraged me a little more each time.

Besides the laying on of hands, I sometimes breathed and sang. I was the first to be surprised by these healing modalities, since I did not really consciously choose them: I only understood their usefulness in retrospect—the breath being a vehicle of life, and the sound an even more subtle way to play with vibrational energy.

The hardest part had been applying them with strangers, for fear of being judged as a weirdo. But apparently my patients accepted these originalities much more naturally—which actually were only original for a Westerner. I regularly discovered that these practices corresponded to the way South American shamans proceeded in their own tradition. Learning it after I had done it spontaneously was always a source of wonder to me, and helped confirm the presence of benevolent entities during my sessions, who continued to guide me and teach me if I let them. I had the impression, during these initiatory journeys in Peru, to have connected with higher consciousness which had not left me since then.

I loved the multiple aspects of this therapy, which varied according to each person's needs and sensitivity. I understood why I had not wanted to limit myself to a specific modality, for example by following a Reiki training or other. I would surely have locked myself into a particular procedure, thus forbidding myself to explore the many facets of healing. Just as in art, its forms of expression are really infinite, and very personal to each of us.

ILLUSIONS

Making a quality video game is very demanding. So much so that almost all my time was swallowed up in this project. I regularly went off track, and had an unfortunate tendency to overwork myself, unable to take the necessary breaks. A kind of feverish anxiety always led me to burnout. The weeks passed inexorably by, and all my secondary activities, such as healing—which I practiced less and less for lack of time—suffered directly from it.

I was typically in an escalation of commitment: The further I progressed in the project, the harder it became for me to consider abandoning it, given all the work and energy I had invested in it. As I felt this growing involvement, I also gradually felt trapped in a situation that was dragging on. It was a vicious circle, of which I was obviously the author, but which made me fear to miss my true "way," which was to develop my healer activity. I was constantly wondering about the direction I was taking my life in, putting myself, body and soul, into the creation of a project whose future was far from guaranteed.

I was sinking deeper and deeper, blaming this project and my partner for my discomfort. Despite my good resolutions concerning the help I wanted to give, I was obviously not clear with my intentions, and felt myself in the situation of one who continues to invest himself only to respect his commitments and not betray his partner. I had to admit, the posture I had decided to adopt did not fully satisfy me. I thought I had understood everything by accepting the role of assistant, but something was still wrong, given my impatience to see this project finish. So I was also missing out on all the pleasure I could have gained from such circumstances, where many interesting and creative aspects were present.

As I confronted myself with this state of tension and rejection towards this situation, I began to glimpse a pattern of thought. And I had the intuition that this pattern, which generated great dissatisfaction in me, was still linked to my habits of labeling certain things as "good" and others as "bad." I had heard regularly about the concept of "Acceptance" with a big A. I knew that many spiritual masters advocated acceptance as the ultimate path to enlightenment. But the concept still seemed vague to me: Did I really have to agree with everything that was happening to me? How could I get a real sense of acceptance, knowing that everything I was going through was positive—or at least relevant? Certainly Ayahuasca had made me grasp the perfection of the Universe and its flawless orchestration. But I was not always able to apply this in a concrete way in my life, nor to reconnect myself to this state: Deep down I continued to think that certain circumstances of my life went against my personal accomplishment.

During a meditation on this subject, I received a message that profoundly changed my perspective on this:

"Absolutely everything you do is You, and nourishes your whole Being."

Again, this message was not a simple statement addressed to my intellect, but rather a concept accompanied by a pure understanding. I knew exactly what it meant: Whatever my activity, it nourished my entire consciousness and had a global effect.

Moreover, all the subjects that interested me revealed a common denominator: understanding and decoding a system, in order to improve, reorganize, simplify and optimize it. When I was programming my game and constantly trying to find the most efficient and elegant technical solutions; when I was treating people and thus trying to help them redefine their beliefs or reorganize their energy field; and even when I was writing this book, always trying to find the clearest and smoothest phrasing... It was all really about the same principles, the same traits of my personality. And as such, I didn't have to put all these activities in competition. In other words, by programming my game impeccably, I trained to be a better healer, thus developing the art of analysis and pragmatism, for example. There was never any waste of time, because all these aspects came from the same source, and were explored by the same person. How could various expressions of myself be fundamentally incompatible, while they came from the same energy?

This simple realization had a very profound impact on me, because it immediately invalidated all my considerations that I was "lost" in projects that prevented me from following the right path. All this had still been the fruit of my ego, of my mind which could only see things separately, trying to compartmentalize all aspects of my daily life. This new perspective helped me enormously to understand that every minute of my life was used one hundred percent, and that none of my actions could thwart a greater goal— even if a minute was devoted to an activity that seemed trivial or apparently disconnected from my long-term goals.

As I further examined this question of "the right direction to follow," I began to have a terrible suspicion: What if these goals, especially my perpetual quest for change, were really only an illusion, a false lead? I kept talking about "my way," "my spiritual path," but was there really a place to go? I had already felt many times the experience of peace when I reconnected myself to the present moment, to the "here and now." Then why did I keep chasing after some ideal?

A dream brought me some answers. It was a recurring dream, linked to studies. I found myself regularly in classes that no longer interested me, to follow a course which I did not really know the purpose of, except that I felt forced to follow it—"just in case..." This time again, I was in French class with Laurent, a former friend from college. I was overcome by a feeling of boredom, as if I were watching a scene already seen a thousand times. After a while, I decided to give up and leave the class. I then began to wander aimlessly, and finally came back to sit in the room, almost out of spite. I then confessed to Laurent that I preferred to do studies that were useless, rather than doing nothing at all—the mere idea of being considered as a lazy person or a dead weight for society was unbearable for me.

My suspicion worsened. Could it be that all this quest for the "Truth" so dear to my heart was a reflection of my dream studies: a pretext to preserve this illusion of hyperactivity, and thus avoid simply Being? Spending my time analyzing, looking for my path, talking about my journey to the point of writing a book about it... All these gesticulations and theories really had only one goal: to make me realize that everything is there, within reach. To be in this state of presence, so simple and yet so powerful. Did my spiritual path consist in running a million times around a chair, when the only sensible thing would have been to just sit on it? Probably.

This long exploration had not been useless, for it had consisted in turning over every single rock, and being sure there were no hidden secrets underneath. But it was more of a verification than a real discovery. When I came to this conclusion and refocused on myself, I felt calm and at peace. As soon as I wanted to theorize this peace, it disappeared. Like a butterfly that one tries vainly to catch. It is by stopping the agitation and by simply remaining seated in stillness, that the butterfly finally comes back beside us and lets us admire its beauty again.

And that's exactly what San Pedro and the Wolf had taught me: to Be, without questioning what it means, or how to reach it. Just let go and reconnect to something that has always been there and that we can't miss: We exist, it's already obvious. All we need to do then is to breathe, and abandon ourselves to this existence, without looking for a method to control it, explain it or rationalize it—it is in fact the best way to get away from it...

Some may say that with such an awareness, one has finally reached a kind of "enlightenment." That wasn't really my case. Because these states of pure inspiration were followed by emotions much more difficult to manage. Maybe it would have been easier if I had gone into exile in a Tibetan monastery, but Parisian life did not leave me any respite, constantly challenging me to apply these realizations. My relationship with Matthieu was still complicated, and after letting go of my decision-making role, my partner tended to become even more overwhelming in the control he wanted to exercise. I realized in the end that it just wasn't fun anymore. Some moments were really painful for me, because it seemed that our project had lost all its exciting potential, and I was losing more motivation every day.

I had always naively thought my quest for Enlightenment represented a kind of Holy Grail, that would then allow me to live an ecstatic life filled with pure endless bliss. But I was beginning to revise this definition. Because I understood that developing one's consciousness does not protect one from negative energies. On the contrary, by becoming more lucid, one sees even more clearly the positive AND the negative. Rather, Illumination becomes the ability to manage this increased perception, this exacerbated sensitivity, by consciously choosing to focus on the positive aspects while respecting the existence of their opposites. Easier said than done, when the old reflexes are still there...

THE BREAK-UP

The tension between Matthieu and me had been very palpable for a few days. And the more I did my best to calm things down, by trying to cozy up to my partner, the more I felt like I was making them worse. When I observed myself, I actually saw my mother, who behaved exactly the same way in the face of my father's inexplicable anger. By trying to reason with him and soften him up, she usually only managed to irritate him even more.

I felt very tense. While I was desperately struggling once again with these old demons, something finally "broke" inside me: I suddenly experienced a truly exceptional clarity of mind. Just absolute Silence. I had the impression I had momentarily rid myself of my personality, like a cumbersome disguise that one takes off. My consciousness was overcome with an almost overwhelming calm: a total absence of emotion, a perfectly empty head, and an increased acuity of perception. Yet another concept described by Castaneda, which I was finally experiencing. He called it "The Place Of No Pity," and I couldn't have found a better name. Suddenly things didn't matter anymore. I could have stood there doing nothing, just enjoying this state of pure confidence. In The Place Of No Pity, as the name implies, there is no self-pity, no feeling of injustice, no victim energy. Just Being.

Thanks to this striking contrast, which allowed me to observe in a neutral way the emotional storm I felt a few moments earlier, I could see how all my problems still came fundamentally from self-devaluation. All the negative emotions I experienced were linked to a belittling of myself, to finally try to please others. But above all, bathed in this neutral observation, I finally understood the purpose I gave to this devaluation: trying to attract the love of others. It was a permanent seduction—at least an attempt, as weakness is not actually appealing: It can attract those who want to consolidate their power or some kind of domination. It can instill pity in those who recognize themselves in this energy. But it does not inspire respect. It does not inspire the desire to share with others, it just inspires the desire to use them—which is understandable in this permanent position of submission. "Use me!" The spine bent and the tail wriggling. That was the image I perceived.

In The Place Of No Pity, I did not feel aggrieved. I was indifferent, and that allowed me to feel a great inner strength. It totally killed the little power games I used to take part in, and the emotional escalation they caused.

When I stood as a victim, I could feel hurt by others' attitudes, even though I was paradoxically the instigator of this situation. I was thus tempted to run back in the opposite direction, trying to dominate or hurt the one who had just slapped me. In this state of deep calm, I finally realized it was much more beneficial to return to myself, in the present moment, to feel my power, to become aware of my strength. The concept of "turning the other cheek" finally took on its meaning, because in this feeling of total power, any aggression became an insignificant matter.

Living through submission was therefore a sterile hell that brought me only false solutions. I had been working extensively on this theme for several months. I finally understood—not intellectually, but fundamentally—that reconnecting to personal power and self-respect was the only valid strategy to lead my life, at all levels.

This state of exceptional clarity had been brief, but its impact profound. Thus, as a reflection of this new direction, a dispute erupted between my partner and me. I then understood I no longer wanted to work with Matthieu under these conditions, even if it meant "losing" the fruit of a year's work.

In my normal state of consciousness, guilt soon resurfaced: "It's an escape. It's an avoidance of your problems. You'll always be confronted with the same lessons all your life if you don't master them..." But by wanting to be always more perfect, I realized I wasn't happy. I took life as a task to be accomplished, to be the best student.

I had misinterpreted the principle of "following my joy:" It didn't mean just observing signs or emotions, to know if I was still on the right track. It was sincerely and willingly seeking to enjoy life, to take care of myself, to have fun—instead of approaching existence from a dead serious angle.

Yes, I could go back to my old company. Yes, I could fight all my career to become indifferent to anything that attacked me. And for what in the end? Brownie points when reaching the gates of Heaven? In this case, why not push the logic further, and go to work in a mine, for example? In short, this reasoning finally seemed absurd to me. The purpose of my life was simply to be happy. If I knew a way to be more so, I shouldn't deprive myself of it on the pretext that it was an easy solution!

And then I had to be honest with myself once again: From the start, I had approached this adventure with apprehension. Even though I had made it a point of honor to fulfill my part of the contract, I had not done so with all the enthusiasm and positivity required for such an ambitious project. In that case, what's the point of giving to others, if it's reluctantly?

I had forgotten myself, and now I had to learn the lessons. If all this meant leaving a situation involving other people, then I would try to find a compromise that ideally satisfied everyone. But now I wanted to stay true to myself, and honor my needs, desires and integrity as a priority.

Of course, this decision confronted me with my eternal fear of being seen as a traitor, a quitter. But I had to admit the obvious: If I didn't want to betray anyone, then I had to start by not betraying myself. Or in other words, "Don't do to yourself what you wouldn't do to others."

Still, I was faced with a big challenge: What was I going to do next? Because my unemployment allowance ended in a few weeks, and if I didn't plan to find a job again in a company, then I could only count on the income generated by our game. But in any case, this revenue would not be collected before several months, and it still had to be a commercial success. As it was also certain now that we would not continue our collaboration on other projects, Matthieu and I found ourselves in an extremely uncomfortable situation. I had a long conversation with my partner, during which we admitted the undeniable benefits of our relationship on our personal evolution. As a result, we felt a mutual recognition of the role we had played for each other. But we had come to the conclusion that this venture could not really work in the long term, and that it seemed wiser to us to take different paths. We were going to finish our game, and leave it at that. Matthieu wanted to find a regular job, exhausted by this long period of pressure and uncertainty, and it was quite understandable.

So I was going to be alone soon, and I had to find a way to generate money. Matthieu was the CEO of the company, and as such, he held the purse strings. I began to worry seriously about my future. I felt I had been too lax about the meagre guarantees I had asked for when we set up our studio, and I was now dependent on my partner's goodwill. When you decide to divorce, even on good terms—which was definitely the case—this is not really the position you like to find yourself in.

The project was still not finished and my anxiety was growing. Working under these conditions was difficult for me, especially since we were regularly falling behind in our deadlines. I now felt like I was putting my energy into a bottomless pit, instead of focusing on concrete things that could bring me income in the shorter term. I had to fight to remain honest and consistent with my decisions, and not panic by scattering myself in all directions.

I was especially afraid that, once our divorce was over, Matthieu would not really care about my situation any longer. We would indeed spend long months before receiving the first royalties, months during which our exchanges would inevitably become rarer. By getting out of his life in this way, I thought he could more easily "forget" my involvement in our company. He could even decide to reinvest the money earned in another game rather than redistributing it among shareholders. Technically, and given his status, he had every right.

It was an opportunity to see how fear is associated with the feeling of depending on the others to survive. When we believe someone has something we absolutely need, then we put ourselves in an alienating position of submission: Whether it is to obtain love, money, recognition... the principle is the same. One is then ready to accept many things, even if it means denying oneself. If I wanted to make my situation bearable, and no longer suffer the fear of being cheated one day by my partner, I had to give up those expectations that were ruining my life. It seemed healthier to me not to hope for anything more from this adventure—rather than to cling to an obligation of result over which I had no control, and which put me in a terribly precarious situation. I had to let go, and consider that everything I could get out of this project, I had already gained: a better understanding of myself, an enriched professional and technical experience, and a clearer vision of what I really wanted to do with my life. Which was an undeniable gift. Gratitude still seemed the most pleasant option. After that, I had to assume the risks of a separation, and come what may.

In this period of great confusion, I then received an unexpected proposal. I was offered a new San Pedro ceremony in Spain. I wondered if it was reasonable to use teacher plants too often to solve my problems. Convinced, however, that there are no accidents, the opportunity finally seemed too good to ignore, and I decided to respond favorably to it.

LIVING IN A MADHOUSE

This time, the two ceremonies I was going to attend would take place in a large Spanish city. I wondered how to live such a contemplative experience in a simple apartment. I reassured myself, however, by telling myself I would mainly go into my inner space, whatever the setting. Moreover, I decided to take the opportunity to ask the San Pedro spirit His vision of our Western way of life. I often wondered about the idea of moving to the countryside—or even to Peru—in contact with nature, far from computers, wifi and mobile phones. It was a good opportunity to explore this contrast with the plant, and to review the clichés that are often evoked about our modern life.

When I arrived, I was surprised to learn that I would be the only one to take the medicine. My host—who had been recommended to me by a mutual friend—would simply be there to assist me. I was a little doubtful, but now that I had made the trip... The first morning, I swallowed the powder diluted in a glass of water, without any real ritual. My intention with the plant was then to ask it for a "critique" of my stressed Western life, with possible suggestions to make it more harmonious and balanced.

I sat quietly in the living room, bathed in the sunlight that passed through the large bay window. My body began to move, visibly doing relaxation exercises to loosen up my joints. I was doing these things completely spontaneously, but it felt good. I knew this physical reaction was a way to show myself that I was too sedentary, and that I wasn't allowing energy to circulate in my body enough. I remained focused on my initial intention, and approached the window.

The first idea that came to me was to throw away a good part of my possessions. My life was cluttered, saturated with useless consumer objects that weighed me down considerably. The message was clear: "Get rid of all that mess you don't need. It will create space in your life, because your apartment and closets are simply a reflection of your inner state."

As I looked outside, I saw the imposing towers of a business district. I immediately had a feeling of rejection towards these buildings, in which I had spent part of my career as an IT executive: soulless chicken coops, kingdom of open spaces, plastic tables, suits and ties. Yet San Pedro showed me a higher perspective, as usual. He told me that this vision of things was only a pure choice on my part. And that I could also see these towers as a celebration of human architectural genius. Only I could decide what label I wanted to put on everything in my life, because in the end, everything was basically neutral.

I stayed a moment with these considerations. So did that mean I could go back to a company and be happy? In absolute terms, it was indeed possible. But the voice of San Pedro told me: "You can watch the river flow, without necessarily drinking from it." I understood the meaning of this sentence: I could be an actor in Western life, and get what I liked out of it, without being forced to put up with aspects I didn't. I could live in an urban environment, without feeling aggressed by it, and without having to follow rules that no longer suited me. I was free. So I didn't have to throw everything away in an emotional reaction.

Part of me objected, nonetheless: "But how can I live in this world and not respect its rules? How could I avoid taking the subway every morning to get to work? I have to pay the bills!"

The answer was immediate, and very powerful in its simplicity: "You think you have needs. You've been conditioned for this."

That was true. My anxiety was related to fear of lack. It wasn't a clearly defined threat, just a diffuse apprehension: the fear of terrible consequences if I didn't play by the rules of society. It wasn't so much the fear of not being able to pay for my cable subscription, my Internet connection, or anything that was my definition of comfort. But rather the terrifying prospect of becoming a pariah if I excluded myself from the system. By refusing to follow the herd and the values of consumer society, I was going to become homeless, starving in the gutter—and in total indifference!

In this state of understanding and lucidity, I noticed all the absurdity of this behavior. I even could have laughed... until I felt in my gut how we were all enslaved by this debilitating mass culture: this permanent conditioning—notably through the media and advertising—which strives to convince us that happiness comes through the possession of the latest car or the latest mobile phone. This vicious circle which pushes us to seek satisfaction in the purchase of material goods, even if it means suffering a hundred times more to earn the money necessary to get them.

More than a wolf, I was a sheep, and I wasn't even aware of it. But that prevented me from living my life to the fullest, imprisoned in a set of requirements I had not even consciously chosen to meet. I had simply been told this was the model to follow, and I had adhered to it without any question.

While in this kind of contradictory state, mixing euphoria and disgust, San Pedro continued His demonstration. He encouraged me even more to throw away my precious possessions, which badly compensated for all the energy and well-being I had sacrificed to obtain them. He told me that, in reality, the very idea of owning property or money was a laughable illusion. Nothing belonged to me, I was only the temporary tenant of this world, and it was only a primary human concept to believe that I could own a part of Creation. When I died, I would take none of this to my grave. Money was just energy, literally flowing through my hands, and I could only choose how to use it. But to accumulate it, penny after penny, with the certainty that it was a definitive achievement, was a totally derisory conception of the Universe, and of the place I occupied there.

The lesson was repeated in a nagging tone: "Give, give, give whatever you have, if you have to. Otherwise it will become your burden—frozen, dead energy that stagnates without anyone really being able to benefit from it. The Universe is an infinite buffet, where everyone can feed from freely! So what's the point of stashing food feverishly inside your pockets?"

Then one last idea came to me: "And don't forget that being hungry once in a while can be more exciting than being full all the time. Also enjoy the moments when you don't yet have what you want, because it will only make it more enjoyable when it finally happens in your life. Without lack, there is no desire. And without desire, there is no sense of accomplishment afterwards. Then stop fearing lack, as if it were the most terrible experience. Just take it as the spark that will make you want to create new things in your life, whetting your appetite!"

This exploration had lasted hours, and the effects of the plant were beginning to fade. Despite the absence of a natural environment, the benefits of this medicine had once again proved extremely impressive.

PASSION AND ADDICTIONS

I took a day to digest these teachings. Anyway, at this time, they did not yet have the full meaning and depth that I give them today. The plants are like wonderful teachers, taking us to a beautiful place of understanding. Then, once the experience is over, it is up to us to find our way back to this particular place, knowing from now on that it exists. Just experiencing it is not enough, we have to reconnect with it on our own. It is after this final step that the lesson is truly integrated, and that our definitions are profoundly changed.

I had planned to have one last ceremony the next day. However, I wasn't sure what to ask San Pedro. I knew I still had bad habits in my way of collaborating with others, with an unfortunate tendency to tie myself up with chains. Even if I had already explored this theme, with many realizations about my internal patterns, I wanted to study it in the most exhaustive way possible. I clearly hadn't cleaned everything up.

I swallowed the gooey substance—whose taste seemed more awful than ever—in the middle of the morning. Then I sat there, waiting for the first effects to manifest. I tried to stay connected to the theme I wanted to work on. I recalled typical scenes of my relationship with Matthieu, which had provoked unpleasant emotional states, such as anger, or the permanent fear of being judged.

A first subtle concept began to emerge. I felt like I was being whispered to: "When you do one thing, you don't have to do ten more at the same time. You scatter and wear yourself out." That was correct. When I was working on my computer, I could both program, respond to my associate's requests by instant messaging, check my e-mails, visit discussion forums, do research... I was hyperactive in front of my screen, showing an exhausting visual and intellectual vigilance. This idea unfolded progressively, and I realized I actually had a tendency to overdo everything I did.

Regarding work, I was a bulimic: I swallowed tasks one after the other, sometimes at a frenetic pace, without taking a break. I could last several weeks, then, when I reached saturation, I "vomited" everything I had accumulated. Once the crisis was over, I went back to work full steam.

Of course, I was already aware of these patterns, but I had never equated them with bulimia. Yet the analogy made perfect sense. When I saw myself like that, I found my attitude absurd and totally unbalanced. I realized my hyperactivity was actually an excuse. Regardless of whether it really provided me with financial security, the most important thing was to look like I had used up all my resources. A kind of protection that would prevent others from calling me lazy or good-for-nothing. No problem if I crashed into the wall, as long as everyone could see how hard I was trying. So my goal was to constantly impress those around me, to prove to them I was a winner.

Moreover, I realized I claimed loud and clear to be totally exhausted by our game project. It was like a badge I was always wearing, a medal to prove I was a good person, determined, hardworking and useful to the world. At least they couldn't blame me, especially not for being a parasite.

San Pedro also showed me how much I felt obliged to finish something once I had started it. Even if it can be seen as a virtue, expressing perseverance and obstinacy, it can also prove alienating when we realize we are on the wrong track: We do not feel the right to change course by leaving a task unfinished. "As when you were forced to finish your plate when you were a kid, you were somehow trained to reproduce this pattern in everything you do, even if it means indigestion when you are no longer hungry. But now you're not a little boy anymore, and no one can force you to finish something, especially if you feel you haven't even chosen the menu..."

This idea of consuming something out of necessity rather than desire led me to the topic of addiction: I had to admit, I was a workaholic and addicted to the other person's assent, to the point of exhaustion. I then asked a question: "I know I have to follow my joy and excitement, but how can I tell the difference between a true passion, and the irrepressible need to fulfill this addiction?"

The answer came in my mind, simple and clear: "The frontier is subtle. But passion feeds you, while addiction empties you." I now had a quick way to assess my psychic state, and identify genuine enthusiasm or disguised anxiety. I thanked the plant, or whatever the source of this information, for this very valuable tool. I knew it would be useful all my life, to test my limits and know when I would cross the line.

I had one last question left: "How can I reconcile my personal desires with what others expect of me? How to avoid conflict of interest?"

And the answer was, "You are confusing asking permission with reaching consensus. The difference between the two postures is the respect you have for yourself when you express your personal needs. If you respect yourself, then you will clearly know what you want, and you will simply be in search of a compromise that ideally satisfies everyone. But you'll always have priority. Otherwise you will just have wishes, hoping that the other will give you permission to access them. It's all a question of vibration, which will determine your position in relation to other people."

It all made perfect sense. All I had to do was assimilate those teachings. However, one last spontaneous message came to me. It told me that I no longer needed teacher plants in the immediate future, and that I was perfectly capable of flying on my own. So I didn't have to hold on to them, as if my progress depended on them. Certainly they could help me from time to time, but if this help became indispensable to progress, then it would be another form of addiction. I understood that this appointment was possibly the last one before a long time, at least until I fully realized my ability to find my own answers.

COMING TOGETHER

Weeks passed inexorably. We had finally finished our game with Matthieu, and my unemployment allowance was over. So I wasn't getting any more revenue, and our project sales, even if they were good, wouldn't be cashable until the end of the year—it was May. I feared a long dry spell...

Without really understanding why, my healing activities had also come to a halt. Yet I was getting good feedback from the people I was treating, but the word of mouth effect seemed to suddenly stop for no particular reason.

I had now assimilated the vision of shamans—and quantum physicists—that "reality" is only an illusion, a dream of a more solid appearance. Whatever approach I used, whether psychological, scientific or spiritual, I always came to the same conclusion: We create our life experience through our own consciousness and personal perspective. I knew that everything I experienced was therefore only a reflection of my inner state, and that the circumstances in which I found myself were a mirror allowing me to better analyze my belief system.

I didn't know why I was so convinced of this now, but I was sure the plants' teachings had helped this realization at an unconscious level. On a daily basis, what surrounded me had now lost a bit its concrete aspect. I sometimes found myself in almost dream-like states of consciousness, exacerbated during my healing sessions, and in which I perceived the very malleable character of everything around me.

But when we abandon our victim posture, and take responsibility for the creation of our life, the mind can still play a new trick on us—which was definitely my case: "If I really create my reality, then what have I done wrong to create this one, which plunges me into a great anxiety and a feeling of precariousness? Why can't I create the security and abundance that would relieve me?"

The answer was, however, simple: If life was only a mirror, then it was the perfect reflection of my lack of confidence and my fear of the Unknown. I had to admit it, without guilt, but reconnect to the certainty that I had the power to change that state. I now had to clearly identify the origin of these long-lasting definitions, which was surely the trickiest part.

Stéphanie was also regularly worried about our situation, as she herself had a long-term story with fear of lack. Besides, we were so connected that I often took her anxieties as my own. It was enough for me to see her depressed to immediately want to comfort her. But my attempts to analyze the circumstances aloud and consider solutions only betrayed my own perplexity at a situation that seemed blocked to me. This had the opposite effect: Instead of reassuring my wife, the exposure of my feelings reinforced her sentiment that we were both lost. It seemed nobody really held the helm, and the boat drifted without a real captain on board. We kept switching roles, and she regularly cheered me up, offering me her precious advice—showing once again that we were both progressing along parallel but extremely similar paths.

Surprisingly, all the projects I tried to launch fell through. Even those I had voluntarily set aside during my association with Matthieu now seemed obsolete. After all these months of hyperactivity, I found myself in the eye of the storm. Days passed, and nothing changed. The more I struggled to find solutions based on my old models, such as IT services, the more everything seemed to stagnate. This situation was, in fact, a great opportunity: It allowed me to put into practice the teachings I had received at my last San Pedro ceremony, especially related to the deep anxiety that motivated my constant need to be active. I had entered a withdrawal process, in spite of myself, and I had every interest in giving it a positive value.

In this profound reorganization of my life, by systematically favoring patience and trust, things gradually improved. However, these readjustments took time, and I was still oscillating between very contrasting emotional states: heightened enthusiasm and creativity, followed by deep depression and confusion. Yet the darkest moments of that period were also the richest, for they forced me to seek answers, and to put together all the pieces of the puzzle. As in every transformative process, it was not comfortable, but necessary.

During this slow process of reconciliation and integration, I even wondered if the fact of not wanting to return to the corporate world was not ultimately an overreaction on my part. This rejection seemed like a dissonant energy, which only fueled my fear of failure. I also realized my mind's inability to imagine alternatives to what it had already experienced: If I did not manage to reinvent my life, it seemed I was necessarily condemned to return to the only environment I had known until now. That was absurd.

I worked every day on these principles of acceptance, because I was intuitively convinced this was the royal road to true healing. After many months of integration, I decided to take a new step and return once again to the Amazon. I felt an irresistible call to work with Ayahuasca again. But this time I decided to go alone. I had the feeling that I was dealing with very deep themes, and in this solitary journey, I wanted to put myself to the test—like a warrior confronted with adversity, I wanted to reveal my unsuspected resources and feel stronger.

It would take too long to describe this adventure in detail, but I did discover a fabulous hidden treasure there. Except that where I thought I would find strength, in a macho and belligerent attitude, I discovered what I really lacked: deep Love and Acceptance of myself. One more time.

My patterns were clearly shown to me in a masterly demonstration, and this revelation had an absolutely shocking impact for me. During extremely intense emotional experiences, I could see that, all my life, I had maintained an energy in me. And that energy was rejection. It was so deep inside me, I wasn't even aware of it. It had been expressed in all possible ways in my life, and I had explored in detail its many facets: the need to be loved, the feeling of being rejected by others, but also the desire to keep people at bay to avoid suffering, and above all, the constant rejection and dissatisfaction of myself. All these aspects actually came from the same source.

I had spent my time constantly judging myself, being ashamed of myself, mistreating myself. All the painful experiences I had had with others were only the reflection of this inner vibration, linked to a deep feeling of devaluation.

Had I "celebrated" myself even once? I was barely celebrating my birthdays, actually. Did I ever welcome myself to this world? I now knew that to reverse this behavior which caused me only suffering, I had to be able to pay homage to my own existence. And if I didn't, no one would do it for me. I then devoted an entire ceremony simply to honoring my presence in this world, and exploring all I could offer myself as a human being. It was an absolutely unforgettable experience. Now I saw why I had such a strong intuition that acceptance—i.e. the reverse energy of rejection—was the key!

In light of this fundamental understanding, I finally grasped why my relationships, especially in my professional life, had been so painful. I was always looking outside for a love I didn't give myself. But it was an endless quest: Ayahuasca had shown me that the only love we can really feel is the one that is within each of us, there, eternally present and accessible.

When someone says to us "I love you," this person cannot concretely "fill" us with love, because she is external to our body and our mind. If we feel pleasure and happiness when we hear these words, it is because we reconnect with the love *within us*: "Someone tells me she loves me, so it must mean I deserve it. I can finally allow myself to feel love without guilt. At least for a while. Then, when that feeling is gone, I will wait for the next external opportunity to give me permission to love myself again." In fact, like a beggar sitting on a pile of gold, I had neglected my own infinite wealth, to go begging others—either for affection, admiration or respect. I was always asking for proof that I was lovable.

So in reality, the circumstances of my old jobs were a false problem. I saw more clearly the patterns I had thus constantly repeated: my tendency to always follow the same model, systematically looking for a person or an institution, to put myself at their service. There had been my various jobs, then my association with Matthieu, and each time this did not really satisfy me. Quite simply because I asked these people to give me what I refused to give myself, even though I was the only one who could really grant it to me. In this hopeless search, I logically only got a reinforcement of my disappointment and my feeling of not being loved.

When I introduced dependency into my relationships, I was necessarily hoping to get something in return. And when I started to be afraid that others wouldn't give me anything at all, then I would give even more. I had sought the company of people to reassure myself, and I realized that on the contrary, it had created a permanent feeling of insecurity. To live a healthy relationship and offer in a fair, balanced, honest and loving way, I had to be able to feel independent and self-sufficient. And to reinforce this autonomy, I needed to reconnect with this consideration for myself, a feeling that had constantly been lacking in me—yet which was the only one that could finally give me a real feeling of strength and freedom. The secret was to cultivate in me the resources that I thought I should receive from others, such as approval and respect.

Now I knew where my happiness lays: inside me. It had always been there, and I had deprived myself of it voluntarily. Sometimes people ask me, "But how do you love yourself?" I then answer that there is no "How," but rather a "Why." You just have to decide it, convinced that any other approach would be as unfair as it would be cruel—and above all, totally absurd!

So I was now going to be my best supporter. The unconditional love for myself, the respect, the openness, the confidence in the perfect orchestration of things... all these benevolent precepts that my shamanic experiences had shown me for years, finally took their meaning in a coherent system. By cultivating them, I would have the foundation and the necessary resources to continue my journey.

It would have taken me a long time to understand all this, but I could finally take a breath and let go. I now knew, in the depths of my being, that this coveted peace could only come through total acceptance: of myself, of course, but also of all eventualities, even the "worse." This unconditional acceptance, so often advocated by many sages throughout history, and which I confused with resignation.

I knew without a shadow of a doubt that anything I would label as negative, anything I would dread, would be ghosts that would haunt me all my life. I refused to be a prey, much less of my own anguish. In the end, the only system I had always been a prisoner of, and against which I had fought all the time, was me...

To be able to move forward without fear, I had to welcome all these possibilities, without seeing them as scarecrows that would slow me down or make me run away. I no longer wanted to be the slave of my fears, and thus sentence myself to life emprisonment. Instead of avoiding them, I would examine them in detail. For fears are *really* like scarecrows: They are frightening only at a certain distance. When we approach them and study them closely, we realize that they are only a bad imitation, often made of old, shabby and mismatched objects. And the illusion is finally fading.

I then reconnected with that German Jewish soldier I had dreamed of, and tried to imagine how his story might have ended. Certainly he could have deserted, and then lived hidden, in permanent apprehension of being found. Was that really freedom? Would he have found the happiness and peace he sought so much? I preferred to invent a different fate for him: a fictional army from which he could have resigned, and with which he would have kept cordial contacts, while remaining external to this system.

Living in constant fear that someone or something can end a fragile happiness is not freedom. It's just a survival situation, a Sword of Damocles permanently placed over our heads. To live fully, I therefore had to accept all eventualities, without exception, including those I had feared most until now. The idea was not to necessarily favor these options, but rather to transform them, to reinvent them—in order to disarm them definitively and thus remove any paralyzing effect. The hardest part was realizing that I had that power, and that I always had it.

I would have had to spend all these years questioning myself, overcoming my fears and doubts, regaining my self-esteem, exploring the darkest corners of my mind—and incidentally vomiting my guts in the Amazon jungle—to come to this simple yet essential awareness. Thanks to this love and total acceptance, the way was finally clear for me to accomplish my full potential, because they not only soothed my professional and material anxieties, but actually healed all my apprehensions. Whatever my future, I would overcome challenges with elegance—and never really fail. Actually, how could I fail when there is no real stake, and when I am free to reorient my life at any time, supported by a magnificent ally: myself?

Free from the fears and chains I had created, I could finally take the great leap, and soar into the Unknown...

EPILOGUE

"Wait, is that it? To be happy and free, you just have to love yourself and accept everything? If that was really the solution to all problems, everyone would already do that! It's a bit simplistic, don't you think?"

Well, I would say it is indeed a fundamentally simple principle by nature, but a real challenge when it comes to applying it in everyday life. First of all, because self-love is not really the first value that our society encourages us to develop. It can be quickly labelled as selfishness or egocentrism, fostering a sense of guilt. Since we do not want to be judged or categorized as "bad people," we often forget ourselves in favor of others.

As for acceptance, it represents a challenge of every moment for an unsatisfied, goal-oriented mind, used to control and label everything. We spend our whole lives being afraid, complaining or rebelling against anything that upsets us, without even realizing that this is also the best way to maintain it.

Let us take a logical approach. If we assume that our inner state defines our reality, then what we focus on necessarily becomes our life experience. To oppose a situation or behavior, to react negatively towards them, means to feed them, thus creating a vicious circle. Common sense should rather naturally push us to look for another perspective, an exit way. Accepting does not mean endorsing, but rather observing in a neutral way what is already there, while focusing on a positive outcome in a creative way. We always take life so seriously that we forget to play with it.

Acceptance is not, therefore, a failure, a lesser evil or a naïve philosophy. But, on the contrary, a strategy that allows us to move forward, and not constantly saw the branch on which we are sitting. It creates a virtuous circle leading to incredible synchronicities. When we realize that acceptance offers us freedom, it becomes an ally that makes us stronger, and not a resigned choice dictated by ethics.

When we begin to practice acceptance, it certainly allows us to welcome external circumstances with grace. But more importantly, it gradually leads us to the key element of true happiness: self-acceptance. To finally be able to present ourselves to the world without shame or false modesty, and to stop denigrating ourselves as we so often do. One can thus access the Holy Grail: sincere and authentic Self-Love. That is why these two principles—love and acceptance—are indissociable and mutually reinforcing.

I wanted this book to represent an experimentation with a pragmatic—almost scientific—approach. After all, in science, we use the following methodology: We try an experiment, we measure its results, we adjust parameters, and we try again until we find a satisfactory formula. This can also apply to a spiritual path.

Acceptance, love and positive thinking are certainly not new concepts, but when they are asserted to us without preamble, they often seem to be abstract, naive or idealistic concepts. I wanted to put them into practice for my own healing, and see what challenges I would face.

The French version of this book was published in 2013. Since then, a lot has happened, but I wouldn't change a line. By concretely applying these realizations, my life changed drastically and improved considerably. As if, by stopping fighting with life and myself, all doors had opened and most of the "obstacles" I came up against had disappeared naturally. My healing sessions have resumed their course. I have developed an activity combining spirituality and computer development, by creating a collection of oracle cards and guided meditations apps[1]. I started my apprenticeship as an ayahuasquero by going back regularly to Peru. I moved closer to Nature by settling in the countryside. I obviously

---

[1] Indie Goes Software, www.indie-goes.com

finished the translation of my book... Everything fell into place, safely and effortlessly, in a coherent whole representative of my various passions and my inner peace. And most importantly of all: I globally feel more balanced, grounded and peaceful.

Stéphanie, for her part, has obviously also learned a lot from her journey, made stronger by all the trials she has gone through, and the worries she has managed to overcome. Always brave, she now feels able to face situations that previously would have seemed insurmountable to her. We have really progressed together, hand-in-hand.

Of course, I have no guarantee about what will happen next, and I will obviously have to face new challenges. But I finally learned to make peace with that uncertainty. Does that mean I never feel fear again? No, of course not! I don't pretend to be a superman disconnected from his emotions. Fear is a natural, useful reflex that gives us the opportunity to identify our bad definitions. But what causes real suffering is *living constantly in fear*. To get out of this hell, I had to realize I was not a victim of my life, and that I was able to take a new direction every time I found myself in a dead end. By reconnecting myself to this love and personal power, I can now accept not knowing where life takes me, for I will always be able to create new circumstances in accordance with my deep nature. In other words, no matter where I go, as long as I know why I do it, and it gives me joy.

I began this book by saying I did not want to present miracle recipes. It seemed more interesting to me to tell a lived experience. However, in conclusion, I would like to quickly summarize the fundamental principles that have enabled me to move forward on this path, hoping that they may also inspire you. Here are the personal behaviors I was able to transform, in order to give them a powerful positive impact.

- **Stopping judging everything.** Judgment is what constantly ruins our lives, based on the principle that there are "good" and "bad" things. The result is the paralyzing fear of a hazardous choice, and of failure. But there is an even worse consequence: By bathing in this energy, we then also apply this principle to ourselves and to others. We constantly judge ourselves, often through an extremely brutal and critical look.

How can I be happy when I spend my whole life with an internal tormentor who regularly condemns me to shame, devaluation and rejection of myself? When I stop judging and labelling everything, I finally give myself the respite to let go and quickly feel genuine happiness and relief.

Don't worry, you have nothing to prove, and you are just perfect as you are!

- **Honoring others, but also myself.** To maintain harmony around us, it is sometimes tempting to forget ourselves in the process. Yet, constantly sacrificing one's personal integrity or well-being is not what will make this world a better place. What will make it better is that people deeply respect themselves, give themselves unfailing support, and inspire this feeling to their fellow human beings. It is finally the most beautiful gift we can give to each other.

- **Being responsible for my life.** If I experience dissonant energies, my responsibility is to change my definition of what blocks me, not to change external circumstances. They are only a reflection, and wanting to change a reflection is absurd. Logically, if I don't like what I see in my mirror, I change my attitude. I start by smiling, so that the reflection smiles in turn. In any case, I am not a victim—nor have I ever been.

- **Having trust, without looking for guarantees.** I have no expectations and I make peace with the unknown. I don't always understand why events happen this way, but I know that the Universe supports me all the time, and that there are blessings in every situation. So I do not have to be afraid and force things to happen in the form that my mind imposes on me. As a result, I can finally stop making plans and forecasts all the time to try to protect myself. I just surrender and go with the flow.

- **Focusing on happiness at every moment.** I follow my joy as a priority, in accordance with my integrity. Joy is my beacon, a true guidance system, and I must trust it even if appearances seem contradictory. When I feel excited, when I am passionate about something, I know I am on the right track.

- **Healing with inner silence.** If I feel emotional difficulties, the priority is to stop the flow of my thoughts. On our path, there will necessarily be ups and downs. Moments of pure bliss, and moments of total discouragement and doubt. In trying situations, the key point is not to feed this negative state—as said earlier, by making the circumstances as neutral as possible, without judgment. The most effective way to do this is to go back to the present moment. To stop this overactive mind which passes constantly from one idea to the other, in an endless torment. Quiet and listen, observe, breathe deeply, meditate, walk, sing... Writing, in a diary for example, is also a very good way to stem this excess of activity, and to put one's ideas in order. Once in the present moment, we reconnect to our true power, and inspiration comes to bring us solutions.

I know it is not always easy to apply these principles, especially during those times of great change. We are human after all, and Life will always find new ways to confront us with our contradictions. But the ultimate goal of this personal evolution is to feel better, not to pressure ourselves with another obligation of results! Let's simply accept ourselves as we are, with humility, for we will continue to learn and evolve all our life, until our last breath and beyond...

***

Finally, to conclude, I would like to share with you a letter I wrote to myself after my second Ayahuasca ceremony in Spain. We had indeed decided to write to ourselves, taking advantage of this extremely clear and inspired state of consciousness: We could then reread it in difficult moments, knowing that it came from a place of knowledge, wisdom and love.

A few days ago, while searching in old papers, I found it "by accident." I was surprised to rediscover this totally forgotten message, and yet it already conveyed the essential. At the bottom of the page was my thumbprint, previously dipped in the sacred brew.

The message, simple and direct, said this:

"Dear Fred,

"I love you, and for that reason, I don't want you to forget all the beautiful things you learned during this journey. That's why I'm writing this note to you.

"Believe me, you don't need to worry about your future, even if it seems unclear right now. You already live in a spiritual world, and this world, All That Is, supports you unconditionally. Don't wear yourself out, things will come at the right time, when you're ready. Focus on what is important to you: the ones you love, your passions, your creativity.

"Allow yourself to follow what excites you, and the Universe will assist you to create that reality!

"Don't try to rush things, take your time. Your journey will be long, even endless. So enjoy every step on your path, because only the path counts. Simply love yourself and others, to make this world a beautiful place to live.

"Trust, believe in yourself, and enjoy the wonderful gift your life is."

In memory of Diego Palma
1967 - 2019

Free As A Wolf

If you want to contact the author, please write
to: freeasawolf@outlook.com

Printed in Great Britain
by Amazon

31746483R00159